THE BIBLE IN ITS WORLD

David Noel Freedman, *General Editor*
Astrid B. Beck, *Associate Editor*

THE BIBLE IN ITS WORLD series offers an in-depth view of significant aspects of the biblical world. Reflecting current advances in scholarship, these volumes provide insights into the context of the Bible. Individual studies apply up-to-date historical, literary, cultural, and theological methods and techniques to enhance understanding of the biblical texts and their setting. Among the topics addressed are archaeology, geography, anthropology, history, linguistics, music, and religion as they apply to the Hebrew Bible/Old Testament, Apocrypha/Deuterocanonicals, and New Testament.

Contributors to THE BIBLE IN ITS WORLD are among the foremost authorities in their respective fields worldwide and represent a broad range of religious and institutional affiliations. Authors are charged to offer fresh interpretations that are scholarly, responsible, and engaging. Accessible to serious general readers and scholars alike, THE BIBLE IN ITS WORLD series will interest anyone who seeks a deeper understanding of the Bible and its world.

Music in Ancient Israel/Palestine

ARCHAEOLOGICAL, WRITTEN, AND COMPARATIVE SOURCES

Joachim Braun

Translated by
Douglas W. Stott

WILLIAM B. EERDMANS PUBLISHING COMPANY
GRAND RAPIDS, MICHIGAN / CAMBRIDGE, U.K.

Wm. B. Eerdmans Publishing Co.
255 Jefferson Ave. S.E., Grand Rapids, Michigan 49503 /
P.O. Box 163, Cambridge CB3 9PU U.K.
www.eerdmans.com

Printed in the United States of America

07 06 05 04 03 02   7 6 5 4 3 2 1

Library of Congress Cataloging-in-Publication Data

Braun, Joachim, 1931-
[Musikkultur Altisraels/Palästinas. English]
Music in ancient Israel/Palestine: archaeological, written,
and comparative sources / Joachim Braun.
p.   cm.
Includes bibliographical references (p. 321) and index.
ISBN 0-8028-4477-4 (cloth: alk. paper)
1. Jews — Music — History and criticism.
2. Music — Palestine — To 500 — History and criticism.
I. Title.

ML166.B7613   2002
780'.933 — dc21
2002040362

This book is a revised, updated, and enlarged version of the German book *Die Musikkultur Altisraels/Palästinas: Studien zu archäologischen, schriftlichen und vergleichenden Quellen* (Freiburg, Switzerland/Göttingen: University Press/Vandenhoeck & Ruprecht, 1999).

For Vivi

Contents

CONTENTS

Contents

CONTENTS

Preface

Neither sound nor musical notation remains of the music of ancient Israel/Palestine. Apart from the sparse written records, the only information we have is that provided by the stone, bone, or metal unearthed by archaeologists.

Yet even musical periods documented much more richly than those of the ancient world can leave us in uncertainty. How were Beethoven's works actually performed? How were the harmony and melody of Corelli's *basso continuo* realized? What was the correct interpretation of neumatic symbols? What about the Jewish *ta'amei hamikra?* With even less information at our disposal, what can we possibly say about the music of the ancient world? This music, the music of ancient Israel/Palestine, is still passed on orally and from father to son. Beginning in this small strip on the eastern edge of the Mediterranean, it has over the course of two-and-a-half millennia spread over the entire globe and assimilated literally hundreds of musical styles.

The present study attempts to assemble a portrait of this past musical world from many small *tesserae*. Because the music itself has probably disappeared forever, the goal obviously cannot be total restoration; we can, however, gain insight into the character of that music, into its "setting in life" and symbolism. Even at best, though, such a mosaic can offer no more than a fragmented, vague imitation of this past world of sound. Given the nature of our sources, we must simply accept that parts of the mosaic will have faded with time; others will have been destroyed entirely. Similarly, even the relationships between what tiny pieces of the mosaic we do have at our disposal may not always be what they seem.

The acoustic restoration of musical events is impossible not only because the source material is absent in the first place, but primarily because the historical situation, the social circumstances, and the listeners' psychological disposition and corresponding reaction to this music are forever beyond our reach. The acoustic ecology of this ancient past was radically different from our own. We today can hardly imagine how in the relative stillness of the ancient world, the rustling of the ornamentation women wore on their arms, feet, and hips was a significant experience of sound, or how the sound of an animal horn or of a trumpet was perceived as a supernatural rumbling.

Although the present study draws from both archaeological and written and comparative ethnological sources, the focus is on archaeological findings. The only real witnesses to this acoustic past are the musical instruments, terra-cotta and metal figures, etched stone illustrations, and mosaics unearthed by archaeologists. And yet even this evidence is often a matter of dispute, or somewhat deceptive.

This book focuses not on "music in the Bible" or on music in "biblical times," but on music in ancient Israel/Palestine. Until now, musical research has been based largely on information from a single source, namely, the Bible. Its status as "Holy Scripture" has typically bestowed upon it a preferential standing among ancient sources. In the following presentation, however, I examine the Bible as one possible written source alongside others in constructing an overall mosaic of the world of ancient music. By including a broader spectrum of sources than is usual in musicological studies, and especially by focusing more sharply on archaeological findings, the study ultimately found reason to call into question or even refute various views long accepted within the traditional "historiography of biblical music."

In assembling this portrait of the music of ancient Israel/Palestine, I have examined historical periods and cultures that doubtless influenced the development of the musical culture of both the region and its populace but which previous comprehensive assessments have largely excluded. The history of music in ancient Israel and Palestine extends from the very beginnings of musical activity in the larger sense in this region up to the Byzantine period; that is, it encompasses periods such as the Stone Age and the Natufian period that hitherto have not been included in more comprehensive assessments. The emergence of local musical culture here involved a far broader spectrum of peoples than previously assumed, including the Canaanite, Judaic, Israelite, Phoenician, Philistine, Samaritan, Nabatean, Idumaic, and other groups, many of whom have never even been mentioned in the history of the region's music. Closer examination and analysis of archaeological evidence raised questions that had never presented themselves before. Why, for example, do all archaeological sources suddenly disappear for considerable periods, or for musical instruments that written sources and convention suggest were quite widespread and were even considered indispensable?

This book is a revised, updated, and enlarged version of my German book *Die Musikkultur Altisraels/Palästinas: Studien zu archäologischen, schriftlichen und vergleichenden Quellen* (Freiburg, Switzerland/Göttingen: University Press/Vandenhoeck & Ruprecht, 1999). Since the German book was completed, five years have passed. No radical changes in the state of research of ancient Israel's/Palestine's musical culture have occurred, no new musical activities or new musical instruments have been discovered, and no new evaluations of the sociomusical landscape have enriched our knowledge. Some new archaeological finds have added to the information on the music of one or another local community or ethnic group without, however, changing the general picture of ancient Israel's/Palestine's musical culture. Certain interpretations and concepts discussed earlier received reaffirmation during the past year. The serious doubts expressed in my study in regard to the biblical descriptions of music, especially musical liturgy, until now considered a *factum notorium* by musicological writing, were strengthened by general studies in the history, archaeology, and anthropology of ancient Israel/Palestine (see the latest studies by William G. Dever, Baruch Halpern, Israel Finkelstein, and others). I see this, however, without being carried away by postmodernist and deconstructionist nihilism.

I am grateful to the always understanding translator from German to English, Mr. Douglas W. Stott, to Eerdmans managing editor Charles Van Hof, and especially to general editor David Noel Freedman and associate editor Astrid B. Beck, who encouraged and supported the publication of this study on music in the biblical-historical series The Bible in Its World.

I would again like to take this opportunity to thank everyone who has contributed to this work, each in his or her own way, with counsel or encouragement, bibliographical suggestions, or photographic materials.

PREFACE

Above all, I would like to thank the archaeologists Prof. Yaakov Meshorer, Prof. Amihai Mazar, Prof. Jan-Baptist Humbert, Prof. Asher Ovadia, Prof. Amos Kloner, Prof. Eric Meyers, Prof. Seymor Gitin, Prof. Itzhag Beit-Arieh, Prof. Ephraim Stern, Dr. Varda Sussmann, Dr. Magen Broshi, Dr. Itzhaq Magen, and Dr. Ze'ev Weiss. I am grateful to Prof. Dr. Othmar Keel for reading my manuscript and offering valuable comments. Staff members of the Israel Antiquities Authority have been consistently helpful, including Dr. Ruth Peled, Dr. Roni Reich, Dr. Baruch Brendel, and Mrs. Hava Katz. I would also like to thank the staff members of the Israel Museum in Jerusalem, the Haifa Museum of Art, the Eretz-Israel Museum in Tel-Aviv, the Oriental Institute of the University of Chicago, the Museum of the University of Pennsylvania, and the British Museum.

It is unfortunately impossible to mention all the cordial and helpful staff members of various libraries and museums without whose help this study would have been impossible.

Financial help from the Bar-Ilan University (Israel) and the Memorial Foundation for Jewish Culture (USA) made this publication possible.

Finally, this work would not have been completed without the daily, patient support of my wife, Aviva Breitbord-Braun, who contributed to this study through critical reading of the manuscript and the execution of the drawings and tables.

JOACHIM BRAUN
Jerusalem 2001

Illustrations

If not otherwise indicated, all drawings listed below are by A. Breitbord-Braun.

CHAPTER II

ILLUSTRATIONS

CHAPTER III

CHAPTER IV

CHAPTER V

Abbreviations

Ancient Works

Church Fathers, Classical, etc.

Ant.	Josephus, *Antiquities of the Jews*
B.J.	Josephus, *Bellum Judaicum (Jewish War)*
Hist.	Tacitus, *Histories*
Paed.	Clement of Alexandria, *Paedagogus*
Vit. Cont.	Philo, *De Vita Contemplativa*

Dead Sea Scrolls

1QH	Thanksgiving Hymns
1QM	War Scroll
1QS	Manual of Discipline
11QPsAp[a] 151	Psalm 151

Rabbinic Writings

'Arak.	*'Arakin*
b.	Babylonian Talmud

Abbreviations

Ber.	*Berakot*
Bik.	*Bikkurim*
Ketub.	*Ketubot*
m.	Mishnah
Qidd.	*Qiddushin*
Roš. Haš.	*Rosh Hashanah*
Šeqal.	*Sheqalim*
Sukk.	*Sukkah*
y.	Jerusalem Talmud

General

Akk.	Akkadian
Arab.	Arabic
Aram.	Aramaic
EE	Expedition Property
Egyp.	Egyptian
Eth.	Ethiopic
h.	height
JB	Jerusalem Bible
l.	length
NJB	New Jerusalem Bible
NRSV	New Revised Standard Version
RSV	Revised Standard Version
Sum.	Sumerian
Syr.	Syriac
Ugar.	Ugaritic
[[ ]]	Unattested or conjectural reading

Institutions, Publications

AAM/AM	Amman Archaeological Museum
AASOR	*Annual of the American Schools of Oriental Research*
ABSA	*Annual of the British School at Athens*
ADAJ	*Annual of the Department of Antiquities of Jordan*
AI	Archaeological Institute

ABBREVIATIONS

AJA	*American Journal of Archaeology*
AM	*Archaeologia Musicalis*
ANRW	*Aufstieg und Niedergang der römischen Welt*
ANS	American Numismatic Society
BA	*Biblical Archaeologist*
BAR	*Biblical Archaeology Review*
BASOR	*Bulletin of the American Schools of Oriental Research*
BCH	*Bulletin de Correspondance Hellenique*
BIF	Biblical Institute, Freiburg/Switzerland
BM	British Museum
BR	*Biblical Research*
CANE	*Civilizations of the Ancient Near East*
CM	*Current Musicology*
EB	Ecole Biblique, Jerusalem
EIM	Eretz Israel Museum, Tel Aviv
HAM/HMAA	Haifa Museum of Ancient Art
HMME	Haifa Museum of Music and Ethnology
HMMAL	Haifa Music Museum and AMLI Library
HSM	Harvard Semitic Museum
HUCA	*Hebrew Union College Annual*
HUHM	Haifa University Reuben Hecht Museum
HU/HUIA	Hebrew University Institute of Archaeology, Jerusalem
IAA	Israel Antiquities Authority
IEJ	*Israel Exploration Journal*
ILN	*Illustrated London News*
IMJ	Israel Museum Jerusalem/*Israel Museum Journal*
IMN	*Israel Museum News*
INJ	*Israel Numismatic Journal*
ISBE	*Insternational Standard Bible Encyclopedia*
JAMS	*Journal of the American Musicological Society*
JAOS	*Journal of the American Oriental Society*
JARCE	*Journal of the American Research Centre in Egypt*
JBL	*Journal of Biblical Literature*
JDAI	*Jahrbuch des Deutschen Archäologischen Instituts*
JNES	*Journal of Near Eastern Studies*
JPOS	*Journal of the Palestine Oriental Society*
JRAI	*Journal of the Royal Anthropological Institute*
JRAS	*Journal of the Royal Asiatic Society*

Abbreviations

LA	*Liber Annuus*
ML	*Music and Letters*
NGD	*New Grove Dictionary of Music and Musicians*
OBO	*Orbis Biblicus et Orientalis*
OI	Chicago University Oriental Institute
PC	Private Collection
PEFQ	*Palestine Exploration Fund Quarterly*
PEQ	*Palestine Exploration Quarterly*
PL	*Patrologiae Latina cursus completus, seria latina*
PRMA	*Proceedings of the Royal Musical Association*
PS	Patrologia Syriaca
PU	Provenance Unknown
QDAP	*Quarterly of the Department of Antiquities in Palestine*
RA	*Revue Archéologique*
RlA	*Reallexikon der Assyriologie*
SBF	*Studia Biblicum Franciscanum*
TA/TAUIA	Tel Aviv University Institute of Archaeology
TDOT	*Theological Dictionary of the Old Testament*
VT	*Vetus Testamentus*
ZA	*Zeitschrift für Assyriologie und Vorderasiatische Archaologie*
UF	*Ugarit-Forschungen*
ZDMG	*Zeitschrift der Deutschen Morgenlandischen Gesellschaft*
ZDPV	*Zeitschrift des Deutschen Palastina-Vereins*

TABLE 1

Archeological Finds Pertinent to Music from Ancient Israel/Palestine: Typological Statistics

In this table, appearing on the following three pages, the finds are divided into three categories: musical instruments (MI); three-dimensional items (3D), such as statuettes and figurines; and two-dimensional items (2D), such as drawings, engravings, reliefs, mosaics, coins, and the like. The musical images on coins and tessarae are counted by the relevant mint. Items of uncertain provenance, chronology, or organological definition are shown in parentheses.

ABBREVIATIONS USED IN THE TABLE

BE	bells	LI	lithophones
BR	bull-roarers	LU	lutes
BW	bone whistles	LY	lyres
CL	clappers	OR	organs
CF	cross flutes	PP	panpipes
CR	clay vessel rattles	RF	round-frame drums
CT	conch trumpets	SC	scrapers
CY	cymbals	SI	sistrums
DH	double-headed drums	SP	single pipe
DP	double pipes	SH	shofars
FC	forked cymbals	SR	strung rattles
HA	harps	TR	metal trumpets
HD	hourglass drums		

PERIOD		STONE AGE before 3200 BC				BRONZE AGE 3200-1200 BC			
Artifact		MI	3D	2D	Subtotal	MI	3D	2D	Subtotal
IDIOPHONES	BE								
	BR	2			2				
	CL					2			2
	CR					26 (10)			26 (10)
	CY					18 (4)			18 (4)
	FC								
	LI					1			1
	SC					(5)			(5)
	SI					1		(1)	1 (1)
	SR	2			2	1			1
	Subtotal	4			4	49 (19)		(1)	49 (20)
MEMBRANOPHONES	DH					(1)			(1)
	HD		1		1				
	RF							1	1
	Subtotal		1		1	(1)		1	1 (1)
CHORDOPHONES	HA			1	1				
	LU						2	1	3
	LY							3	3
	Subtotal			1	1		2	4	6
AEROPHONES	BW					1 (1)			1 (1)
	CT								
	DP							1	1
	HF								
	OR								
	PP								
	SH								
	SP								
	TR							1	1
	Subtotal					1 (1)		2	3 (1)
	Total	4	1	1	6	50 (21)	2	7 (1)	59 (22)

PERIOD		IRON AGE 1200-586 BC				PERSIAN AGE 586-332 BC			
Artifact		MI	3D	2D	Subtotal	MI	3D	2D	Subtotal
IDIOPHONES	BE	10			10				
	BR	2			2				
	CL								
	CR	51 (12)	1		52 (12)				
	CY	3	1		4				
	FC								
	LI								
	SC	(10)			(10)				
	SI		(1)		(1)		1		1
	SR								
	Subtotal	66 (22)	2 (1)		68 (23)		1		1
MEMBRANOPHONES	DH								
	HD							1	1
	RF		15 (1)	28 (14)	43 (15)				
	Subtotal		15 (1)	28 (14)	43 (15)			1	1
CHORDOPHONES	HA								
	LU								
	LY		2	9 (2)	11 (2)				
	Subtotal		2	9 (2)	11 (2)				
AEROPHONES	BW	8			8	1			1
	CT	3			3	(1)			(1)
	DP		9	1 (1)	10 (1)			1	1
	HF								
	OR								
	PP								
	SH								
	SP								
	TR								
	Subtotal	11	9	1 (1)	21 (1)	1 (1)		1	2 (1)
	Total	77 (22)	28 (2)	38 (17)	143 (41)	1 (1)	1	2	4 (1)

PERIOD		HELLENISTIC-ROMAN AGE 332 BC–324 CE				
Artifact		MI	3D	2D	Subtotal	Total
IDIOPHONES	BE	65		1	66	76
	BR					4
	CL					2
	CR					78 (22)
	CY	25 (3)		1 (3)	26 (6)	48 (10)
	FC			7	7	7
	LI					1
	SC					(15)
	SI	1 (1)	1		2 (1)	4 (3)
	SR			(2)	(2)	3 (2)
	Subtotal	91 (4)	1	9 (5)	101 (9)	223 (52)
MEMBRANOPHONES	DH					(1)
	HD			(2)	(2)	2 (2)
	RF					44 (15)
	Subtotal			(2)	(2)	46 (18)
CHORDOPHONES	HA		1 (1)	2	3 (1)	4 (1)
	LU		1 (1)		1 (1)	4 (1)
	LY	(3)		12 (7)	12 (10)	26 (12)
	Subtotal	(3)	2 (2)	14 (7)	16 (12)	34 (14)
AEROPHONES	BW	1	(2)		1 (2)	10 (3)
	CT	5 (3)		1	6 (3)	9 (4)
	DP		1	13 (2)	14 (2)	26 (3)
	HF			3	3	3
	OR			5	5	5
	PP		2	5 (7)	7 (7)	7 (7)
	SH			16 (12)	16 (12)	16 (12)
	SP	3 (4)	1 (1)	3 (1)	7 (6)	7 (6)
	TR			1	1	1
	Subtotal	9 (7)	4 (3)	47 (22)	60 (32)	86 (35)
	Total	100 (14)	7 (5)	70 (36)	177 (55)	389 (119)

TABLE 2

Lyre Contours from
Israel/Palestine Artifacts

Unless otherwise indicated, numbers in parentheses refer to illustrations in this book; the Roman numeral indicates the chapter, and the number following the period indicates the illustration within that chapter. DA signifies doubtful authenticity.

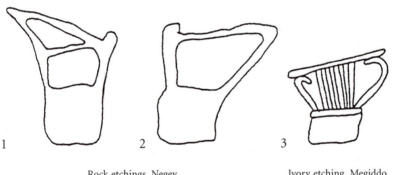

Rock etchings, Negev,
early 2nd millennium B.C. (III.1)

Ivory etching, Megiddo,
13th/12th cent. B.C. (III.16)

Table 2

4

5

6

Jar drawing, Megiddo,
11th cent. B.C. (IV.21)

Clay stand, Ashdod,
10th cent. B.C. (IV.32)

Seal, Ashdod,
10th-8th cent. B.C. (IV.25)

7

8

9

Terra-cotta figurine, Ashdod,
8th cent. B.C. (IV.33)

Seal, Tell Batash,
10th cent. B.C. (IV.24)

Jar drawing, Kuntillet ʿAjrud,
8th cent. B.C. (IV.23)

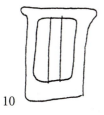
10

11

12

Seal, PU,
10th-8th cent. B.C. (IV.26)

Seal, Nebo,
10th-8th cent. B.C. (IV.27)

Seal, PU,
10th-8th cent. B.C. (IV.28)

TABLE 2

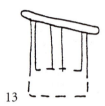

13

Seal, Tell Keisan,
9th-7th cent. B.C. (IV.29)

14

Seal (DA), PU, 9th-7th cent.
B.C. (see Braun 1999, IV/3-10)

15

Seal, PU, 9th-7th cent.
B.C. (IV.30)

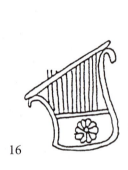

16

Seal (DA), PU, 9th-7th cent.
B.C. (see Braun 1999, IV/3-11)

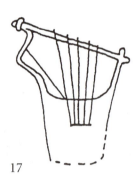

17

Samaritan coin, PU,
4th cent. B.C. (V.46)

18

19

Terra-cotta plaque, Petra
2nd-1st cent. B.C. (V.16)

20

Basalt etching, Harra Desert,
1st cent. B.C. (V.18)

xxxiv

Table 2

21

22

23

Acco coins, PU,
125-110 B.C. (V.56)

Tessarae, Caesarea,
2nd-3rd cent. (V.59)

24

25

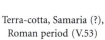

26

Terra-cotta, Samaria (?),
Roman period (V.53)

Bar-Kokhba coins,
2nd cent. (V.57)

27

28

Intaglios, PU,
1st cent. (V.60c, d)

TABLE 2

29

31

Gems, PU,
2nd-3rd cent. (V.61a, b)

Mosaic, Gaza,
3rd-4th cent. B.C. (V.41)

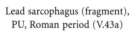

32

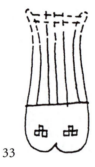

33

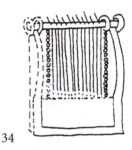

34

Lead sarcophagus (fragment),
PU, Roman period (V.43a)

Mosaic, Sepphoris
synagogue, 5th cent.
(Weiss Netzer 1996, 27)

Mosaic, Gaza,
6th cent. (V.45)

CHAPTER I

INTRODUCTION

O f all pre-Christian cultures, none has a music history as burdened by one-sided and subjective perspectives and prejudices as that of ancient Israel/Palestine. Research into other high cultures of the ancient world has never been as plagued by a neglect of scientific principles or by unscientific arguments as is the case with this region. Indeed, until the mid-twentieth century, the entire assessment of the music of ancient Israel/Palestine was based on a single source, namely, the Bible; although this source was clearly of a mythological nature, its theological significance elevated it to the status of a historical document. This one-sided focus prompted an attitude of fetishism with regard to what the Bible actually recounts about instruments, musical events, and music in the larger sense, and led scholars to disregard completely all cultural entities and tendencies within ancient Israel/Palestine besides the specifically Israelite.

Not surprisingly, then, a genuinely new history of music in this region is emerging only now, at the turn of the third millennium. This new assessment has been made possible by an examination of the only sources capable of ensuring an objective discussion based on factual material, namely, archaeological and iconographic evidence from ancient Israel/Palestine itself.

The history of music in ancient Israel/Palestine transcends the boundaries of purely musical interest. Musical findings illuminate for the historian certain social processes that otherwise cannot be perceived in quite

1

the same way, or allow the historian to rectify misunderstandings that neither the natural nor the social sciences can really address.

Scholars today generally accept that music is an expression of certain socially shaped aspects of human behavior. Because the ancient civilizations of the Mediterranean always viewed music this way themselves, the history of ancient music invariably reveals much about these civilizations that we might otherwise entirely miss.

Interest in the history of music in ancient Israel, often misidentified as "music in the Bible," began during the period immediately following the conclusion of the Greek version of the Old Testament (the Septuagint; third/second century B.C.). Because for centuries musicologists viewed the Bible as the only primary source, it became by default the only material actually studied; even though the Septuagint itself also qualified as such a source alongside the Hebrew version, in reality it represented the first interpretation of the original biblical texts. Even at that early stage, though, different translators interpreted the text differently and were otherwise often insecure about the various terms; the confusing result was that they translated the names of musical instruments quite inconsistently. This insecurity becomes even more pronounced in another pre-Latin translation, namely, the Syrian Peshitta. By contrast, and despite many deviations, the Latin Vulgate is much more consistent in this regard, though its consistency probably derives more from the disciplined system of translation itself than from a more accurate understanding of the material.

Although Roman authors do indeed add certain secondary details, their discussions do not contribute much to clarifying hard facts. Flavius Josephus, Philo of Alexandria, Plutarch, and Tacitus function as more or less reliable eyewitnesses who provide various tangential comments concerning Jewish music during the Roman period.

The tractates of the Mishnah and Talmud (second to sixth centuries) function as both sources and interpretative efforts, the former primarily for contemporary circumstances, the latter on the basis of a lengthy oral tradition. Although both works sometimes provide excellent descriptions of musical reality, some of their traditions cannot be taken seriously. Care must be taken, for example, when considering the tradition of the Jerusalemite *magrēpah*, an instrument allegedly capable of producing one thousand tones (*b. Sukk.* 5:6), whose sound could be heard as far away as Jericho (*m. Tamid* 3:8).

Because the influence of Augustinian thought and its permutations

2

was so pervasive, the *scientia musicae* of the Middle Ages tended to view the music of ancient Israel from a primarily allegorical perspective, ignoring the *musica practica* of the Bible and focusing instead on the spiritual symbolism of the biblical musical instruments themselves. Focus on the instruments produced the equivalent of an inventory of ancient Israelite/ Palestinian instruments, and focus on the symbolism became the central area of research. Neither, however, contributed anything of substance to genuine research into the music of ancient Israel; the discussion centered mainly on daily circumstances involving admissible or forbidden instrumental performance.

The earliest historiographical writings on the music of ancient Israel appeared almost simultaneously in the circles of the Jewish-Italian Enlightenment and the German Reformation. The first of these is [[*shiltey hagiborim*]] (Heb. *Shield of the Heroes* [Mantua, 1612]) by Avraham Portaleone (1547-1612), based on biblical and Talmudic texts. Although Portaleone does indeed try to follow the biblical texts in reconstructing a history of temple music, his tendency mirrors that already discernible in the Septuagint and even in the Hebrew Bible itself. Like many scholars before and after him, he tries to accommodate the biblical information anachronistically to his own musical present, in this case the late sixteenth century, interpreting most of the instruments as replicates or at least analogues of instruments of his day (e.g., the *minnîm* as the clavichord, the *ʿûgāḇ* as the *viola da gamba*). Nonetheless, this work was cited as late as the nineteenth century.

Michael Praetorius's (1569?-1621) encyclopedic opus, *Syntagma musicum* (vols. I and II [Wittenberg, 1614]), offers the best description of biblical musical instruments of its day but does so independently of Portaleone. Divine grace, Praetorius asserts, has insured the continuity between Jewish and Christian music. Unfortunately, he then elevates the exclusive use of these textual sources into an explicit principle, asserting that "in Palestine, Asia Minor, and Greece, no more vestiges of older instruments exist" (vol. II, fol. 4), an unsupported assertion that was maintained as late as the *New Oxford History of Music*. Since Praetorius, virtually every work on the history of music has included a discussion of ancient Israelite or Jewish music based on biblical texts, and only in isolated instances have authors drawn on archaeological material as well in attempting to illuminate ancient Israelite music (the first being Carl Engel, then also Curt Sachs, Ovid R. Sellers, and especially Bathia Bayer).

3

1. Geographical, Chronological, and Cultural Parameters

Given the specific historical, geographical, and cultural parameters of the discussion, I have chosen the expression "ancient Israel/Palestine" in identifying the book's content.

Geographically this study focuses on the present-day state of Israel and on a small area in Jordan. In isolated instances, I also examine archaeological evidence from southern Syria and Lebanon and incorporate artifacts from the Near East at large as comparative material.

Chronologically, the earliest musically relevant archaeological evidence of interest in this context dates to the tenth millennium B.C., and the latest extends down to the early Byzantine period (ca. fourth/fifth centuries). The internal division of this overall period derives from the traditional archaeological designations for epochs (Stone Age, Chalcolithicum, etc.). Historical cultural periods in antiquity, however, cannot be assigned to specific years. In reality, they constituted lengthy processes of change. In the history of music, this situation applies particularly to changes in style and standards, which can appear later or even earlier than concomitant socio-political changes, functioning either as stragglers or as premonitory signs of such changes. Melodies, modes, and musical instruments themselves can hang on tenaciously for centuries and outlive even profound sociohistorical changes. On the other hand, they might change quite independently of social processes, or a particular type of performance might undergo an unexpected stylistic change; unfortunately such changes are often difficult to identify with historical precision.

The geography and the historical development of the cultural sphere of inhabitants of ancient Israel/Palestine resulted in a peculiar chronological heterogeneity, Professor Helga Weippert (1988) has described as "non-simultaneity within simultaneity." Because of the tripartite division of the local population into "city dwellers, village dwellers, and nomadic shepherds," the signs of a new epoch occasionally are already manifesting themselves in one group while the earlier culture continues in another, separate group. This phenomenon is especially striking in the musical culture. In one and the same historical period, the most primitive noise devices can appear alongside sophisticated string instruments, as when primitive rattles were used alongside lyres during the Iron Age. On the other hand, some musical instruments outlive historical periods without undergoing even the slightest alteration in form or material. That is, the

4

material or physical musical culture might remain quite unaltered, with genuine changes apparently affecting only the mode of performance or presentation of the music (e.g., cymbals).

The present study is the first to incorporate ethnicity as part of local music history, with several different sections discussing the Philistine, Phoenician, Nabatean-Safaitic, Idumaic, and Samaritan musical cultures. Insufficient archaeological material unfortunately prevented more than a peripheral mention of Edomite, Moabite, Ammonite, and Amorite music.

The musical culture of ancient Israel/Palestine was quite clearly influenced by both ethnic and religious factors. If we view it primarily as culture, and only secondarily also as music in the strict or more exclusive sense, we find that it is both complex in its homogeneity and uniform in its heterogeneity, and that perhaps the most revealing way to examine it is as a rich and diverse mosaic dominated by syncretistic tendencies. Just as the element of "non-simultaneity within simultaneity" characterizes the development of ancient Israel/Palestine in general, so also does the element of "heterogeneity within homogeneity" and vice versa characterize the development of music in ancient Israel/Palestine.

The extraordinarily small dimensions of this country may well have influenced this process of cultural and musical syncretism; such syncretism was doubtless also encouraged by the peculiar local cultural dynamic — also a function of geography — of the ongoing amalgamation of the local peoples. Only such a constellation of geographical and cultural factors can explain how such homogenous musical styles and types of musical instrument could have developed from the various local but otherwise extremely heterogeneous musical phenomena. It is obvious now that ancient Israel/Palestine generated an autochthonous local musical culture which in many aspects was congenial to the great neighboring musical cultures of Egypt and Mesopotamia/Babylon.

2. Sources

The most reliable primary source for information about the musical culture of ancient Israel/Palestine is doubtless the archaeological-iconographic evidence. Unlike so many previous musicological studies, which largely neglected this evidence or had insufficient access to it, the present study incorporates as many of these findings as possible in trying to clarify our understanding of the technical, socioanthropological, and symbolic aspects of this lost musical culture. Indeed, thanks to archaeology, occasionally even the timbre of certain instruments has been preserved although the actual form of the music itself has disappeared forever.

Given the shortcomings of previous studies, modern research must redirect its attention to the local Canaanite-Israelite-Palestinian musical culture and examine above all the local archaeological-iconographic evidence. Recent studies confirm this presupposition insofar as they now view the most important regional changes in the thirteenth through eleventh centuries B.C. as "long-term socio-economic transformation followed by the collapse of the city-state system" (McGovern, 1987, 270), and only in part as the result of conquest or infiltration. Again, however, we keep discovering that the musical culture must be viewed largely as a local development. Scholars have long recognized the polytheistic nature of the first half of the first pre-Christian millennium in ancient Israel/Palestine. It now seems this polytheism also generated a polystylistic musical culture. This very musical culture, however, can be examined only on the basis of local archaeological evidence.

Puzzled by the apparent absence of iconographic evidence, scholars even up to the present have explained this phenomenon by citing the biblical injunction against images, noting its enduring and clearly deleterious effect on iconographic research into the musical culture of ancient Israel/Palestine. More recent studies, however, after considering both the archaeological-iconographic evidence on the one hand, and Old Testament historiography on the other, have found that neither the ancient Israelite culture as such nor ancient Israelite religion in particular was always and everywhere iconoclastic. The intensity of artistic activity discernible in Israelite/Judaic history is a function both of the internal social and cultural processes and of integration and acculturation with neighboring cultures. Archaeological-iconographic evidence is thus indeed available, and the question has now become just how one is to assess and classify it typologically against the sociocultural background of the region (see Table 1, p. xxviii). At the same time, however, great care must be exercised when selecting these archaeological-iconographic sources, and written sources should be juxtaposed only with historical-geographically relevant archaeological evidence.

The Old Testament remains the most important, albeit most disputed written source for the region of ancient Israel/Palestine. Interpreting that

6

written source, of course, is the task of biblical exegesis. Hence any musicological study that wants to draw from these texts in explaining or examining the musical culture of this region during the period in question here must naturally also take its cues from the current status of biblical criticism. Moreover, the only authentic source in this sense is the biblical text in its original language, namely, Hebrew. Quite apart from modern translations into English, German, French, and so on, even the Septuagint, the Peshitta, and the Vulgate are, as suggested earlier, of questionable value. For example, the Septuagint translates the terms *kinnôr* and *'ûgāb* in Gen. 4:21 as *psaltérion* and *kithára* while the Peshitta translates them as *kinorā'* and *zᵉmārā'*, and the Vulgate as *cithara* and *organo*. Even in one and the same language, a single instrument can have several different renderings. The Septuagint renders the term *kinnôr* as *kithára*, *kinýra*, *psaltérion*, and *órganon*, the term *'ûgāb* as *psalmós*, *kithára*, and *órganon*. Information offered by biblical texts concerning instrument manufacture is sparse, with only three passages actually mentioning the material out of which instruments are made (Nu. 10:2; 1 K. 10:12; 1 Ch. 15:19). By contrast, the "setting in life" of music can be identified fairly precisely.

Biblical texts in the strict sense are by no means the only sources of information in this regard. Scholars can also consider, again while exercising the requisite caution, written auxiliary sources such as the canonical postbiblical writings (Mishnah, Jerusalem or Babylonian Talmud), the apocrypha, writings of the church fathers, and rabbinic *responsa;* the latter are actually collections of questions posed by the congregation with answers given by the rabbis concerning Jewish beliefs, and date primarily from the eighth to the fourteenth centuries. Nor do even these sources exhaust the material available. Indeed, comparative studies are indispensable for any musicological assessment of ancient Israel/Palestine and can be carried out on a number of fruitful levels, including textual, etymological, archaeological-iconographic, and ethnological.

In this capacity, Langdon (1921) examined Sumerian sources early in the twentieth century, and recent scholarship has confirmed their significance (Foxvog/Kilmer, 1980). Similarly, Ugaritic research has provided complementary evidence for the inventory of instruments in the form of instrument names dating back as early as the fourteenth through thirteenth centuries b.c. (*mzltm*, cymbals; *tp*, drum; *knr*, lyre). In some cases biblical musical terminology reaches back to the third millennium b.c. (for example, the term *kinnôr; see pp. 16-19). The significance of such comparative etymological observations becomes obvious when their findings prove to be not only useful but sometimes even crucial, as in the case of the terms *kinnarātim* and *ʿûgāb*.

Nor should one ignore archaeological material from neighboring regions. Especially if the Israelite/Palestinian provenance of the iconographic material can be confirmed, such material can be extremely valuable; this is definitely the case with the Semitic lyre player from the Beni-Hasan tomb (chap. III/1), the captured Jewish lyre players from Lachish (chap. IV/3A), and the trumpets depicted on the Arch of Titus (chap. V/2). Again, though, extreme care should be exercised. For example, the recent comparison of royal lyres from Ur with the *kinnôr* of the Bible in the first volume of the *Neues Handbuch der Musikwissenschaft* is highly questionable since it ignores the historical and sociopolitical circumstances of the two countries. Nonetheless, within those particular geographical areas of concern to the study of instruments in ancient Israel/Palestine, comparative ethnomusicology can definitely offer additional insights; one example in this context is the parallel suggested between the double pipe illustrated on a stone inscription from Nabataea and the modern *arghul*.

Anne Caubet's study (1994) is one of the most successful recent studies employing comparative or interdisciplinary methodology in this field. Her examination of archaeological evidence from Ugarit convinced her that the emergent overall picture does indeed permit us to identify those particular elements that are constitutive for the musical universe of the Levant at the end of the second millennium, a universe that differentiated itself discernibly from those of the more familiar countries of the surrounding world such as Egypt, Mesopotamia, and pre-Hellenic Greece. In my own recent studies, I have tried to implement a similar method, one incorporating the entire spectrum of source material into my historico-musicological analysis (see the bibliography).

3. Musical Instruments in the Bible

Meaning

Unfortunately, from the beginning down to our own period, the only documentary aids available for interpreting biblical references to music were the names of the musical instruments found in the Bible itself, that is, the common technical expressions used there; as a result, both exegetical and musicological studies have always focused on these expressions. Roman authors were among the first to try to explain and explicate the meaning, significance, authenticity, and symbolism of the biblical names of musical instruments, though Mishnaic and Talmudic tractates as well as the church fathers also engaged in such early discussions. The original source itself, however, namely, the Hebrew text, is unfortunately multilayered by nature, and because its contextual relationships constantly shift, the entire question of its interpretation in this regard is extremely difficult and controversial. Even the Hebrew terms are ambiguous. Although the text may well refer to instruments belonging chronologically to the events in question, it is also possible that it refers instead to instruments used during the time of the narrator, that is, to instruments familiar during the period of the emerging oral tradition; or it may refer to local instruments contemporaneous with the time at which the tradition was finally committed to writing. The thorny and sometimes exasperating question then becomes whether the meaning of a particular instrument's name changes independently of the biblical text that mentions it and how one might discern that change. Similarly, must instruments in the relevant chronological and geographical context necessarily be supported by archaeological evidence in order to be viewed as historically factual? Clearly, questions such as these complicate the historian's task.

A semantic interpretation of biblical musical instruments can be carried out at various levels, the theoretical framework being supplied by anthropological, etymological-linguistic, semiotic, archaeological, iconographic, and organological (organology: the science of musical instruments) models that have been modified to accommodate the specific needs of musicological studies.

The first stage of any semantic interpretation is an organological-historical examination of the material. This includes a basic, presemantic and preiconographic identification of the original meaning of the names of the instruments themselves (Panofsky, 1955), a task that in many cases is still incomplete insofar as the names of many biblical musical instruments have not yet been unambiguously deciphered (e.g., *ʿûgāḇ*) and others are still disputed (e.g., *nēḇel*). All subsequent interpretations, however, depend on precisely this determination of meaning or definition. Similarly, the determination and clarification of the names of instruments attested by archaeological evidence and of those illustrated or otherwise depicted on artifacts are of equal significance. Already at this early stage, the historian must juxtapose and take stock of the written, archaeological-iconographic, and comparative sources that are now accessible for further study (e.g., an early assessment of this sort reveals that the historian has no real archaeological evidence of harps for any subsequent interpretation of the *nēḇel*).

The next level is that of textual-iconographic analysis in the narrower sense. The task here is to clarify the topos, the context of the individual motifs, and the historical, mythological, or theological themes at work in the text (e.g., the context surrounding David's healing of Saul, 1 S. 16:23). Here, however, the investigation is already easing into the third stage, namely, that of determining or clarifying the symbolism of musical instruments. The Old Testament makes it quite clear that music, personified by singing or the playing of instruments *(zmr)*, is synonymous with praise of God *(hll)*: "I will praise *(hll)* the Lord as long as I live; I will sing and play *(zmr)* to my God all my life long" (Ps. 146:2). In its own turn, this symbolic significance influences the theological significance of instrumental music or even of the instruments themselves. Faith, and even theophany, takes many forms; music is one of those forms that through performance and its accompanying joy and beauty enters dimensions no faith can do without (Casetti, 1977).

The final, highest level of semantic interpretation discloses the "intrinsic meaning" of the text or of the work of art or musical instrument, that is, "those underlying principles which reveal the basic attitude of a nation, a period, a class, a religious or philosophical persuasion" (Panofsky, 1955). Although the symbolism of musical instruments ultimately goes back to the early historical period and to the high cultures of antiquity, it is also anchored in the texts of the Old Testament itself. Passages do occur, albeit not in numbers as great as the historian might wish, that clearly point in this direction: "Therefore my heart moans for Moab like a *ḥālîl*. . ." (Jer. 48:36). Symbolism and allegory play a considerable role in the Hellenistic-Jewish philosophy of Philo of Alexandria as well, which was, significantly enough, deeply bound to the religion; the seven-stringed lyre is the earthly reflection of the celestial harmony, and the soul is compared to a well-tuned lyre (*De Opificione Mundi* 42/126). These considerations of the symbolic significance of instruments did ultimately have a profound effect on later views, since from the time of the early church writers "a specific symbolism of musical instruments developed in the sense of a closed system that became a fixed constituent part of Christian exegesis" (Giesel, 1978); as such, the system laid a foundation affecting the understanding of this symbolism all the way to the present.

Classification

We can no longer determine whether any internal, culturally specific ("culture-emerging/natural," cf. Kartomi, 1990) classification of biblical musical instruments ever existed, though the oral tradition fixed in the written text of the Old Testament suggests as much. Closer examination does in any case reveal a biblically specific symbolism of musical instruments or sociomusical semantic classification that may or may not reflect such a fixed system. Biblical writers view the *šôpār*, for example, as the only double musical symbol "of the human-earthly as well as of the spiritual-transcendental" (Gerson-Kiwi, 1980), and as such as the musical instrument *par excellence*. Furthermore, Chronicles seems to be grouping the musical instruments of the priests (*ḥᵃṣōṣᵉrâ*) and of the Levitical clans or musical guilds *(kinnôr, nēḇel, mᵉṣiltayim)* together in a way that might reflect such a system (1 Ch. 15; 16; 25; 2 Ch. 5; 7).

This manner of classifying instruments according to a sociomusical principle has been incorporated into the work of various scholars. E. Gerson-Kiwi (1957) focuses on the two musical instruments in Genesis (Gen. 4:21) as symbolizing the legend of how music arose and then identifies three groups of biblical musical instruments in the larger sense: (a) sacerdotal instruments *(šôpār, ḥᵃṣōṣᵉrâ)*, (b) Levitical instruments *(kinnôr, nēḇel)*, and (c) lay instruments *('ûḡāḇ, ḥālîl, 'abbîḇ, [[magrefah]])*. H. Avenary (1958) offers a variation of this classification, subdividing them thus: (a) magical instruments of the nomadic period *(šôpār, ḥᵃṣōṣᵉrâ, tōp, mᵉṣiltayim)*, (b) artistic instruments of the city cultures during the monarchy *(kinnôr, nēḇel, ḥālîl)*, and (c) temple instruments *(šôpār, ḥᵃṣōṣᵉrâ, ḥālîl, kinnôr, nēḇel, mᵉṣiltayim)*. These classifications unfortunately cannot be sustained with systematic rigor insofar as overlappings and doublings do indeed occur, though both Avenary and Gerson-Kiwi silently pass over such inconsistencies, prompted probably not least by the Old Testament itself (*kinnôr*, for example, appears in 1 Ch. 25:1 and 3 as a Levitical and temple instrument, and in Gen. 31:27 as a secular instrument of joy). By contrast, C. Sachs prefers a quasi-historical classification based on the succession of instrument names mentioned in the Old Testament (Sachs, 1940).

Most scholarship until now has been based on an observer-imposed/artificial schema (Kartomi, 1990) reflecting the thinking of the time rather than the thinking intrinsic to the Old Testament itself. Portaleone's work was probably the first of this type, following Renaissance models in classifying its thirty-six musical instruments and musical terminology in general into two groups: (a) those suitable for artistic music, and (b) those unsuitable for such music because of their inferior quality or harsh, crude sounds. Praetorius (1614/15) seems to emphasize musical instruments of the psalms (*nᵉĝînôṯ, ʿal-māḥᵃlaṯ, gitît, ʿûĝāḇ*), stringed instruments and cymbals, tympani, and a few other groups. In the seventeenth century, the usual division was "de instrumentis poliochordis, de pulsatilibus" and "de instrumentis pneumaticis" (Kircher, 1650), and since Pfeiffer (1779) and Forkel (1788), the tripartite division into strings, wind, and percussion instruments continued into the twentieth century. Modern musicology accetps the Hornbostel/Sachs (1914) system, which divides the musical instruments according to the sound: idiophones, membranophones, chordophones, and aerophones. Slight variations toward a "culture-emerging" system have appeared in recent scholarship (e.g., Foxvog/Kilmer, 1980), dividing wind instruments into two groups: horns/trumpets and woodwinds.

4. The Instruments

ʿᵃṣê ḇᵉrôšîm

This expression occurs only in 2 S. 6:5 and represents the plural form of *ʿēṣ ḇᵉrôš,* "cypress tree, wood." Actually, the entire expression reads *ḇᵉkōl ʿᵃṣê ḇᵉrôšîm,* "with all kinds of cypress wood." Oddly, the parallel passage 1 Ch. 13:8 replaces the term with *ḇᵉkol-ʿōz ûḇšîrîm,* "with all their might and with songs." The Septuagint clearly identifies it as one of the six musical instruments providing orgiastic music for David and the people as they transport the ark back to Jerusalem (four of the instruments are idiophones and membranophones). Many modern translations prefer 1 Ch. 13:8, probably because it seems to play down the notion of secular music in the scene and to replace it with that of more organized cultic performance, and although some contemporary scholars correctly identify these instruments as clappers made of cyprus (Avenary, 1958; Sendrey, 1969b), most simply ignore the reference (Kolari, 1947; Gerson-Kiwi, 1957; Werner, 1980). Archaeological finds include Hathor-clappers made of bone dating to the late Bronze Age in Canaan. During the monarchy (twelfth-eighth centuries B.C.), cypresses were still plentiful in Israel, and the people probably played clappers made of this wood during the great cultic and paracultic festivals.

ḥālîl

This term occurs in 1 S. 10:5; 1 K. 1:40; Isa. 5:12; 30:29; Jer. 48:36 (bis).

The root *ḥll*, "to hollow out, pierce," is a common and widespread Semitic root, occurring as Eth. *ḥel(l)at*, "hollow stick"; Akk. *ḥālilu*, "a pipe"; and Arab. *ḥalla*, "to pierce, wound." It can also refer to something profane or reprehensible (Koehler/Baumgartner, 1967), and in the Old Testament usually means "to profane, desecrate" (*TDOT* IV, 410f., 417). In the Old Testament, it appears in connection with the joyous anointing of the king (1 K. 1:40), victorious celebration (Isa. 30:29), and prophetic ecstasy (1 S. 10:5), though it could also symbolize lament (Jer. 48:36) and be associated with the excessive revelry of sinners (Isa. 5:12). The Septuagint and Vulgate translate this term fairly consistently as *aulós* (an oboe- or clarinet-type instrument; as "dance," 1 K. 1:40) and *tibia*, while the Peshitta and the Targum stumble about in utter confusion, translating as "drum" or "cymbal" (1 S. 10:5; 1 K. 1:40) or as "stringed instrument" or "wind instrument" (Jer. 30:29). Unfortunately, some modern translations identify the *ḥālîl* incorrectly as a "flute" instead of as a "pipe" (NRSV). As a matter of fact, however, much of what one finds concerning this instrument in the Septuagint and the Vulgate already suggests that it was a kind of "clarinet" or "oboe," with either a single or double reed, a point Talmudic literature seems to corroborate (*b. ʿArak.* 10.1; *m. ʿArak.* 2.3). In general, modern scholarship has come to view the *ḥālîl* as a "clarinet" (Werner, 1980), "double clarinet" (F. Galpin in Stainer, 1914; Bayer, 1968c), "oboe" (Stainer, 1914), and "double oboe" (Sachs, 1940; Marcuse, 1975), though some prefer "flute" (Pfeiffer, 1779; Kolari, 1947), or "double flute" (Keel, 1972). Still others pick up on suggestions made by the Talmud (*y. Sukk.* 55.c) that the *ḥālîl* is actually a collective designation for wind instruments in general (Gerson-Kiwi, 1957; Sendrey, 1969b).

Various materials could be used to make the *ḥālîl*. Talmudic texts suggest that it could be made of bronze or copper as well as of reeds (*m. ʿArak.* 2.3; *m. Kelim* 11.6) or bone (*m. Kelim* 3.6), and general consensus held that the bronze instruments sounded a bit harsher, the bone or reed instruments a bit sweeter. According to the Talmud, overlaying a *ḥālîl* made of reed or bone with bronze caused it to lose that sweetness of tone (*b. ʿArak.* 10.2). Archaeological finds have confirmed these manufacturing methods (see chap. V/4), though the only wind instrument from Israel's Iron Age supported by archaeological evidence is the double pipe (see chap. IV/2).

In general, scholars tend to identify this instrument as a kind of oboe. On the other hand, a great many examples of the aulos have been found dating from the Hellenistic-Roman period, primarily from Jerusalem and Samaria (Sebaste), where they may have been manufactured locally (see chaps. V/4 and V/6).

Talmudic sources offer several bits of information concerning how and when the *ḥālîl* was used. Rather than being a regular cultic instrument, it was played before the altar only twelve days in the year (*y. Sukk.* 55a), and the temple orchestra was to include no fewer than two but no more than twelve of these instruments (*m. 'Arak.* 2.3). This, however, contradicts the Old Testament, where none of the five verses mentioning the *ḥālîl* relate to liturgical music or to music in the temple. By contrast, it was used frequently at paraliturgical or secular occasions such as the sacrifice of the first fruits (*m. Bik.* 3.3-4), during pilgrimages (*m. 'Arak.* 2.3), and at burials (*m. Ketub.* 4.4). Significantly, although the *ḥālîl* was definitely associated with the temple as mentioned above, it was also used in connection with ecstatic or orgiastic activities, a fact attested by sources both archaeological (Dionysian mosaics from ancient Palestine; also Braun, 1994) and written (Sendrey, 1969b; *m. 'Arak.* 2.3). The *ḥālîl* thus emerges as an instrument characterized by a peculiar dualism or symbolism even into the present; on the one hand, it was associated with the sacred activities of the temple, and on the other with the secular music of sinners or with events celebrating joy or lamenting disaster (cf. Avenary, 1971).

ḥªṣōṣᵉrâ

This term occurs thirty-one times in the Old Testament: Nu. 10:2, 8-10; 31:6; 2 K. 11:14(bis); 12:14; Hos. 5:8; Ps. 98:6; Ezra 3:10; Neh. 12:35, 41; 1 Ch. 13:8; 15:24, 28; 16:6, 42; 2 Ch. 5:12(ter), 13; 13:12, 14; 15:14; 20:18; 23:13(bis); 29:26-28.

Of uncertain etymology, the term *ḥªṣōṣᵉrâ* possibly derives from a root meaning "to wail, shout" (Finesinger, 1926; Arab. *ḥṣr*) and may reflect an onomatopoeia. The Septuagint and Vulgate seem quite clear concerning the identity of this instrument, translating it consistently as *sálpinx* and *tuba* respectively. It occurs only three times in preexilic literature (twice in 2 K. 11:14 and Hos. 5:8) as an instrument associated with war, though also with celebration and even festivals (Kolari, 1947); atypically, at least for this period, it was played by the people rather than, for example, by cult officials. Following the exile, however, the *ḥᵃṣōṣᵉrâ* became a cultic and priestly instrument.

Moses — so the Bible tells us — received instructions concerning manufacture and use of the *ḥᵃṣōṣᵉrâ* from God himself (Nu. 10:1-10), and from this point on, the instrument was played only by priests (Nu. 10:8; Neh. 12:35, 41). Its uses were many, and included events associated with the temple (2 K. 12:14), summoning the congregation (Nu. 10:2), festivals (Nu. 10:10), the transport of the ark (1 Ch. 15:25; 2 Ch. 5:12), and the administering of oaths (2 Ch. 15:14). As earlier, it could still be used in time of war (Nu. 10:2, 9; 2 Ch. 13:14; 20:28), though also at ceremonial occasions such as enthronement (2 Ch. 23:13) or the laying of the temple's foundation (Ezra 3:10). Two terms are used to describe the actual sound of the instrument (cf. Nu. 10:1-7). The *tᵉqî'â* was a powerful, sustained sound used when assembling the camp or its leaders. The *tᵉrû'â* was a shorter blast used for breaking camp, attacking the enemy, or in connection with admonishment by God.

The *ḥᵃṣōṣᵉrâ* is the only instrument for which the Old Testament provides fairly detailed information concerning both construction and material. It was definitely a trumpet made of beaten or hammered silver (Nu. 10:2) about a cubit long (40 cm.) with a narrow body and a broad, bell-shaped end (Josephus, *Ant.* iii.12.6).

The two well-known archaeological witnesses for the *ḥᵃṣōṣᵉrâ*, namely, the Arch of Titus in Rome and the Bar Cochba silver denarii, cannot be considered reliable (see chap. V/2). New evidence of the use of the trumpet in the context of an Egyptian settlement in Beth-shean (thirteenth century B.C.) was discovered (see chap. III/3). This commends the thesis that the *ḥᵃṣōṣᵉrâ* was actually borrowed from Egyptian models as attested especially in the bronze and copper trumpets from the tomb of Tutankhamen (1347-1338 B.C.). However, one cannot exclude the possibility of western Greco-Roman or even Philistine-Phoenician provenance (see the Idumaic trumpet mural, chap. V/2). This instrument was used in many different situations extending from daily life to the cult and to war. We are fortunate to have several different sources of information concerning its use, including the Old Testament itself, postbiblical writings (*m. Roš Haš.* 3.3; *m. 'Arak.* 2.5), and especially the apocalyptic War Scroll from Qumran, "The War of the Sons of Light against the Company of the Sons of Darkness," with its "rule for the trumpets of summons and the trumpets of alarm according

15

to all their duties" (1QM 2:15; 3:11; 7:9; 9:9). The War Scroll subdivides the *ḥᵃṣōṣᵉrâ*-signals even further, with every stage of daily life and of holy war being accompanied by six groups of trumpets. Several other details provide additional information about these instruments. For example, they are engraved with various expressions probably alluding to incantations or to their actual functions: "The Called of God"; "The Princes of God"; "The Mighty Deeds of God Shall Crush the Enemy, Putting to Flight All Those Who Hate Righteousness and Bringing Shame on Those Who Hate Him"; references are made to the "trumpet of summons," the "trumpets of ambush," and the "trumpets of pursuit," and so on (1QM 3). A similar degree of precision is provided concerning the actual tones to be sounded at various occasions; such include a "sustained blast," a "soft and sustained signal," a "shrill staccato blast," and a "mighty alarm to direct the battle."

In discussions of the meaning and symbolism of instruments, interpreters unfortunately often confuse the *šôp̄ār* (see chap. V/8) and the *ḥᵃṣōṣᵉrâ*. Given the similar functions and symbolism associated with the two instruments, one can probably say that a certain continuity of tradition does obtain between them. At the same time, the *ḥᵃṣōṣᵉrâ* was clearly a cultic instrument and a symbol of the institutionalized, sacral-secular and autocratic power of the second temple, while the *šôp̄ār* was from time immemorial an instrument associated with the magical and mystical phenomenon of theophany.

kinnôr

This term occurs in Gen. 4:21; 31:27; 1 S. 10:5; 16:16, 23; 2 S. 6:5; 1 K. 10:12; Isa. 5:12; 16:11; 23:16; 24:8; 30:32; Ezk. 26:13; Ps. 33:2; 43:4; 49:5; 57:9; 71:22; 81:3; 92:4; 98:5(bis); 108:3; 137:2; 147:7; 149:3; 150:3; Job 21:12; 30:31; Neh. 12:27; 1 Ch. 13:8; 15:16, 21, 28; 16:5; 25:1, 3, 6; 2 Ch. 5:12, 9, 11; 20:28; 29:25.

The *kinnôr* is of central significance among the instruments mentioned in the Old Testament. The term as a reference to a musical instrument is attested throughout the ancient Near East long before the Old Testament occurrences (probably in the middle of the third millennium B.C.) and represents "a cultural term of unknown origins that transcends geographic and linguistic boundaries" (*TDOT* VII, 199). An eighteenth-century letter from the archives at Mari mentions lyres as $^{gis}kinnarātim$, the plural form of $^{gis}kinnaru$ (Ellermeier, 1970a, *kinnaruḫli,* "lyre player/master"), though the root was also incorporated into the names of deities such as Canaanite, Phoenician, and Cypriot *kinýras,* [[*kinnaras, kuthar,*]] as well as Akkadian and Ugaritic *knr* appearing in [[*kinarum*]]. Finally, the root also appears in toponyms such as *kn-n3-r'-tw* (= *knnrt*) from the great name inventory list of Thutmose III of Karnak (*TDOT* VII, 199), Chinnereth of Josh. 19:36, and the Sea of Chinnereth (= Sea of Galilee, Sea of Gennesaret in Nu. 34:11). Additionally, as a designation for wood (also [[*kunar*]], "lotus wood") the term can be traced back to the 18th/19th Egyptian Dynasty, where *knwrw* as a Semitic loanword clearly refers to a lyre (*TDOT* VII, 198).

From its forty-two Old Testament occurrences, one discovers that the *kinnôr* was used in an unusually wide variety of situations. In the first chronological (though not earliest written) mention in Gen. 4:21, it symbolizes the profession of all who were musicians by lineage, as members of guilds, or as "bards." The *kinnôr* also provided music during secular celebrations (Gen. 31:27; Isa. 24:8), in times of lament or mourning (Job 30:31), of praise, and even at the transport of the ark (2 S. 6:5; 1 Ch. 15:16; Ps. 43:4; 98:5; 149:3; 150:3). Yet it could also be used by prostitutes and the wicked (Isa. 23:16; Job 21:12), in connection with miraculous healing (1 S. 16:16, 23), and with prophetic ecstasies (1 S. 10:5). The Septuagint seems not to have been entirely certain of the correct translation, using the terms *kithára, kinýra, psaltḗrion,* and *órganon.* The Vulgate was a bit more certain, rendering the term as *cithara, lyra, psalterium,* and *organum.* Despite this uncertainty, and despite the traditional association of the *kinnôr* with "David's harp" through the centuries both in written (e.g., Forkel, 1788) and iconographic (e.g., Psalter, twelfth century; NGD 2000, 7:44) sources, contemporary scholars are quite certain that the *kinnôr* was a lyre. At the same time, however, we must acknowledge that the form of this instrument doubtless changed over the centuries. As far as construction material is concerned, we know that during the Solomonic period almug timber was imported from Lebanon (an otherwise unknown kind of wood, possibly sandalwood; 2 Ch. 2:7) for use in building the *kinnôr* and *nēḇel* (1 K. 10:11-12; 2 Ch. 9:11). According to Josephus, there were "musical instruments, and such as were invented for the singing of hymns, called Nablae and Cinyrae, which were made of electrum" (*Ant.* viii.3.8), probably a silver and gold alloy serving either as the actual construction material or possibly (?) as decoration. It is not until the postbiblical period that we learn anything about the number of strings on the *kinnôr*. According to Josephus, it had ten (*Ant*. vii.12.3), according to Jerome six (*PL* xxvi.969), and according to *b. 'Arak*. 13.b seven. Sources in any event agree that the *kinnôr* had fewer strings than did the *nēḇel*. It was generally played with a plectrum (Josephus, *Ant*. vii.12.3; St. Basil in McKinnon, 1987), though it could also be played simply by hand to achieve a more soothing sound, e.g., as when David played when comforting Saul (1 S. 16:23).

The identification of the *kinnôr* as a lyre is amply confirmed by archaeological evidence since, with the exception of a small number of finds (and even these are chronologically irrelevant in this context), no other stringed instruments besides lyres have been found in the areas that once comprised Canaan, ancient Israel, and ancient Palestine. Scholars now have at least thirty representations of lyres from which to draw information, and these can be subdivided into four main types (see Table 2, p. xxxii): (a) large, asymmetrical lyres with diverging arms and rectangular resonators (nos. 1-4); (b) smaller, symmetrical lyres with rounded or rectangular resonators (nos. 5-10 and 23-24); (c) asymmetrical lyres with parallel side arms and rectangular resonators (nos. 11-17); and (d) symmetrical lyres with horn-shaped side arms and rounded resonators (nos. 18, 22,and 25-32). This rich inventory can be amplified by two additional witnesses of Semitic-Judean provenance, namely, the nineteenth-century fresco in an Egyptian tomb at Beni Hasan depicting a lyre player (illust. III.3), and the lyre players among the prisoners from Lachish on an early-seventh-century Assyrian relief depicting Sennacherib's conquests in Israel (from the southern palace at Nineveh, 704-681 B.C.; illust. IV.22). Unfortunately, it is still difficult to determine whether and how these lyres might also be classified according to local ethnic considerations, though the ancient Israelite/Palestinian lyres are clearly related to neighboring cultures (cf. illust. III.2a-2l). As far as the various historical-social functions of the *kinnôr* are concerned, iconographic sources offer as rich a testimony as do the Old Testament texts themselves. The *kinnôr* was used at remarkably varied occasions, including incantation and cultic dances (Table 2, nos. 1-2), at the cultic ceremonies involving animals or trees (no. 4), in connection with the music performed for the Philistine cult of Cybele (no. 10), the Judean lunar celebration (nos. 11, 12), and the cults of both Nabataean (nos. 23, 24) and Jewish sects (no. 7). Nor do these examples exhaust its use. Lyres also appear in connection with victory celebrations (no. 3), as a symbol of independence and liberation (nos. 20, 21), as a secular sign of general significance (no. 22), as a symbol of the middle classes (nos. 18, 19), and as an attribute of Dionysus (nos. 30, 32).

Not surprisingly, the use of the *kinnôr* in such a wide variety of situations and functions also influenced its symbolism. The Old Testament passage in Gen. 4:21 asserts that "his [Jabal's] brother's name was Jubal; he was the ancestor of all those who play the *kinnôr* and the *'ûgāb*," beginning a history of rich symbolic associations for the *kinnôr* as a musical instrument. The seven-stringed lyre was viewed as a reflection of the celestial harmony, and the soul itself was seen as a well-tuned lyre (Philo of Alexandria); the Christian understanding of the *cithara (kinnôr)* as a symbol of the human being as such, of the soul, and of the body (Giesel, 1987) has continued into the present.

mᵉnaʿanʿîm

This term occurs only in 2 S. 6:5 in connection with the transfer of the ark to Jerusalem, and even then only in the plural, deriving from the verb *nwʿ*, "shake, tremble." Although the Septuagint and Vulgate both agree it was an idiophone, translating it as *kýmbala* and *sistra* respectively, the *Pistis Sophia* (a Coptic gnostic writing) and the Targums both translate as [[*rviyin*]], "drum." Various interpretations have been put forth, including even "trumpet" (Pfeiffer, 1779). Others suggest it should be identified more generally as a sistrum (Kolari, 1947), clapper, rattle, or sistrum (Foxvog/Kilmer, 1980), or a bone or metal rattle (Werner, 1980). A consideration of the archaeological evidence, however, suggests that B. Bayer (1964) is probably correct in identifying it more specifically as a clay rattle, since over seventy intact instruments of this sort have been found for which one can provide a definite provenance (see chap. III/5). A comparison of 2 S. 6:5 with the parallel passage in 1 Ch. 13:8 is even more revealing. The Chronicler tellingly replaced the *mᵉnaʿanʿîm* and other noisemakers in the passage (see chap. III/5; III/6) with more "respectable" instruments such as the trumpet, and with a reference to singing. The social function of the *mᵉnaʿanʿîm* as reflected in 2 S. 6:5 represents a pagan remnant from Canaanite culture, and this cultural context seems to justify their singular mention in the Old Testament.

$m^e \underline{s}iltayim$, $\underline{s}el\underline{s}^e l\hat{\imath}m$

The term $m^e \underline{s}iltayim$ occurs in Ezra 3:10; Neh. 12:27; 1 Ch. 13:8; 15:16, 19, 28; 16:5, 42; 25:1, 6; 2 Ch. 5:12, 13; 29:25; $\underline{s}el\underline{s}^e l\hat{\imath}m$ occurs in 2 S. 6:5; Ps. 150.

The form $m^e \underline{s}iltayim$ itself is dual deriving from the onomatopoeic root $\underline{s}l\underline{s}l$, "to ring, tremble," and appears only in postexilic texts, primarily in Chronicles. The Septuagint and Vulgate translate it as *kýmbalon* and *cymbala* respectively, and scholars today concur that the reference is to cymbals. The dual form, of course, also suggests as much, as does its mention in Ugaritic sources (cf. Caubet, 1987).

The $m^e \underline{s}iltayim$ were clearly ceremonial cultic instruments, and in that capacity were considered instruments of the guild of Levites. Ezra 3:10 and 1 Ch. 16:5 identify these players as the "sons of Asaph"; 1 Ch. 15:19, 16:42, and 2 Ch. 5:12 as the singers Heman, Asaph, and Ethan. In any event, the $m^e \underline{s}iltayim$ were never played by women, at least in the Bible. They were often used together with other cultic instruments, but only in connection with cultic events such as the transfer of the ark (1 Ch. 15:28), the dedication of the temple and presence of God (2 Ch. 5:13), and to accompany burnt and sin offerings (2 Ch. 29:25). Unfortunately, only two contemporary witnesses actually describe the $m^e \underline{s}iltayim$ that appear in the Old Testament. 1 Ch. 15:19 speaks of "brightly ringing bronze [NRSV] $m^e \underline{s}iltayim$," while Josephus tells us that "the cymbals were broad and large instruments, and were made of bronze" (*Ant.* vii.12.3).

The word $\underline{s}el\underline{s}^e l\hat{\imath}m$ is a plural form, and actually first appears in the Old Testament significantly earlier than does $m^e \underline{s}iltayim$. David tries unsuccessfully to transfer the ark to Jerusalem after retrieving it from the Philistines, and in a scene still brimming with pagan intoxication, both he and the people are said to have danced before Yahweh while playing these cymbals along with other instruments (2 S. 6:5). Interestingly, the parallel passage 1 Ch. 13:8 replaces $\underline{s}el\underline{s}^e l\hat{\imath}m$ with $m^e \underline{s}iltayim$ (cf. also chap. III/6). Similarly, the Septuagint avoids the word $\underline{s}el\underline{s}^e l\hat{\imath}m$ altogether and replaces it with *aulós*. The rejoicing people play $\underline{s}el\underline{s}^e l\hat{\imath}m$ in Ps. 150:5, though the expressions here are $\underline{s}il\underline{s}^e l\hat{e}$-$\check{s}\bar{a}ma^\varsigma$, "clanging cymbals" (NRSV; "sounding," so RSV), and $\underline{s}il\underline{s}^e l\hat{e}\ t^e r\hat{u}^\varsigma\hat{a}$, "loud clashing cymbals" (NRSV). Since the occasion here is at least a paraliturgical one, we find that the $\underline{s}el\underline{s}^e l\hat{\imath}m$ always appear in connection with a cultic mass event whose syncretistic features derive from the pagan past. Sachs believes Psalm 150 is actually alluding to the two forms of cymbals characteristic of Asiatic cultures, namely, cymbals that were held horizontally and struck only lightly, and those held vertically but struck much more forcefully (Sachs, 1940).

With the information currently available, it is difficult to pinpoint the exact difference between the *ṣelṣᵉlîm* as instruments played more by the people at large and at occasions still betraying a more intoxicating pagan past, and the *mᵉṣiltayim* as ceremonial and liturgical instruments of the Levitical guild. It is quite possible that the *ṣelṣᵉlîm* represent a different form of struck metal idiophone, perhaps a kind of clapper with a handle or slap cymbals (forked crotala), but probably not castanets.

We are fortunate to have a great deal of archaeological evidence for cymbals. At present, finds include at least twenty-eight cymbals in two different sizes ranging from a diameter of 7-12 cm. on the one hand, and 3-6 cm. on the other, coming from fourteen different cities in Canaan, ancient Israel, and Palestine. Two different chronological groups seem to be represented, the first from the late Canaanite period between the fourteenth and twelfth centuries B.C., the second from the Hellenistic-Roman period. The surprising archaeological gap extending from the eleventh to the third centuries B.C. and covering almost a thousand years is difficult to explain at present. Were these instruments not used at all during the monarchy in ancient Israel? In any event, the two different cymbal types attested archaeologically may correspond to the two types that seem to be mentioned in Psalm 150. The finds include gently rounded discuses with a small metal loop attached at the center to which a handle made of wood or some other material was then attached. Acoustic tests on intact cymbals have revealed that these instruments were capable of producing broad, resonating sounds. The archaeological evidence considered together with the mention of *mᵉṣiltayim* exclusively in postexilic Old Testament writings suggests inconsistencies concerning how these cymbals fit into the reality reflected by the written Old Testament tradition. For example, the elimination of the *ṣelṣᵉlîm* from 1 Ch. 13:8 (in contrast with 2 S. 6:5) might suggest that later authors introduced the *mᵉṣiltayim* retroactively into the description of worship in the first temple (prior to 586 B.C.).

The symbolism associated with cymbals evolved during the following centuries from the Hellenistic notion of the instrument as indicative of youth (Virgil) to that of an instrument associated with the Dionysian-Bacchic celebrations, and then to the abstract ecclesiastical understanding articulated by Clement of Alexandria, who interpreted the cymbals as representing human lips and as a *corpus sanctorum*.

nēḇel, nēḇel ʿāśôr

These terms occur in 1 S. 10:5; 2 S. 6:5; 1 K. 10:12; Isa. 5:12; 14:11; Amos 5:23; 6:5; Ps. 33:2 *(nēḇel ʿāśôr);* 57:9; 71:22 *(kᵉlî-neḇel);* 81:3; 92:4 *(ʿāśôr* and *nēḇel);* 108:3; 144:9 *(nēḇel ʿāśôr);* 150:3; Neh. 12:27; 1 Ch. 13:8; 15:16, 20, 28; 16:5 *(kᵉlê nᵉḇālîm);* 25:1, 6; 2 Ch. 5:12; 9:11; 20:28; 29:25.

The etymology of this word is ambiguous, since the root *nbl* can be vocalized in two different ways, namely, either as *nāḇāl* or as *nēḇel*. The relationship or even possible overlapping between the two terms is not entirely clear, and various arguments can be adduced in favor of separating them entirely or associating them with one another. The Hebrew and Akkadian derivative *nāḇāl* can mean "to degenerate; ritually impure, wicked, obscene; villain; carcass," as well as "flame." Moreover, Heb., Ugar., and Syr. *nēḇel* (also *neḇel*) can mean "jar, leather sack or vessel for liquids, stringed instrument" (1 S. 10:3, 4). Such associations between musical instruments and idioms of scorn or disparagement occur in other contexts as well. For example, the Latin term *ambubaia* refers to a Syrian-Roman prostitute who also played the *ʾabbûḇ* or *tibia* (reed pipe). Similarly, the French term *un violon,* reflected in the English version *fiddlingman,* refers to a con artist or thief. Interestingly, this particular instrument or its name may well have developed locally in the area of ancient Israel/Palestine, since although the exact etymology is ambiguous, the Semitic or possibly even Phoenician-Sidonian origin of the word *nēḇel* seems fairly certain (Gk. *nábla, TDOT,* IX, 172; see Sachs, 1940; Kolari, 1947). In this context, a recent discovery by the Greek archaeologist Dmitrios Pandermalis in Dion (Greece) offers indirect but convincing evidence for the interpretation of the biblical *nēḇel* as a lyre. He discovered a funerary stele from the Roman period on which for the first time we have a text accompanying *nēḇel* iconography. On this stone, a lyre in relief is juxtaposed next to an engraved encomium to the *nábla* (Pandermalis, 1997).

Significantly, of the twenty-eight occurrences of the *nēḇel* in the Old Testament, twenty-two are associated with the *kinnôr* as well. Not surprisingly, its function was similar to that of the *kinnôr* as an instrument specific to the Levitical guilds (1 Ch. 15:16, 20; 25:1, 6); it was then also an instrument played when the ark was transferred (2 S. 6:5; 1 Ch. 13:8), at the dedication of the wall (Neh. 12:27), during victory celebrations (2 Ch. 20:28), and as an instrument of ecstatic prophecy (1 S. 10:5). It was also, however, an instrument associated with hostile royal power and hostile religions (Amos 5:23; 6:5) and with the revels of the wicked (Isa. 5:12). It was made of the same material as the *kinnôr*, namely, of almug wood (1 K. 10:5), and was probably plucked by hand (Amos 6:5).

The Septuagint and Vulgate unfortunately do not translate this term consistently, using a panoply of terms including *nábla, psaltérion, órganon, kinýra, psalterium, lyra, nablium,* and *kithára/cithara,* and even though the majority of passages suggest that translators understood the instrument as a *psalterium,* this rendering does not really justify its interpretation as a harp. Nor do we learn much in the way of complementary information from the various later authors who mention this instrument, including the Greeks Sophocles and Philemon, apocryphal writings (Ps. 151; Sirach; Maccabees), and the Qumran writings (1Qs; 1QH). Among later authors, only Josephus addresses the differences between the *nēbel* and the *kinnôr,* asserting that the former had twelve strings and was played or struck with the fingers rather than with a plectrum, as was the *kinnôr* (*Ant.* vii.12.3). The Mishnah offers several bits of interesting information about these instruments as well. It limits the number of *nēbel* instruments in worship to "no fewer than two and no more than six," but "never fewer than nine *kinnôrôt,* and more may be added" (*m. ʿArak.* 2:5). The strings of the *nēbel* were made of a sheep's large intestine, those of the *kinnôr* of its small intestine (*m. Qinnim* 3:6). Another interesting point is made with regard to the purity of the instruments played by Levites and women: those of the Levites were clean and thus suitable for use in worship, while those of women were unclean (*m. Kelim* 15:6). Finally, Isa. 14:11 tells us that the sound of the *nēbel* could be a powerful drone. By contrast, later Christian authors probably had no real idea which instrument they were calling a *psalterium,* nor were they really in a position to identify it with the Hebrew *nēbel.*

Even though various interpretations have been put forth for the *nēbel,* ranging from lyre, bagpipe, lute, or stringed instrument in general, most scholars understand it as a harp (from Sachs, 1940 to *TDOT*). At this point, however, archaeological evidence certainly gives one reason to reconsider, since no harps dating to the pre-Hellenistic period have yet been found in the territory of Canaan and ancient Israel. Given this contradictory status of scholarship and archaeological evidence, Bayer's (1968b) hypothesis seems to be the most persuasive. In her view, the *nēbel* was a particular kind of lyre of local Near Eastern provenance, yet one that was not really Hellenized, or was Hellenized only very little. Since it had more numerous and thicker strings than the *kinnôr,* it was probably capable of being played quite loudly even though it was played without a plectrum. Its resonator was probably similar in shape to a leather bag or container for water or wine, whence perhaps also its name (*nēbel,* "waterskin"). Finally, given its thicker strings and deeper tone, the *nēbel* probably served as the tenor or bass instrument in the orchestra of the second temple (from the end of the sixth century B.C.). The larger lyre depicted on the Bar Cochba coins is probably a *nēbel* (see chap. V/7, illust. V.57c, d).

Among the secondary expressions, the *nēbel ʿāśôr* is generally interpreted as a *nēbel* instrument with specifically ten *(ʿāśôr)* strings. Ps. 92:4, however, does mention the *ʿāśôr* and *nēbel* as separate instruments. Finally, the *kᵉlê nᵉbālîm* in 1 Ch. 16:5 and the *kᵉlî-nebel* in Ps. 71:22 can probably be understood as different types of stringed instruments, with *kᵉlê* referring to the instruments, and *nᵉbālîm* as the plural of *nēbel* qualifying them.

paʿᵃmôn

The term occurs in Ex. 28:33, 34; 39:25, 26.

The Semitic root *pʿm* is attested in Ugaritic, Phoenician, and Hebrew as "foot, step, time (point in time)," and occurs quite frequently in the Old Testament. A much less frequent meaning is "bump, strike," and though the derivation of *paʿᵃmôn* is still uncertain, this particular semantic variation apparently influenced its association with the musical instrument (Kolari, 1947). The term occurs only four times in the Old Testament, though Sirach 45:9 and Zech. 14:20 are also of interest in this context. The Septuagint renders the term as *kódōn,* the Vulgate as *tintinnabulum.* The reference is actually to golden bells that alternate with blue, purple, and red cloth pomegranates fastened to the bottom of the high priest's robe (Ex. 28:33ff.; see chap. V/1). Sirach recounts that their ringing was pleasing (45:9), and Josephus describes the alternation of fringes and golden bells as "a curious and beautiful contrivance" (*Ant.* iii.7.4). The significance attaching to these bells resonates clearly in Exodus 28:35, which stipulates that "its sound shall be heard when he [Aaron] goes into the holy place before Yahweh, and when he comes out, so that he may not die."

Extrabiblical sources also mention such bells as a part of priests' garments (cf., e.g., Plutarch, *Quaestiones convivales,* 672a), and we even have access to iconographic materials providing extrabiblical parallels. The portrayal of an Assyrian emissary from the fifteenth century B.C. includes such bells (Grace, 1956; fig. 2), as does the statue of a high priest found at Hierapolis/Bambycé in northwest Syria wearing a row of bells near the hem of his garment (Seyrig, 1939). The oldest bells unearthed by archaeologists in ancient Israel date to the ninth and eighth centuries, and from this period forward they were an integral part of the world of sound in ancient Israel/Palestine (see chap. V/1).

The function of such bells as musical instruments in the strict sense, of course, is questionable, and the Old Testament texts themselves already allude to the primarily apotropaic and prophylactic function of bells in connection with exorcisms. Josephus explains that the sound of the golden bells on the priest's garment symbolized thunder, while the pomegranates symbolized lightning (*Ant.* iii.7.7) For Philo, they symbolized the cosmic harmony, and for Rabbi Jonathan penitence. Even in later centuries these bells were always associated primarily with their symbolic apotropaic function, and occasionally were even identified exclusively as objects for use in exorcisms. Israel's/Palestine's archaeological evidence clearly reveals the provenance and development of bells from the tradition of Bronze Age clay-rattles (*mena'an'im;* see illust. III.25), and places them among the instruments of the pagan cults, particularly the Dionysian (see chap. V/5, illust. V.41d).

qeren hayyôḇēl

This expression occurs only in Josh. 6:5.

The word *qeren* derives from a common Semitic and Indo-European root and as such dates to the earliest stages of culture (Kolari, 1947; *TDOT*). The ordinary Hebrew term refers to an animal horn, and appears in this meaning more than seventy times in the Old Testament. At the same time, other meanings contribute to the semantic field of the root *qrn* as well. Exodus 34:29 says that Moses' face "shone"; Hab. 3:4 speaks of "rays" coming forth from God's hand; and Ezk. 29:21 speaks of "redemption." It is mentioned only once as a musical instrument. At the mythical destruction of the wall of Jericho, it appears in the expression *qeren hayyôḇēl,* "horn of a ram," and even here its semantic field is expanded by the ambiguity naturally attaching to the word *yôḇēl,* "ram," since the latter can also refer to an anniversary, whence also the English term "jubilee" (the root in question being *ybl,* "to lead, conduct; leader of the flock"). Because the expression occurs only once in the Old Testament, textual analysis offers no real possibility for distinguishing typologically between this *qeren hayyôbēl* on the one hand, and the *šôpār* or *hayyôbēl* on the other. Gerson-Kiwi (1980) suggests that a deeper musical-genealogical meaning may be providing the basis for the reference to Jubal in Gen. 4:21 as well as for the scene depicting Abraham's sacrifice of Isaac in Gen. 22:13 (with the appearance of the ram). Perhaps, so Gerson-Kiwi, the horn of the ram, that is, of the sacrificial animal that replaces human sacrifice, when used as a musical instrument came to symbolize the emergence of monotheism.

šôpār and *šôpᵉrôt hayyôbᵉlîm*

These terms occur in the following Old Testament passages: Ex. 19:16, 19; 20:18; Lev. 25:9; Josh. 6:4, 5, 8, 9, 13, 16, 20; Jgs. 3:27; 6:34; 7:8, 16, 18-20, 22; 1 S. 13:3; 2 S. 2:28; 6:15; 15:10; 18:16; 20:1, 22; 1 K. 1:34, 39, 41; 2 K. 9:13; Isa. 18:3; 27:13; 58:1; Jer. 4:5, 19, 21; 6:1, 17; 42:14; 51:27; Ezk. 33:3-6; Hos. 5:8; 8:1; Joel 2:1, 15; Amos 2:2; 3:6; Zeph. 1:16; Zech. 9:14; Ps. 47:6; 81:4; 98:6; 150:3; Job 39:24, 25; Neh. 4:12, 14; 1 Ch. 15:28; 2 Ch. 15:14; *šôpᵉrôt hayyôbᵉlîm*, Josh. 6:4, 6, 8, 13.

With seventy-four occurrences, the *šôpār* is the most frequently mentioned instrument in the Old Testament. Interestingly, it is also the only instrument to have survived within Jewish liturgy essentially unchanged from biblical times, and as such has attracted the most voluminous scholarly attention in the form of monographs and discussions. The word *šôpār* may derive etymologically from Akk. *šappāru*, itself considered a loan from Sum. *šegbar*, "ibex" or "wild goat." Even though this etymology has been favored from the inception of nineteenth-century comparative studies in Hebrew and Aramaic, it is still uncertain, since more recent studies have called this derivation in question. As recently as 1967, the authors of the Koehler/Baumgartner lexicon limited their own assessment to saying that the origin of *šôpār* remains obscure.

General consensus holds that this instrument is to be identified as a naturally occurring horn, in this case the horn of either a goat or a ram. The Septuagint and Vulgate clearly misunderstood the reference, and translated it as *sálpinx* and as *tuba*; unfortunately, the modern versions that followed them have also gone astray, and only the NJB translates unambiguously as ram's horn. The longer expression *šôpᵉrôt hayyôbᵉlîm*, the plural of *šôpār hayyôbēl*, occurs four times in connection with the destruction of the walls of Jericho (Josh. 6:4, 6, 8, 13), and has generally been viewed as the equivalent of the single expression *šôpār*. Although one cannot be entirely certain, the addition of the qualifier *yôḇēl* here may have something to do with the special significance of the event, especially considering that the city's walls were allegedly destroyed as the result of some supernatural power attaching to the use of the horns in the episode. In this context, the additional word may attach some symbolical meaning to the simpler term.

We must turn to postbiblical writings for information concerning how the instrument was actually made (see chap. V/8). The Talmud tractates *m. Roš Haššanah* and *b. Šabbath* together with various Qumran writings (1QM VII, VIII, XVI) offer the most detailed accounts. Two forms of the shofar were used: a straight or linear horn at the New Year, whose mouthpiece *(piyah)* was covered with gold, and a curved one covered with silver on the day of fasting. Portrayals from the Roman period show a separate mouthpiece. Great care was to be taken whenever working on, repairing, or otherwise decorating one of these horns, since its natural tone was to be preserved at all costs; still, a text could be carved into it under certain circumstances. Considerable attention, however, seems to have been given to the quality of the tone itself; whether it be "thin, thick, or dry," it was still considered "clean" or "pure" as long as it was natural (*b. Roš Haš.* 27:1-2). The Old Testament first mentions instruments made of naturally occurring horns in Ex. 19:13, 16, 19; in the ancient Near East at large, however, iconographic evidence dates back far earlier, with examples from Mari dating to the eighteenth century and Carchemish to the ninth-eighth century B.C. (Keel, 1972, illust. 456, 457). It is not until the Roman period that we have any iconographic evidence for the *šôpār* in the Israelite-Judean context, and even then, care must be taken in interpretation insofar as the instrument has already become part of symbolic groupings. It appears first together with the *mᵉnôrâ* (seven-branched lampstand) and *maḥtâ* (incense pan; see illust. V.62b and c), and then later also with the *lûlāḇ* and *'eṭrôg* (palm branch and citrus fruit, two of the four plants blessed at the Feast of Succoth [V.68]). Although the horns could also be softened in hot water and straightened, only the bent horn is attested iconographically. In any event, a survey of these artifacts reveals that at this point, the *šôpār* was viewed as a symbol of national and ethnic identity and was capable of functioning in both sacral and secular contexts (see chap. V/8).

In sixty-nine of its seventy-four Old Testament occurrences, the *šôpār* appears as a solo instrument, reflecting its unique position in the biblical world of sound. Similarly, its tonal capacity was appropriate to a particular socioacoustic role insofar as the character of the two or three tones it was capable of producing (second and third overtones) could function as a signal of alarm whose quavering blast is described as a "voice" *(qôl)*, "trumpet blast" *(tᵉqîʻâ)*, shout *(tᵉrûʻâ)*, or "sobbing, moaning" *(yabbābâ)*. This descriptive series suggests that the sound of the *šôpār* could accommodate itself to a variety of situations, evoking a magical or even eschatological atmosphere, or functioning symbolically. Unfortunately, none of the older sources provides any information regarding the character of the *šôpār* signals themselves. The Mishnah says only that the tones were to be "long," "short," "calm," "sustained," and "quavering" (*m. Roš Haš.* 3.3-4; *m. Sukk.* 4.5), and the Qumran War Scroll mentions only a "mighty alarm" (1QM 7:10). Nor do the rabbinic writings agree concerning just how the *šôpār* signals were to sound. Around the fourth century, Rabbi Abbahu of Caesarea fixed the terms *tᵉqîʻâ* as a long tone, *tᵉrûʻâ* as a quavering blast, and *šᵉbārîm* as a broken tone (*b. Roš Haš.* 33:2–34:1-2; *m. Sukk.* 4.5). The "Order of Blowing" from the Talmud then tried to establish the relationship among these three signals by using an order based on multiples of three. The *tᵉqîʻâ* was to be the length of three *tᵉrûʻôt* (pl. of *tᵉrûʻâ*); the *tᵉrûʻâ* was to be the length of the three [[*yᵉbābôt*]] or as long as three [[*šᵉbārîm*]] (*ibid.*, and *m. Roš Haš.* 4.9). The rabbis thus apparently equated the latter two designations, and understood the relationship between the three possibilities in terms of triplets. Curt Sachs (1940) has suggested that this description may possibly be related to the *modus perfectum* of the Middle Ages. The tenth-century Siddur (prayer book) of Saadiah Gaon and the thirteenth-century Codex Adler (illust. V.81a-b), the oldest known graphic representations and descriptions of the *šôpār* signals, might give us some idea of these signals during the Roman period. Today, *šôpār* use in contemporary synagogues generally follows these written sources (see illust. V.83).

The wide variety of functions this instrument fulfilled is reflected in both cultic and secular contexts within the Old Testament. Within cultic contexts, it appears as an omen of transcendental powers (Ex. 19:13; Ps. 47:6), on the day of atonement (Lev. 25:9), at the feast of the new moon (Ps. 81:3), and on the day of penitence (Joel 2:1). Within secular or quasi-cultic contexts, it accompanies the transfer of the ark (2 S. 6:15), engagement in war (Jgs. 3:27; 6:34; Josh. 6:4-20; 2 S. 2:28), the celebration of victories (1 S. 13:3), and coups (2 S. 15:10). These dual contexts also provide the approximate lines of development for the *šôpār* in the Old Testament. The first involves the *šôpār* as an instrument of communication during times of war, a function and line of development the exile, of course, brings to an abrupt end. The second involves the *šôpār* as a cultic instrument, and this line continues even into the present. In summary, this is an instrument with deep roots in the world of the Old Testament, and its presence and use in so many contexts — both cultic and secular — profoundly affected its symbolic significance in Jewish spiritual history.

tōp

This term occurs in Gen. 31:27; Ex. 15:20; Jgs. 11:34; 1 S. 10:5; 18:6; 2 S. 6:5; Isa. 5:12; 24:8; 30:32; Jer. 31:4; Ps. 68:26; 81:3; 149:3; 150:4; Job 21:12; 1 Ch. 13:8.

The Ugaritic root *tp* ("drum") is attested in the fourteenth century B.C. and is probably onomatopoeic. The root is widespread, providing the basis for a *verbum denominatum* (drum — drummer — to drum) extending from Sum. [[*dub*]] to Akk. [[*dadpu*]], Aram. [[*tupa*]], Arab. [[*duff*]], Phoenician [[*mtpp*]], Egyp. [[*tbu*]], Ugar. [[*dob*]] (Koehler/Baumgartner 1967). The interpretation of the *tōp* as a drum seems secure in all 16 Old Testament occurrences, and the Septuagint and Vulgate translate the term consistently as *týmpanon* and *tympanum*. It is often women whom we encounter playing the *tōp* (Jgs. 11:34; 1 S. 18:6; Jer. 31:4; Ps. 68:26), the quintessential scene being the crossing of the Red Sea (Ex. 15:20), where the prophet Miriam takes a *tōp* in her hand, and "all the women went out after her with [[*tupîm*]] and with dancing." Even today, Yemenite women of Jewish heritage continue this tradition. It is not quite correct, however, to assert that the *tōp* was an "exclusively woman's instrument" (Werner, 1980), since although women do seem to be the only ones who play it as a solo instrument, it was played by both males and females when accompanied by other instruments. Unlike the *šôpār*, however, it is never mentioned in connection with temple music (cf. 1 Ch. 25:6), though it seems always to appear whenever cultic dances are performed (Ex. 15:20; 1 S. 18:6 etc.), cultic hymns sung (Ps. 149:3; 150:4), feast days celebrated (Ps. 81:3), and processions organized (2 S. 6:5; 1 Ch. 13:8). In cultic processions, the female drummers seemed to have come second, after the singers, but before the other instrumentalists (Ps. 68:26). The instrument appears in more secular contexts as well, and this function as an instrument of rejoicing (Gen. 31:27) and ecstasy (1 S. 10:5) apparently belongs to the older strata of the instrument's tradition.

The Old Testament itself nowhere really provides information about the size or shape of this type of drum. Modern interpretations, however, generally agree that it was a drum whose round frame was made out of wood and measured approximately 25-30 cm. and resembled what we today refer to as a tambourine or timbrel, though unlike the familiar modern tambourine, the *tōp* had no metal jingles attached to its sides. Although the rounded form seems to have been applicable to this particular instrument, interpreters have considered other shapes as well, including that of an hourglass or a square or rectangle. Although postbiblical sources, including *m. Qinnim* 3:6, tell us that the membrane was made from the leather or hide of a ram, we do not yet have archaeological evidence indicating unequivocally whether any of the Near Eastern frame drums were covered on both sides as has been suggested (Nixdorff, 1971). The evidence we do have relating to this instrument in ancient Israel/Palestine, however, is fairly uniform. Even as early as the Canaanite period, this particular, rounded frame drum appears to have been the only membranophone in this region; two different terra-cotta versions (see chap. IV/1) attest it as an explicitly local iconographic topos of ancient Israel during the Iron Age, though it is difficult to determine the precise cultural provenance and significance of these terra-cotta examples. In any event, the *tōp*-topos itself is doubtless of local provenance and represents a characteristic product of the musical world of ancient Israel. These terra-cotta examples seem commensurate with the Old Testament witness insofar as they, too, synthesize the sacral and secular in a way apparently also commensurate with the actual use and function of the instruments. The figures may be household icons or amulets (cf. the *tᵉrāpîm* in Gen. 31:19, 34), though scholars have given them interpretations ranging from deities to toys (Winter, 1983). In any event, and quite apart from their actual meaning, the form and quantity of these terra-cottas attest how widespread this particular percussion form and its performance were in ancient Israel/Palestine.

As in other musical cultures as well in which the drum is associated with women, so also is the drum in the Old Testament a sexual symbol. In Jgs. 11:34, Jephthah's daughter bewails her virginity with the drum. The nude and decorated terra-cottas of the Israelite period clearly document this element of fertility and eroticism, the attendant iconography also contradicting the official, orthodox faith. Later Old Testament books sublimate this sexual and erotic element by employing the metaphor "virgin Israel," as in Jer. 31:4: "O virgin Israel! Again you shall adorn yourself with the *tōp̄*, and go forth in the dance of the merrymakers."

ʿûg̱āb̲

This term occurs four times in the Old Testament: Gen. 4:21; Ps. 150:4; Job 21:12; 30:31.

The *ʿûg̱āb̲* is one of the Old Testament instruments whose exact identity is still a matter of considerable discussion. Its etymology is still unclear, though the root *ʿg̱b̲* is associated with the Hebrew-Arab term *ʿᵃg̱āb̲â*, "ardor, sensual desire, lust" (Koehler/Baumgartner 1967; cf. Ezra 23:5, 7, 9). The nominal form *ʿûg̱āb̲* is thus referring to contemptible features and thus to a musical instrument somehow associated with a contemptible lifestyle. In any event, the Septuagint already did not quite know what to make of this instrument, and used various terms, including *kithára*, *órganon*, and *psalmós*. Although the Peshitta follows the Septuagint in this regard and exhibits thus the same degree of uncertainty, the Targums and Vulgate seem to be much more consistent, translating as *'abbûb̲ā'* (an oboe-like instrument) and *organum*, and this may suggest that as early as the postbiblical period, the exact identity of this instrument was already uncertain. At the same time, and especially given the etymological associations discussed above, the Targums may be translating according to their own contemporary reality, and the other two translations may well reflect simply an attempt to disguise a banned or otherwise severely disparaged instrument.

Already in Gen. 4:21, a passage mentioning the first musical instruments and as such establishing the unique status of the *ʿûg̱āb̲* in the Old Testament, we read that Jubal "was the ancestor of all those who play the *kinnôr* and the *ʿûg̱āb̲*." Peculiarly, however, whereas the *kinnôr* is the most often mentioned Old Testament stringed instrument (see chap. IV/3), the *ʿûg̱āb̲* is mentioned only three more times in the entire Old Testament: as an instrument of lament in Job 30:31 together with the *kinnôr*, as an instrument of the wicked in Job 21:12, and in the concluding doxology in Ps.

150:4, though here outside the temple and together with the *tōp* and danc-ing. Although a Hebrew version of the apocryphal Ps. 151 found in the Qumran scroll 11QPsAp^a 151 is of interest in this context, its singularity and extremely late provenance, dating as it does to the mid-first century A.D., make it difficult to assess. It associates David, the builder of instru-ments, with the *kinnôr* and the *'ûgāḇ*, (vs. 2), which the Septuagint trans-lates as *órganon* and *psaltérion*. This early Christian source may be associ-ating *'ûgāḇ* as a "(water) organ" with an understanding of David as a Christian Orphic figure. As attested iconographically in ancient Palestine around the second to third centuries, the Talmud also understands the *'ûgāḇ* as a hydraulic device (*y. Sukk.* 55c). In the meantime, the Aramaic Targum translation clearly equates the *'ûgāḇ* with the *'abbûḇā'*, the instru-ment played by the Roman *ambubaia*-girls, pipe players whom Roman au-thors describe as prostitutes (Horace, *Satires* i.2; Suetonius, *Nero* 27). On the other hand, *m. 'Arak.* 2.3 equates the *'abbûḇā'* with the *ḥālîl*.

The lack of clarity and uniformity surrounding our sources of infor-mation concerning the *'ûgāḇ* has also resulted in a wide variety of interpre-tations for the instrument. Some see it as a purely symbolical musical in-strument (Werner, 1980), others as a wind instrument in the general sense, others as an instrument resembling the panpipe, others even as a kind of bagpipe, or as a lute or harp. Most of these interpretations, however, are neither historically nor etymologically tenable, and C. Sachs (1940) still offers the only plausible interpretation given the present inventory of sources for this instrument. Because many flute-like instruments are asso-ciated with the onomatopoeic vowels *u-u*, and because flutes are so often associated with features involving love, desire, ardor, and the like, Sachs believes the *'ûgāḇ* was a kind of long flute, an instrument widely attested in the neighboring cultures of Egypt (as the [[*ma't*]]) and Sumeria (as the [[*tigi*]]), and later in the Near East (Israel/Palestine) as well (as the *nay*).

5. Instruments in Daniel

The book of Daniel, composed between 167 and 164 B.C., mentions instru-ments in Dnl. 3:5, 7, 10, 15.

All four passages enumerate a group of musical instruments in virtu-ally the same form, now often called the "orchestra of Nebuchadnezzar." "When you hear the sound of the *qarnā'*, *mašrôqîtā'*, *qayṯerōs*, *sabbᵉkā'*, *pᵉsanntērîn, sûmpōnᵉyâ,* and *kōl zᵉnê zᵉmārā',* you are to fall down and worship the golden statue that King Nebuchadnezzar has set up," failure to do so resulting in a person being "thrown into a furnace of blazing fire" (Dnl. 3:5-6). Although the passage is written in Aramaic, the names of the musical instruments are a mixture of Greek, Aramaic, and Hebrew.

The *qarnā'* is the Aramaic form of Heb. *qeren,* referring to any naturally occurring horn, though in this passage it is probably referring to a metal or clay trumpet. In the New Babylonian Kingdom, cylindrical trumpets between seventy and ninety centimeters long with gently conical ends were used as signaling instruments (Rashid, 1984, illust. 143, 144), and during the period when the book of Daniel was composed, trumpets about fifty centimeters long (made of clay) with broad bells were used at festive occasions in the Parthian Kingdom (Rashid, 1984, illust. 196).

An apotropaic effect is often ascribed to the *mašrôqîṭā'* (from the Heb. root *šrq,* "to whistle, hiss"); such a *šᵉrîqâ* is otherwise used to describe the sound of a shepherd's pipe (Jgs. 5:16; see Koehler/Baumgartner 1967). Hence the Septuagint translation as *sýrinx* may possibly be correct, an instrument that during the Seleucid period represented a large, double-bound instrument (cf. Rashid, 1984). Considering the acoustic relationships in Daniel 3, one should probably interpret this instrument as a reed instrument, possibly played in an ensemble together with trumpets and other festival instruments at mass events.

The *qayṭᵉrōs* is a borrowing from Gk. *kithára.* The lyre forms familiar to the author of Daniel were the small, symmetrical Hellenistic lyres measuring approximately 50 × 25 cm., and used in both cultic and secular contexts. Babylonian tradition included a kind of military ensemble composed of lyre instruments together with drums and cymbals; this particular ensemble type was continued later as well (e.g., in connection with the cult of Dionysus) and would have been suitable as a musical ensemble to accompany the kind of mass celebrations associated with the worship of a statue as suggested in the Daniel story.

The term *sabbᵉkā'* is a loan from Gk. *sambýkē* (Vulg. *sambuca*), though its further etymology suggests a Near Eastern, perhaps Phoenician derivation. Although it has often been identified as a lyre, Sachs (1940) has suggested, probably correctly, that it was instead a small, angular harp that was held vertically. A similar instrument is attested in written sources (Arnobius) as an instrument of revelry, the *sambucinae* of prostitutes; imported from the Phoenicians, its shape resembled the form of a ship or a nautical siege-engine. The only form attested during the Seleucid period, the one familiar in ancient Palestine during this period, is probably also the one intended in the text of Daniel. In general, the harp was an integral part of the local musical culture in Mesopotamia, and in this case was probably a vertical angular harp and a resonator that was held vertically against the shoulder (Rashid 1984, illust. 176-83).

The p*esantērîn* is also a loan from the Greek, from *psaltérion,* but appears in this language only after the sixth century B.C. whereas Sachs (1940) traces it back to a kind of ancient Greek harp. Kolari (1947) suggests interpreting it as a small zither played with sticks. This view is problematical, however, insofar as apart from a ninth-century ivory pyxis from Nimrud, zithers are in fact not attested in Babylonia. The situation in Daniel more closely evokes a religious occasion at which the masses also participated, and for such an occasion the p*esantērîn* would more likely be something like the large angular harp attested in the New Assyrian Empire of the seventh century B.C., held horizontally and beaten with sticks (Rashid, 1984, illust. 141). Because the beating technique of the Assyrian harps was passed down and applied to the later, hammered *psalterium*-instruments as well, interpreters probably confused the harp and *psalterium;* this confusion in its own turn resulted in later translators (e.g., Luther) identifying this instrument as the *psalterium.*

The term *sûmpōn*e*yâ* is doubtless also a loanword from the Greek, and may not be an instrument at all. Its meaning has long been a matter of intense dispute, and until the mid-twentieth century it was generally thought to be a kind of bagpipe. The general meaning in Greek itself, however, and remarks made by Jerome that the *symphonia* referred to a "consonant harmony" rather than to an actual instrument, prompted a change of view. Since the work of Sachs (1940), scholars have accordingly interpreted this word as referring to "an entire ensemble." The structure of the eastern [[*maqam*-]] and [[*taqsim*]]-form seems to support this interpretation insofar as solo improvisation by individual instruments was usually followed by a performance of the entire ensemble. In this context, however, the structure of the verse in Daniel presents its own problems, since there the *sûmpōn*e*yâ* is listed within a series of other instruments and separated from "all other z*emārā*'" (see below) by an "and." Mitchell and Joyce (1965) suggest that *sûmpōn*e*yâ* may be a translation of a dialect variation of the word *týmpanon,* and thus identify it as a drum, the missing instrument in Nebuchadnezzar's orchestra.

Oddly, not much attention has been paid to the expression *kōl z^enê z^mārā'*, especially since, as the conclusion to the verse, it is of great interest. Strictly speaking, *kōl z^enê* refers to "all kinds" (Koehler/Baumgartner 1967), even though the expression is usually translated as "all other instruments." The other term, *z^mārā'*, derives from the Akkadian root *zmr* and is quite widespread in the Semitic languages, including Ugaritic, Hebrew, Aramaic, Syrian, and Arabic. In general, the Old Testament associates the root with musicians and singers, though also with a summons to praise, song, and even song with instrumental accompaniment (*TDOT*, IV, 93f.). Coincidentally, the only text directly associated with an iconographic document from ancient Israel/Palestine contains the word *zmrt* (see chap. V/3). A stone drawing from the late-Hellenistic/early Roman period shows a female double pipe player and is accompanied by the Sippaite inscription "the beautiful woman *zmrt* the pipe." The translation thus seems to be that the girl is "playing a (wind) musical instrument," or is "making music with the pipe." If the translation "musical instrument" is also to be applied to Daniel 3, then *sûmpōn^eyâ* probably does not mean "the entire ensemble." But if *z^mārā'* is referring to song, praise, or music generally, then what we may have here is first a series of musical instruments mentioned individually, then a reference to the entire ensemble, and finally to all kinds of songs, praise, and music in the larger sense. The above-mentioned Sipparite inscription indicates rather the interpretation "to play a wind instrument." There is certainly no reason to imply primarily stringed instruments (cf. Smith, 1998, 255).

It seems obvious that the author of Daniel is attempting to describe a specifically Seleucid group of musicians even though some of the instrument names may well go back to an earlier tradition. Among all the instrument names in the Old Testament, these in Daniel are the only ones deriving from a non-Israelite musical culture. All these instruments exhibit foreign names, possibly even in corrupted forms. Because none of these names has appeared yet in other sources, it is very difficult to draw on historical sources in clarifying or confirming their identity. At the time the book of Daniel was written, the confrontation between the Jewish and Hellenistic cultures was becoming increasingly severe. At such a time and in a climate of such increasing cross-cultural hostility, these enigmatic musical instruments — which the author introduces four times in his work almost like a threatening ostinato — evoke for the Jewish readers the presence of an alien, even hostile musical culture.

6. Collective Expressions — Typological Terminology

Old Testament expressions include: *kēlîm* (1 Ch. 23:5); *kᵉlê*-David (2 Ch. 29:26, 27); *kᵉlî-neḇel*, *kᵉlê-nᵉḇālîm* (Ps. 71:22; 1 Ch. 16:5); *kᵉlê-ʿōz* (2 Ch. 30:21); *kᵉlê šîr* (Amos 6:5; 1 Ch. 15:16; 16:42; 2 Ch. 5:13; 7:6; 23:13; 34:12; Neh. 12:36); *minnîm* (Ps. 45:9[?]; 150:4).

The term *kᵉlî* probably derives from the verbal root *klh-kwl*, meaning "to contain, surround" (Koehler/Baumgartner, 1967), and in the Old Testament refers primarily to implements, objects, vessels, containers, tools, weapons, objects of art, and jewelry (*TDOT*, VII, 169ff.). In connection with temple service, the *kᵉlî/kēlîm* (pl.) was understood as a cultic object, for example, as the altar of burnt offering, the seven-branched lampstand, or the Table for the Bread of the Presence (e.g., Ex. 25:9; 2 K. 14:14; 2 Ch. 28:24). When referring to musical instruments, it is with one exception (1 Ch. 23:5, "instruments . . . for praise") used only as an addendum and in the plural. Combinations include the *kᵉlê*-David, the "instruments of David"; *kᵉlê-neḇel/nᵉbālîm*, "*nebel*-instruments"; *kᵉlê-ʿōz*, "mighty (loud) instruments"; and *kᵉlê-šîr*, "instruments of song." These appellatives appear eleven times as Levitical temple instruments, and three times in other functions, including praise to the king (2 Ch. 23:13), prayer (Ps. 71:22), and as instruments made by David (Amos 6:5).

The understandings of the Septuagint and Vulgate essentially concur, though their translations do offer different nuances in each passage mentioning this term. In 1 Ch. 15:16, for example, they translate *kᵉlê šîr* as *en orgánois* and *in organis musicorum*, and in 2 Ch. 7:6 as *en orgánois ōdṓn kyríou* and *organis carminum Domini*. The Talmud often simply replaces these collective expressions with the expression *kᵉlê*-[[*zemer*]], "instruments of music and song" (*m. ʿArak.* 2.4; *m. Kelim* 15:7-8), from which derives the term *klezmorim* (Yiddish plural of *klezmer*), referring to folk musicians from eastern and central Europe. The expression *kᵉlê-nᵉḇālîm* refers twice to stringed instruments, and as a result has often been interpreted exclusively as such. These collective expressions, however, can in some instances also refer to wind or percussion instruments (1 Ch. 15:16; *m. Sukk.* 5:4).

The singular appellative *minnîm* (pl.) is related to Syr. *minā* and Akk. *manānu*, "hair, cord, string" (Koehler/Baumgartner 1967-1990). The word has since Pfeiffer (1779) been understood as a collective name for stringed instruments.

Apparently a radical change took place in the cultural and musical life of postexilic Israel, since it is only in postexilic Old Testament books that the collective expressions for musical instruments are found. The musical culture was subject to a new process of rationalization, and as a result musical instruments were now classified according to a more artificial schema.

7. Terminology in the Psalms and Unresolved Questions

Most of the one hundred seventeen psalm superscriptions use musical terminology. Unfortunately, textual analysis is our only means of interpreting these expressions, and that analysis is itself made more difficult by the considerable exegetical, linguistic, and musicological problems which confront it. As a result, these expressions are among the most obscure and difficult in the Old Testament, and have unsurprisingly generated a long and complicated history of interpretation (see Sachs, 1940; Sendrey, 1969b; Bayer, 1982a; Werner, 1989).

Contemporary scholars generally agree that these superscriptions primarily represent performance notes or guidelines, and at present can contribute little to our understanding of musical instruments as such. Foxvog/Kilmer (1980) accordingly discuss the psalm superscriptions in their chapter on musical performance, subdividing the discussion further under (1) titles (functional and social considerations), (2) performance, and (3) catchwords concerning songs (allusions to familiar melodies or songs recommended for the performance of any given psalm).

More recent scholarship (since Sachs 1940) has refuted Langdon's attempt (1921) to develop a parallel between the Sumerian-Babylonian-Assyrian material on the one hand, and the Old Testament psalms on the other based on classification of specific instrument groups. Scholars have argued persuasively in this connection that not a single word interpreted as a musical instrument actually appears with this meaning in the Old Testament. A more likely parallel to consider would be that between the Old Testament psalms and the Arabic [[*maqam-*]] or Indian *raga*-designations, which include place names, numerals, and substantives.

As early as antiquity itself, the meaning of these superscriptions had already become rather obscure, and the result was a plethora of differing translations even in the first Greek and Latin versions, which cannot agree concerning even the most frequently occurring words. One example is the expression *lammᵉnaṣṣē(a)h*, which occurs fifty-five times (as well as in the subscript of Hab. 3) and actually derives from the word meaning "victory" ([[*niṣaḥôn*]]). Modern translations generally translate this expression as "for the choirmaster," though also as "to be sung" (Luther) even though Aquila's second-century Greek translation reads "for the master of victory" and the Septuagint and Vulgate as "to the end." In any case, the expression *lammᵉnaṣṣē(a)ḥ* does not appear to possess any particular musical meaning. By contrast, the title designation *mizmôr*, occurring fifty-seven times itself, derives from the root *zmr* (see discussion above) and is generally understood to be referring to singing with instrumental accompaniment. Clearly, one's understanding of this term would have had considerable consequences for the performance of these particular psalms.

Of interest in this context is the recent research on Old Testament canticles by John Arthur Smith (1998). Although the discussion concentrates on the well-known canticles from the books Exodus (song of the sea, Miriam's song), Judges (song of Deborah and Barak), 2 Samuel (David's lament and song of thanksgiving), Isaiah (Isaiah's hymn of praise), and others, the observations of the author may equally well be applied to certain aspects of the performance of the Psalms. So, for example, Smith's conclusions on the performance of the two basic forms of singing — responsorial and corporate (pp. 232-235):

> The first was executed in five ways:
> a. by the congregation repeating each unit after the leader;
> b. by the congregation repeating a standard refrain after each verse of the leader;
> c. by the congregation completing the second half of the unit started by the leader;
> d. by the leader singing the incipit of each unit and the congregation repeating the incipit and completing the unit, and
> e. by the leader singing the entire song and the congregation repeating it.
> The corporate performance could have been executed in two ways:
> a. by the entire congregation;
> b. by the leader of a certain gender singing the incipit and the congregation of the same gender singing the next part of the song.
> c. by a congregation of mixed genders, which actually does not differ from the first form.

We should take into consideration that although "it is probably safest to assume a time within the Second Temple period" (Smith, 1998, 252), the main source for the analysis of the actual performance of the canticles, as well as the Psalms, is Talmudic texts, and only partly biblical texts proper. On the use of musical instruments together with singing (*n'gina* and *zimra*), see above, pp. 34-35 and below, p. 40.

Expressions from these superscriptions that may be of organological significance are always used relationally, that is, with the prefixes *bi*, *'al*, *'el*; as a result, their meaning is also colored by the semantic scope of these prepositions, which varies according to context with meanings such as with, upon, according to, and so on.

1. The expression *'al-'ᵃlāmôt* is found in Ps. 46:1 and has, as a plural form, been associated with the sg. *'almâ*, "young woman," or "young woman of marriageable age" (Gen. 24:43). Interpretations are quite varied. Some adduce the expression *binᵉḇālîm 'al-'ᵃlāmôt* in 1 Ch. 15:20 in understanding it as an expression indicating a particular tuning for a stringed instrument, in this case perhaps in the high soprano register characteristic of a young girl's voice, or as a wind instrument related to the Greek *aulós* (Sendrey, 1969b). Others adduce the expression *'ᵃlāmôt tôpēpôt* in Ps. 68:26 in understanding the reference as a female musician or female drummer, a common phenomenon in ancient Israel. Still others think the reference is to a female musician trained for a specific stringed instrument of the sort familiar from Egypt (Sachs, 1940). Finally, some scholars have thought some connection may exist with the octave or eighth tone or mode.

2. The expression *'al-haggittît* in Ps. 8:1; 81:1; 84:1 is apparently a musical *terminus technicus* and is often linked with the city of Gath *(gat)*, where David stayed with his troops (1 S. 27:2). If this connection is correct, then the expression would mean "in the style of Gath" or "upon the instrument-of-Gath," an interpretation supported by the use of the definite article *ha-*. Another possible source of the term is *gat*, "wine-press," following the Septuagint and Vulgate, which understand the reference as being to the "song of the pressers/treaders of wine" *(hypér tôn lēnôn, pro torcularibus)*. The underlying reference may even be to the harvest festival *sukkôt*, something possibly suggested by the content of Psalm 81.

3. The expression *'al-māḥᵃlat* (Ps. 53:1; 88:1) was already presenting problems to the earliest translators. Some understood it as referring to dance *(maḥôl)*, others as referring to a pipe (from *ḥll*). Pfeiffer (1779) sug-

gested that *maḥôl* was referring to flutes elsewhere in the Old Testament as well, e.g., in Ex. 15:20; Jgs. 11:34; 21:2; Ps. 150:4. Following Herder (1783), however, interpreters have suggested a syncretistic interpretation that includes music, poesy, and dance. More recent studies have even interpreted this expression as meaning "to the accompaniment of wooden wind instruments" (Sendrey, 1969b), as a round dance, or as an indication that the psalm is to be performed with a quiet or depressed sound (Foxvog/Kilmer, 1980).

4. *binᵉgînôṯ, ʿal-nᵉgînaṯ* (Ps. 4:1; 6:1; 54:1; 55:1; 61:1; 67:1; 76:1). The root *ngn* was associated with someone who plays musical instruments, that is, with the musician, but also was understood as referring simply to music or songs in general. This variety is also reflected in the early translations. The Septuagint renders as *en hýmnois*, the Vulgate as *in carminibus*, and the second-century Greek Aquila translation as *en psalmoís*. Interestingly, however, the Septuagint also draws on the meaning "song, music" in using other translations as well, such as *psaltérion* in Ezra 33:32 and *kithára* in Job 30:9; of further interest in this context is the nuance of "instrumental music" in Ezra, and yet "mocking song" in Job. Still other meanings are evoked as well, including "drunkard's song" in Ps. 69:13, *kinnôr*-player in 1 S. 16:16; 18:10, and professional instrumentalist in Ps. 68:26; 2 K. 3:15. Most of these examples suggest that the reference is to some type of instrumental playing or music; there is some indication, however, that the reference may sometimes be to vocal performance as well. Unfortunately, in most cases we do not have the additional information necessary to decide between the two. This quandary prompted Sachs (1940) to understand the *nᵉgînâ* as an early form of the later *nigûn*, "melody, melodic formula, mode."

5. The expression *ʾel-hanᵉḥîlôṯ* occurs in Ps. 5:1, and is now generally associated with the root *ḥll*, by extension with *ḥālîl*, and translated "for the flutes." Unfortunately, this interpretation contradicts not only the Septuagint, but also the Vulgate and all other early versions, including even Luther. They associate the word with the meaning "heir" and thus do not think it has any musical reference at all. Hence Koehler/Baumgartner (1967) simply acknowledge this uncertain state of affairs and understand the word as a hymnic or musical *terminus technicus* that we cannot identify more closely until additional information comes to light.

6. The expression *ʾal-haśśᵉmînîṯ* in Ps. 6:1; 12:1 derives from *šᵉmînîṯ*, meaning "eighth." When used in this way with the definite article *ha-*, it is

understood as an instrument with eight strings or as an instrument playing an octave removed from the basic tone. Ps. 6:1 associates *'al-haššᵉmînît* with *binᵉgînôt* (see above), and in 1 Ch. 15:20-21 David organizes his own Levites according to the various groups of instruments, including *binᵉbālîm 'al-ᶜᵃlāmôt* (see above) and *bᵉkinnôrôt 'al-haššᵉmînît*. This juxtaposition of instrumental groups associated with string performance and the reference to various string tunings — probably in octaves — may well be alluding to octave performance in ancient Israel. The heptatonic scale is now known to have been in common use in Ugarit (Foxvog/Kilmer, 1980), and this suggests that octaves were used in ancient Israel as well. Similarly, Athenaeus confirms that the flageolet was also employed (*Deipnosophistes,* xiv.638f.).

7. The expression *'al-šûšan* occurs in Ps. 45:1; 60:1; 69:1; 80:1, and derives from *šûšan,* "lily," though some Old Testament scholars translate as "water lily" or "lotus." Since the present context is a Near Eastern one, this interpretation seems cogent. Twice this expression is used together with the word *'ēdût,* "testimony" (*'al-šôšannîm*). Early versions do not take this expression as having any specifically musical reference, the Septuagint translating as "which are altered," Aquila as "upon the testimony of the flower," and Jerome as "upon the lily of testimony." Today most exegetes and musicologists believe that this expression is to be understood in the same context as that of many other psalms, namely, as the beginning of a song for contrafacts of once familiar lyrics that had long since fallen into obscurity (Werner, 1989). A few authors adduce the witness of late medieval rabbinic literature in interpreting *šûšan* as a musical instrument shaped like a lily (Gesenius, 1906).

Several other Old Testament terms similarly seem to be of significance for our understanding of musical instruments, but their interpretation, like that of the psalm superscriptions, remains unresolved.

1. The plural form *šālîšîm,* which occurs only in 1 S. 18:6, "has been the most disputed musical term of the Hebrew language" (Sachs, 1940). This Old Testament verse recounts how after the victory over the Philistines "the women came out of all the towns of Israel, singing and dancing, to meet King Saul, *bᵉtupîm* (with drums), *bᵉśimḥâ* (with joy), *ûbšālîšîm* (and with *šālîšîm*)." Some interpreters incorporate the meaning of the Hebrew root for "three," *šlš,* in identifying the expression as a reference to a musical instrument characterized by three particular features, either as a sistrum with three horizontal rods, as a lute with three strings, as a

41

triangle, as three-part castanets, or as a triangular harp. Cymbals may also be a possibility from the perspective of onomatopoeic considerations, and indeed, the Septuagint translates *en kymbálois.* Sachs (1940) adduces Latin *tripudium,* German *Treialtrei,* and Austrian *Dreisteyrer* in understanding the expression as referring to a specific dance. The flow of the text itself seems to support this interpretation, since the women are described as coming out *b^etupîm b^esimhâ ûbsālîsîm,* namely, with drums, joy, and *sālîsîm;* given this progression, the *sālîsîm* probably are not referring to yet another musical instrument. Latest research in Akkadian-Sumerian studies, however, has clearly revealed that in the many-sided interpretations of *sālîsîm* the Sumerian etymological provenance is decisive. In a hymn for King Suligi (2094-2047 B.C.) the term *GIS sa.es-dar* refers to a musical instrument, quite new to the king and his surroundings, which had three strings, was built from wood (GIS), and had a resonance body (Eichmann, 1996). The only instrument that fits this description both in terms of chronology and organology is the lute. The word *sa.es* is related to the Hebrew *salos,* and it seems that the term *sālîsîm* from the biblical verse is the best candidate for the name of the lute.

2. The expression *ûn^eqābekā,* "and with your *n^eqābîm* (pl. of *neqeb,* hole, perforation)," occurs only in Ezk. 28:13. It is the position of *tûpîm* and *n^eqābîm* in the enumeration of jewelry in Ezk. 28:13 that has prompted interpreters since Luther to translate this as "pipe." Though no genuinely cogent reasoning supports this interpretation, it has nonetheless become entrenched (e.g., Fétis, 1867). In reality, until additional information comes to light, this verse remains incomprehensible.

8. Instruments in the New Testament

The New Testament mentions instruments in Mt. 6:2; 9:23; 11:17; 24:31; Lk. 7:32; 15:25; 1 Cor. 13:1; 14:7, 8; 15:52; 1 Th. 4:16; Heb. 12:19; Rev. 1:10; 4:1; 5:8; 8:2, 6-8, 10, 12, 13; 9:1, 13, 14; 10:7; 11:15; 14:2; 15:2; 18:22.

Musicological studies have only rarely drawn on the New Testament as a source, particularly for information about instruments. Kraeling/Mowry II (1960), for example, does not mention a single New Testament instrument. Research has come primarily from polemical patristic sources, focusing especially on vocal performance as this relates to the Christian liturgy and on problems relating to instrumental performance (Werner,

1960; Smith, 1962; McKinnon, 1968; Smith, 1984), the only exception being the brief survey presented in Foxvog/Kilmer (1980). It is not without reason, however, that musicologists have exhibited only limited interest in the instruments mentioned in the New Testament. In the first place, not many are mentioned. Whereas the Old Testament has proven to be a rich source of information about the musical culture of ancient Israel/Palestine, the New Testament mentions instruments only twenty-nine times; yet even that number is deceptive, since of those twenty-nine, twelve in Revelation are almost verbatim repetitions. Similarly, the New Testament does not offer any variety even in those twenty-nine occurrences, since only four different instruments can be discerned. Nor is their value very great from an organological perspective, and is restricted largely to performance and sociomusical issues.

In any event, the New Testament writings mentioning these four instruments were probably all composed originally in Greek, and contemporary scholarship dates them with high probability to the second half of the first century A.D. Significantly, the Latin version composed contemporaneous with the Vulgate gives these terms consistent renderings.

1. The New Testament uses the term *aulós* (Lat. *tibia*) to refer both to an instrument (1 Cor. 14:7; see also chap. IV/3) and to a profession (Mt. 9:23; Rev. 18:22). In every instance, the reference is to the single or double *aulós* familiar during the Roman period and richly attested by archaeological finds from Hellenistic-Roman Palestine. The Sepphoris mosaic (see chap. V/5) offers the best representation of one of these instruments for the Roman period. In both the Old and New Testaments, this reed instrument is played at laments for the dead (Mt. 9:23) and at weddings (Mt. 11:17).

2. The New Testament mentions the *kithára* (Lat. *cithara*) five times as an instrument (1 Cor. 14:7; Rev. 5:8; 14:2; 15:2), and three additional times as a profession (1 Cor. 14:7; Rev. 14:2; 18:22), though its references to the *kithára* are usually of a symbolic nature. It is God's instrument (Rev. 15:2), and its sound is used to characterize the "voice from heaven" (Rev. 14:2). This same passage is also of interest because it compares the sound of the *kithára* to the rushing of "many waters" and with the rolling of "loud thunder." Twice the *kithára* players are said to be singing "a new song," and in one of those passages those players are identified more closely as the "twenty-four elders" (Rev. 14:3; 5:8). The sound of the Roman *kithára* may have changed during this period, and as a result the lyre may have devel-

oped a new tonal quality. As artistic virtuosity as well as the quality of the instruments themselves developed further (Fleischhauer, 1964), it is quite possible that listeners may have perceived the sheer power of the instrument to be somewhat overwhelming, thus prompting the comparisons in Rev. 14. It seems more likely, however, that it is now God's own instrument that is to symbolize the spiritual power of the "new song" of Christianity. Given this symbolical perception of these instrument names, it is quite plausible that the instruments in the New Testament "like the *aulós, kithára* may have been used loosely to refer to more instruments of a general class" (Smith, 1962).

3. The New Testament mentions the *sálpinx* (Lat. *tuba*) twenty-two times (Mt. 6:2; 24:31; 1 Cor. 14:8; 15:52; 1 Th. 4:16; Heb. 12:19; and sixteen times in Rev.). In the New Testament, the *sálpinx* is an instrument used for communication and signaling. It now possesses supernatural powers, usually of an apocalyptic nature. It is even "God's trumpet" (1 Th. 4:16). At the beginning of Revelation, John tells us that the "loud voice" he heard behind him was "like a trumpet" (Rev. 1:10). And more: "Now the seven angels who had the seven *sálpinges* made ready to blow them" (Rev. 8:6). Clearly, the *sálpinx* has become an even more imposing instrument. The Old Testament already alluded to the eschatological significance of the *sálpinx* in Ex. 20:19; Isa. 58:1, and the New Testament now picks up on this feature as well as on the theophanic dimensions of the instrument's sound, which it even equates with God's own voice; all these features the New Testament now carries to the extreme. The *sálpinx* is now the supreme instrument of divine praise and veneration, and is transformed into the *tuba mirum terribilis* (1 Cor. 15:52; 1 Th. 4:16) of both the resurrection and the last judgment. Indeed, it is now a sound or even a voice "whose words made the hearers beg that not another word be spoken to them" (Heb. 12:19).

4. The *kýmbalon* (Lat. *cymbalum*) is the familiar Greco-Roman cymbal. It is mentioned but once (1 Cor. 13:1), in this passage together with the *chalkós échôn* (Lat. *aes sonans*), literally "sounding/booming brass." This expression is usually also taken as a type of musical instrument, for example, as a gong, a trumpet, or a kind of kettle drum. More recent scholarship (Harris, 1982), however, understands this as an unequivocal reference to a resonating vase made of brass of the sort that was placed at the rear of Greek amphitheaters and resonated sympathetically to the various pitches of the actors' or singers' voices, providing a kind of acoustic amplification.

This also accords well with Paul's metaphor in this passage, in which he compares the person who speaks without love and deeper understanding to a noisy cymbal that is amplified only artificially. It is an over-interpretation, however, to adduce this metaphor as evidence of a hostile attitude toward any sort of instrumental music during this period, as does Werner (1960).

5. The *symphōnía* (Lat. *symphoniam*) is mentioned only in Lk. 15:25, and refers unequivocally to instrumental music. Moreover this passage is the only one using a collective term in reference to such performance, in this instance in connection with a joyous festival with dancing.

Finally, the three most important musical instruments (see 1., 2., 3. above) are mentioned together in a New Testament passage (1 Cor. 14:7-8); in its own turn, this passage adds a feature quite singular in the Bible by focusing on the articulation and clarity of the sounds made by these instruments: "It is the same way with lifeless instruments that produce sound, such as the *aulós* or the *kithára*. If they do not give distinct notes, how will anyone know what is being played? And if the *sálpinx* gives an indistinct sound, who will get ready for battle?" In repeatedly emphasizing the importance of the clarity of musical performance and comparing it with the comprehensibility of the spoken word, this passage suggests that the actual practice of music had perhaps become subject anew to reflection and that a focus on a certain degree of competency and quality of performance was being articulated. Similarly, this would reflect a new articulation of what music had come to mean, a new articulation of its significance. To a certain extent, one might view this passage as reflective of a larger situation in which the beginnings of the modern western aesthetics of music and performance were emerging.

These musical instruments were an integral part of the New Testament world, so much so that the author of Revelation evokes the image of the *kithára*, the *aulós*, and the *sálpinx* going silent to symbolize the demise of an entire civilization (Rev. 18:22).

CHAPTER II

THE STONE AGE

(Twelfth Millennium-3200 B.C.)

The Stone Age encompasses a rather broad temporal span, extending from the time when ancient Israel/Palestine was first settled by what we now call modern human beings about 700,000 years ago up to the Bronze Age.

Unfortunately, we have uncovered no direct evidence of any acoustic activity from the more distant cultures such as those of the cave dwellers of Tabun or Yabrud from the middle to late recent Acheulean Age (ca. Sixtieth-Tenth millennium B.C.). One can assume, however, that people did engage in organized musical activity during this extended period now known as the "pebble-tool" culture. In lieu of musical instruments in the strict sense, people probably used various objects, both natural and man-made, including tools and even their own bodies, to produce music.

This assumption is plausible enough considering the basic forms of music-making or even noise-production familiar even today from many parts of the world, including the clapping of hands, stamping of feet, beating on one's chest, or slapping one's thigh. As effective as such activity is for producing primitive rhythms, it still leaves behind no tangible material witness. Hence the comparative method offers us the best hypothesis to date for describing the beginnings of music production, an activity that for millennia was a basic component of human culture. Such activity was doubtless also part of the Stone Age culture.

The Natufian Culture occurs considerably later, ca. 12,000-8500 B.C.; it

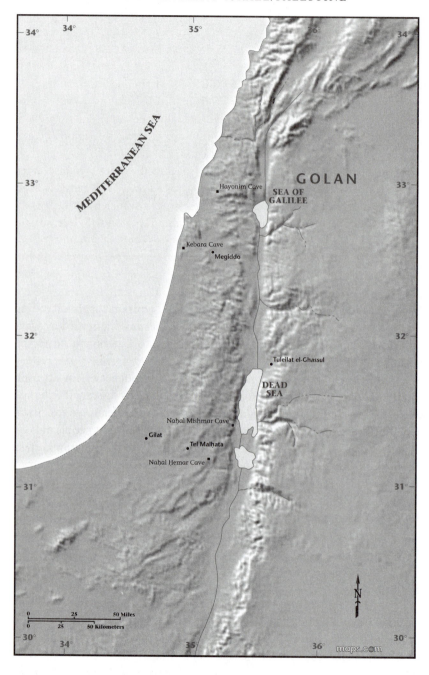

was during this period that the hunter-gatherer culture was replaced by the beginnings of agriculture and animal husbandry. These developments were part of long-term processes that included what is now known as the "neolithic revolution" or, by another designation, the "agricultural revolution," depending on one's focus. Microlithic production developed in this context, and for the first time we find material witnesses to emergent music- or noise-production as well as to an understanding of religion and art associated with intentional acoustic effects.

The historian is handicapped with respect to the Stone Age insofar as source material is still accumulating only very slowly. The result is that scholars must draw conclusions after assessing insufficient evidence, in this case only ten archaeological finds (see Table 1, p. xxviii). While we can deal with most of the historical periods of musical culture in ancient Israel/Palestine on the basis of chronological, geographical, and cultural considerations, the Stone Age does not offer sufficient material for such treatment. Isolated examples must suffice for an admittedly incomplete survey of the period as a whole, and even such a survey is hampered by the difficulty in assessing the often virtually indiscernible changes that took place in Stone Age musical culture over extremely long periods of time. An analogy to such changes might be the hand-axe, which some believe represented the main item of human production for hundreds of thousands of years (Brentjes, 1968). So also did the main noisemakers remain the same for millennia. Especially with regard to the most conservative area of cultural and artistic activity during the Stone Age, namely, cultic music, scholars universally concur that no real changes, or only quite minor ones, took place during this period. Millennia passed before the basic methods of producing noise or sounds changed.

It is during the "neolithic revolution" that the first archaeological finds identifiable as noisemakers or musical instruments appear, suggesting that the new age involved changes not only at socioeconomic and political-intellectual levels, but also with regard to the world of sound. Indeed, these changes were apparently radical enough to be called revolutionary.

The peculiar chronological heterogeneity described earlier as "non-simultaneity within simultaneity" (see p. 4 above) endured for millennia and with unusual tenacity in the musical culture of the Stone Age. Certain musically-related objects of the Natufian culture persisted in various forms for millennia without leaving behind any discernible traces, though idiophones (pendant rattle ornaments) did make their first appearance during the Natufian culture. One characteristic change during this period involved the use of new materials, such as mussels and stone, and even new methods of production and new combinations. Materials were now linked together, given a polished finish, or even adorned with carvings. Indeed, what we seem to have are syncretistic decorative objects such as necklaces of bone or stone whose musical effects resulted from various body movements and emotional expressions; these could include spirited movements during dances, while worshiping the deity, or during work. Such objects functioned on at least two different levels. They were not only noisemakers in the narrower sense, but also broadly accepted cultic objects, personal valuables, or even implements of work attesting a polyaesthetic culture dominated by functional audio-visual values.

Several millennia pass (seventh millennium B.C.) before we find evidence of the mystical "whirring sticks," commonly known as bullroarers, associated with ancestral cults. During the Chalcolithic period, however, the period straddling the transition between the Stone Age and Bronze Age in the fourth millennium B.C., a different revolution takes place, one qualifying as a genuine "organological" or "acoustic" revolution in the sense that new musical instruments appear. It is during this period that we find the first evidence of the hourglass drum and of a new generation of stringed instruments, namely, the harp.

1. Natufians (ca. 12,000-8000 B.C.)

Syncretism of Work, Cult, Adornment, Sound

The more than one hundred cave tombs from Kebara and Hayonim on Carmel, 'Eynan in Galil, and Naḥal Hemar in the Judean Wilderness have yielded the first material evidence of musical activity from the Natufian culture. The findings show that these Stone Age inhabitants had a lifestyle that included intentional acoustic features. The various objects found at these sites include artistic miniatures and jewelry, exhibiting characteristics suggesting independent local provenance and also indicating that this culture experienced an extremely rich period of artistic and intellectual activity. Of the more than two hundred skeletal remains that have been examined from these tombs, approximately twenty had been richly adorned with jewelry made of Dentalium mussels, bones, or animal teeth. These necklaces or chains doubled as objects that could be rattled, and as such attest a syncretistic culture in which work, the cult, jewelry, and sound were often interrelated or even coincided. Such syncretism has been attested in many other parts of the world as well, including Egypt, from the Paleolithic period to the present. Hans Hickmann has called such audiovisual objects or idiophonic jewelry "dance jewelry" or "dance adornment." These syncretistic objects were an integral part of the inhabitants' equipment in their daily struggle for existence, including their attempts to deal with the various problems confronting them in their social lives, their struggles for power, their religious concerns, and their tribal dealings.

One classic example of such objects was found in the Yonim Cave/ Mugaret el-Hamam on Carmel (11,000-9000 B.C.). *In situ*, a female pelvic bone was adorned with a chain belt made out of fox teeth (illust. II.1). Because the belt itself functioned clearly as both adornment and as a means for producing a rattling sound, it qualifies as such idiophonic jewelry. This grave was unusually large, and also contained hundreds of perforated

II.1. Pelvic bone with fox teeth string rattle, Hayonim Cave, IAA 79.536

Dentalium mussels apparently functioning both as adornment and status symbol. That this reflects a genuine cultural tradition is suggested by two skulls that were similarly decorated with crowns made out of these mussels. In any event, this ancient tradition of women, especially dancers, adorning their hips is still practiced in the Near East. This particular woman may have been a prominent figure in Natufian society and was accordingly buried with the symbolic attributes of her position. When we recall that only ten percent of these skeletons were actually thus adorned, we can say with some certainty that such idiophonic jewelry, although certainly not a rarity, nonetheless was restricted to persons belonging to a specific social class.

The Hayonim Cave has yielded objects with considerably more acoustic potential. The bone pendants found here exhibited forms ranging from oval to rectangular to breast- or castanet-shaped (illust. II.2). Hundreds of these

(a)

(b)

II.2. Bone pendant — "castanet form," Hayonim Cave, Carmel, HUIA, H201 etc: (a) a pair; (b) on a cord

unique, finely polished pendants have been discovered. Usually found in pairs, they are without archaeological parallel and exhibit an extremely high degree of craftsmanship. These pairings, along with the identical size and flat interior sides, suggest they were ideal for striking against one another as paired or dual-idiophones. The castanet form seems particularly suitable for such clapping sounds, since their lower parts are somewhat thicker and thus quite resonant. I tried out these Stone Age castanets for myself and found they were capable of producing a pure, transparent, but pitchless sound.

Because Natufian architecture appears first in the northern part of Palestine and is attested there more comprehensively than elsewhere, some scholars believe it also originated there (Weippert, 1988). The idiophonic jewelry just discussed presents a similar situation. The overall evidence of architectural finds, graves, *art mobiles* and jewelry-rattles from the Natufian period suggests that these rattles also originated in the northern part of the country and represent the basic noisemakers of an autochthonous, syncretistic audio-visual culture.

Archaeological finds from this period (tenth-seventh millennium B.C.) include several objects one might call bullroarers (illust. II.3), usually

(a)

(b)

II.3. Bullroarer. (a) Kebara Cave, Carmel, IAA 33.85; (b) Naḥal-Ḥemar Cave, Wilderness of Judah, IAA 84.1745

small pieces of wood with scalelike or comblike ornamentation. Such pieces were tied to the end of a cord and then swung in a circle to produce a wailing or sirenlike sound whose pitch got higher the faster it was swung (illust. II.4). Such devices are familiar from the Paleolithic period onward and even today are still used in many parts of North and South America, Africa, and Australia. Their various symbolic features are related to local Near Eastern cultic traditions. The deepest layer generally involves sexual totemism, with the whirring bullroarer accompanying ritual circumcision; its wailing is understood as the voice of one's ancestors, or, later, of spirits. In any event, this device has always been associated with the world of the supernatural, and in neolithic Israel/Palestine, too, was apparently an auditory cultic device used by the shaman priest. It is probably no accident that the same stratum of the Naḥal Hemar excavations that yielded such whirring devices also yielded various other attributive cultic objects such as a life-size limestone mask (IAA 84-407, THL, illust. 6, 48-49). One can easily imagine a scene in which the Semitic shaman, the sun-god/Shamash priest, whipped his congregation into a religious frenzy by wearing such a mask while swinging these wailing devices in a terrifying display of cultic gesticulation.

II.4. Bullroarer in action (imaginable drawing)

54

2. The Chalcolithic Period (ca. 4000-3200 B.C.)

A. Music in the Dumuzi Cult

Around 4000 B.C., the first objects made of copper appear, and a new period begins: the Chalcolithic period. Discovery of the copper artifacts from the Naḥal Mishmar Caves, with their artistically sophisticated, imaginative shapes, excited the world of art while simultaneously embarrassing scholars in several other scientific disciplines (THL, 72-86). The period also yielded a great many bone, ivory, and wood carvings. Although these finds reflected the artistic and intellectual atmosphere providing the backdrop to this culture, other archaeological artifacts were of much more decisive significance for musicological research. The most splendid examples from the Chalcolithic period include the Gilat figurine with a drum (see below) and the drawing of the Megiddo harp player (see 2B) — both of which attest the real acoustic-organological "revolution" that took place during this period.

In 1975, David Alon uncovered two terra-cotta figures in Gilat (northern Negev) in a building that was either a temple proper or part of a temple (Alon, 1976, plates 33-34). Concerning these two figurines, the so-called Gilat woman and a bizarre sheep figurine, both without archaeological parallels, Alon emphasizes that "the main raison d'être of these vessels was undoubtedly their meaning and cultic function."

Of these two finds, the nude female figurine is of particular interest to us (illust. II.5). She is sitting on an hourglass-shaped stool and is holding a similarly shaped object under her left arm. The vessel she holds on her head with her right hand has been described as a container for butter or milk of the sort Bedouin still use today to hold liquids. The figure itself is portrayed with short, thin legs, a swollen body, and clearly accentuated sexual organs. The entire figure, including the face and hair, is decorated with a red banded or striped pattern. As in many other local finds, the nose is strongly emphasized. The milk container and especially the accentuated genitals indicate the figurine was associated with a fertility rite, and Ruth Amiran has convincingly explicated the cultic significance of the Gilat figurines by drawing attention to their association with the early agrarian Dumuzi cult and myth from Mesopotamia whose basic concepts include milk, juice, fertility, seeds or grain, and blood (Amiran, 1976).

The object the woman is holding under her left arm, however, is of particular interest in our present context. Can this possibly be construed as

II.5. Terra-cotta figurine, Gilat, female with drum, IAA 76.54

an hourglass drum? Most archaeologists have interpreted it as a "bowl" (Alon, 1976), a "high-footed bowl" (Tadmor, 1986), a "vessel" (THL, 65), or as a "stand" of some sort (Hanbury-Tenison, 1985). David Frankel alone adduces a Cypriot figurine from the Bronze Age with a frame drum (British Museum) in suggesting that the object the Gilat woman is holding might well be a drum (Frankel, 1977). The so-called scar-men from Fasa (southern Iran), dating to the late fourth–early third millennium B.C., offer an even more convincing parallel (Paris, Louvre AO 21.104; Berlin, Museum für Vor- und Frühgeschichte XIc 3936/1965). These small, steatite figurines holding small, cylindrical drums under their left arms are generally understood to represent prisoners who must beat their drums in honor of their conqueror (Nadel, 1968; I express gratitude to Professor R. Eichmann for drawing my attention to this source).

Much commends understanding this object as a drum rather than as a bowl or other utensil. First, the shape of the object itself resembles the classic shape of the Near Eastern hourglass drum *(darabukka)* familiar from Old Babylonian seals from the early third millennium B.C. on (Rashid, 1984). Further afield, an hourglass drum dating to 1700-1400 B.C. was unearthed within a Phoenician cultural context on the Iberian peninsula (Cuesta, 1983), and an almost identical small hourglass drum from the Walternienburg-Bernberger culture (2700-2400 B.C.) has now been shown to be of Near Eastern provenance (Seewald, 1934). This chain of parallels strongly suggests that these drums originated somewhere in the Near East, possibly in ancient Israel/Palestine.

A consideration of the way the Gilat woman is actually holding the object is also revealing. Strictly speaking, she is not holding the object in a way familiar from any cultic context. Cultic objects generally were not held under one's arm in this way. Similarly, it is difficult to imagine why household utensils such as goblets or jugs would have been carried or certainly depicted this way. The only object broadly attested as having been carried thus under one's arm is the hourglass drum. Yet even though cultic objects as such were not normally carried in this position, still the most persuasive consideration commending the interpretation as a drum is the cultic context evoked by the figurine's overall symbolism. The elements of milk as evoked by the container on the figurine's head, fertility as evoked by the accentuated genitalia, and blood as evoked by the red ornamentation, all place the figurine squarely within the context of the Dumuzi cult. The very presence of the drum as well as its association with women fit effortlessly into the Dumuzi cultic context, since the instrument itself has deep roots within that cult. It is generally acknowledged that blood, as the magical element of life, and rebirth play an enormous role in the understanding of the drum (Sachs, 1965), and that drums were an integral part of Sumerian mythology. One need only consider "Inanna's Drum Song" and the Sumerian vocabulary at large (Winter, 1983; ANET, 639; Kutscher, 1990).

B. The Appearance of the Harp

The drawing reproduced in illustration II.6a, b was found during excavations in Megiddo (Tell el-Mutesellim) in the northwestern Valley of Jezreel. The location itself was of considerable strategic significance, situated as it is some 40-60 meters above sea level and with a commanding view of the entire surrounding area. From the Chalcolithic period onward, through the Bronze and Iron Age and into the Hellenistic-Roman period, Megiddo played an important role as an international crossroads along the Via Maris in the eastern Mediterranean. It was here that the high powers of the ancient world encountered each other in peace and confronted each other in war, with cultural exchange taking place along a broad spectrum ranging from politics to trade to religion. Megiddo is not mentioned historically before the fifteenth century b.c., during the reign of Thutmose III, who attacked and took the city after a seven-month siege because of its role as an alleged center of a rebellion involving several Canaanite cities. Even before this mention, however, from the fourth millennium on Megiddo had a rich and turbulent history.

Precisely because of this rich history, Megiddo became one of the most important archaeological sites in Israel during the twentieth century, and continues to be of central significance to historians. During the period in question here, the late Chalcolithic period, Megiddo had approximately one thousand to fifteen hundred inhabitants, qualifying it as a smaller to mid-sized city of the Early Bronze Age. Several archaeological finds have shown it had a fairly advanced form of architecture during this period, including the well-known double or "twin temple" attesting the presence of cultic activity involving the worship of twin or even of multiple deities. The Canaanite culture thus shows evidence of relatively early urbanization coinciding with the first Egyptian dynasty as well as with the Uruk IV culture of Mesopotamia.

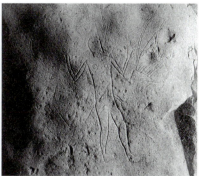

II.6a, b. Etching, Megiddo,
female harpist, IAA 38.954.
Left: (a) entire stone;
above: (b) fragment

Archaeologists have found approximately twenty floor stones, dating to 3300-3000 B.C., with carvings of human beings, animals, and various ornamentation. This dating coincides with the transition from the Chalcolithic to the Early Bronze Age, and although both eastern-Babylonian and western-Egyptian influences are clearly present in these materials, de Vaux has suggested in the *Cambridge Ancient History* that "the Early Bronze Age civilization [of Palestine] can be explained only by the influx of a new population . . . [which] came from the north, perhaps by way of the Jordan valley. . . . Their settlement was effected by peaceful infiltration and not by way of conquest . . . [they] brought with them new crafts, especially an established tradition of architecture and urban life." Recent excavations, however, have revealed that local traditions may have endured in greater continuity than earlier believed, and that precisely these traditions were of considerable cultural significance (Richard, 1987).

These stones were part of an interior courtyard surrounded by several rooms, one of which contained an altar *(bāmâ)* as part of a shrine or sanctuary. The earliest iconographic evidence of drawing in ancient Israel/ Palestine thus stands in immediate proximity to a sacred place.

The nine figures appearing in these carvings (Loud 1948, 271-80) include warriors or hunters, dancers, a female harpist, and possibly a drummer (illust. II.6a, b, 7a). Their physical attributes and clothing are similar, including long noses, pointed headgear, and belts, all of which probably represent local ethnic characteristics. Several features of these carvings suggest that the figures were part of the magical environment of the cult, perhaps even part of a sacrificial rite. The belted nude bodies, hands raised in worship, and especially the proximity of these drawings to a sanctuary all evoke such a context. Moreover, both the animated portrayal of the animals and the dynamic gestures of the human figures show that a remarkably realistic aesthetic sensibility was at work here.

The harpist is an unmistakably female figure with accentuated breasts, and more likely represents a dancer or praying woman than a musician, since her hands are raised and she is not really holding the instrument in any case. Hardly a single bibliographical source does not include a reproduction of the stringed instrument shown in this drawing, and yet the drawing itself has been inaccurately reproduced (see illust. II.7b). As a result, the drawing has proven difficult to interpret and has given rise to the

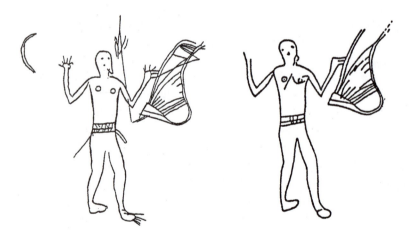

II.7a. Etching, female harpist, copy by   II.7b. Etching, faulty copy by Stauder,
Loud, 1948, fig. 143   1961, fig. 11

60

legend that it actually represents an early version of the lyre, a notion probably going back to Sybil Marcuse, who describes the instrument as "harplike" or "possibly a very large lyre." The same reproduction also appears in two different articles in the *Reallexikon der Assyrologie und Vorderasiatischen Archäologie,* namely, in the articles on the "harp" and on the "lyre."

The drawing from Megiddo unmistakably depicts a triangular harp. Its resonator, also clearly discernible and shaped like a three-sided pyramid, forms the instrument's horizontal base. Two side-arms, one fairly straight and the other elegantly curved in toward the first, are attached to this base; drawn here with double lines, together they form a three-cornered frame. The eight or nine strings are strung between the resonator and the curved side arm of the frame (several horizontal marks at the upper end probably represent attempts at corrections). The harp is about 90 cm. high, and Vorreiter (1972/73) investigated its ergonomic design by reconstructing the instrument itself on the basis of the sketch. The shorter strings are located on the side furthest from the player, a feature incommensurate with the bowed harp or angular harp but certainly typical of the triangular harp. Significantly, the harp is depicted on the stone at a distance from the female player rather than in her hands, suggesting that the artist was intent on underscoring its symbolic character rather than portraying an actual playing situation. It is equally significant that the drawing contains not a single feature associated with the lyre; this instrument is clearly a triangular harp.

At the end of the third millennium B.C., harps with this shape recur within the Cycladic cultural sphere, where the classic triangular harp is attested with the characteristic swan's head (illust. II.8b). While it is true that the authenticity of the marble figures from the Cyclades is still disputed,

II.8a, b, c, d. Megiddo, Cycladic, Georgian, and Abchasien
triangular frame harps, copies

recent research by Martin van Schaik (1998) has shown that some of them are genuine. A stone drawing of a similar triangular harp was discovered in Anatolia dating to a somewhat later period, namely, to the early second millennium B.C. (Bachmann, 2000). These findings in the eastern part of the Mediterranean show that this particular instrument type doubtless represents an important stage in the development of the harp, and that the triangular harp may be considered an ancient Near Eastern typological phenomenon. The Cycladic figure playing the harp is depicted in a sitting position, and here, too, the strings seem to be strung between the horizontal resonator and the curved side arm, and the shorter strings are thus on the side opposite the musician. In fact, during the nineteenth century, an identically shaped and constructed triangular harp was still in use, namely, the *ayum'a* of Abchasien in the northwestern Caucasus. This instrument was played in just this position and closely resembled the Georgian *changi,* itself an instrument that still could have features of an animal's head at the upper end analogous to the swan's beak on the Cycladic harp (see illust. II.8c, d). This particular type also includes the *top-saplyukh* from the Yakutia region of northeastern Siberia, an instrument used to accompany vocal recitation and usually constructed with a bird's head; indeed, its name actually means "wooden craneneck." Seventy to ninety centimeters high, it has five to nine strings; like the Cycladic harp, it is played while positioned on the right knee (see Sadokov, 1970, illust. 6), the left hand playing the melody in the higher registers and the right thumb playing the accompanying drone strings in the lower registers. These instruments from the Caucasus and Siberia are useful for comparative purposes, since they may demonstrate the way the Megiddo harp itself was actually played and, as successor harps, justify viewing it as a prototype of the triangular harp.

On the other hand, a contemporaneous pictograph from Uruk IV ("balag" symbol) and several seals from the Mesalim period (ca. 2500 B.C.; Rashid, 1984) show a development involving the Babylonian crescent harp which the Megiddo harp also seems to have incorporated. The lengthened triangular resonator retained its shape, as did the string holder; but because the number of strings was reduced and the string holder itself lengthened, the third side became superfluous, and was accordingly eliminated. In Egypt as well, a balance within the string arrangement was maintained in the later crescent harp by enlarging and extending these features (Hickmann, 1961, illust. 2-4).

The extensive spread of the Megiddo harp's influence to the northeast and southwest corresponds to the migration patterns also discernible during this period, suggesting that this instrument may well have originated locally. As such, the Megiddo harp seems to be yet another witness to the highly developed, original artistic tradition in ancient Israel/Palestine that evolved from "indigenous urbanization processes in Early Bronze I" (Richard, 1987). This unique phenomenon represents what at present must be regarded as the earliest known iconographic witness to the triangular harp.

Because this harp is obviously a rather advanced instrument for this period, it must already have passed through a long period of development. Unfortunately, no examples of its transitional forms have come to light. It doubtless began as one of the simpler chordophones, including the musical bow, ground zither, and similar string musical instruments, before arriving at the more complicated static construction now attested by the Megiddo harp. During the Canaanite urbanization, however, which occurred during the fifth-fourth millennia B.C., an enormous variety of culture influences converged to produce, among other things, an impressive acoustic revolution involving the musical instruments themselves. The context suggests that this harp may itself have been an indigenous development. Indeed, the Megiddo harp may be understood as one indication among others that a new, autochthonous culture was emerging during this period, a development first pointed out by Anne Caubet (1994) in connection with the northernmost part of Canaan (Ugarit). A more extensive assessment of the overall musical culture in Canaan, however, confirms that this development extended to the entire geographical-cultural and musical Canaanite sphere, and was a phenomenon common to the entire Near Eastern musical culture.

That the cultic drum and harp inaugurated a new world of sound in this region, however, is not quite the whole story. Because representations of these instruments were found in the immediate proximity of an active cult locale, they also attest the emergence of a musical culture of (actually, female) priests. Moreover, the first evidence of this culture shows that even in the musical sphere, individuals now became the focal point. That is, music in this world was now socially stratified and professionally compartmentalized, apparently with only select professionals actually engaged in its praxis. Both they and their instruments were now subject to extraordinary veneration or even apotheosis, and what emerged was a phenomenon akin to the modern cult of celebrity and stardom.

It is of some consequence that musical instruments and related activities appear with a considerable time lag in artistic representations. Indeed, the more distant the historical epoch, the greater this temporal lag. In Chalcolithic iconography, this phenomenon pushes the actual time line back several centuries. Similarly, advanced musical instruments such as the Megiddo harp do not simply appear out of nowhere. Unfortunately, however, the missing link connecting this particular harp with its precursors among neolithic string instruments in ancient Israel/Palestine has not yet come to light; we can only surmise that such a link was an early form of the musical bow or a more primitive form of the harp itself.

The musical culture during the Chalcolithic period culminates in the terra-cotta female drummer from Gilat and the first drawing of a harp from Megiddo. Developments in the musical culture, however, were part of a larger development within Natufian culture at large whose main features included what was apparently the first real burgeoning of emphatically indigenous intellectual and artistic activity. Does the presence of such unique autochthonous artistic development in the larger sense not also suggest that a similarly autochthonous musical style developed concurrently? In any event, do these isolated archaeological finds allow us to say anything substantive about the musical culture of the epoch?

As sparse as the information admittedly is, certain conclusions can be drawn concerning the nature of this musical world. A certain corpus of artifacts does after all stand at our disposal, and some attempts have been made at reconstructing both the instruments themselves and the sounds they produced. Considered together with comparative methodology, this material does allow certain characteristics to emerge.

In many instances, the dynamic power of the music produced during this period was by contemporary standards quite modest. Nor could it be otherwise in Natufian villages with between sixty and at most two hundred inhabitants whose only instruments were the idiophonic jewelry discussed earlier. In larger, collective performance, such instrumentation in all likelihood produced an overall effect dominated by clanking sounds of indefinite pitch.

Moving up the social ladder of the musicians themselves, the sounds and resulting music became more sophisticated, primarily as regards dynamics and timbre. The most important consideration for musical formulas was the rhythmic models of functional activities such as work and ritual. That is, music was tied to social and professional situations, with specific social situations prompting the development of "pathogenic" music (Curt Sachs, 1968) in an otherwise more consistent sound environment.

Although the earlier Natufian musical culture was apparently centered in the northern Carmel region, the organological revolution that produced the more advanced forms of the membranophone and chordophone probably took place in various locales all over the country, with a *terminus post quem non* probably around the late or waning Neolithic period (ca. fifth millennium).

The bullroarers mentioned above represent the first signs of an emergent musical culture whose protagonists were the priestly class. This emergence was part of the overall "acoustic revolution" that took place during the Chalcolithic period and in whose wake individuals developed virtuosity as professional players of certain instruments, in this case as drummers or harpists.

CHAPTER III

THE BRONZE AGE

(3200-1200 B.C.)

S everal factors prompted the musical culture of ancient Israel/Palestine to move on to the next stage. The socioeconomic situation changed, with urban culture replacing the Stone Age village culture in many parts of the country. As a result of this development, more and more inhabitants moved into the new urban centers, and rapid demographic changes took place. Because the smaller cities now had up to a thousand inhabitants, and the larger ones between six and eight thousand, musical life in them required more differentiated and more sophisticated sound production than was earlier the case. Earlier instruments no longer served the needs of the inhabitants of these emergent cities, and so the instruments themselves were subjected to change and further development. By and large, these changes prompted the development of musical instruments capable of producing a higher volume of sound.

The musical culture of Canaan reached an astonishingly advanced stage of development during the Bronze Age. Moreover, like its two larger neighbors, Egypt and Babylonia-Assyria, it did so at a unified autochthonous level. Scholars have often asserted that the musical culture in Canaan or ancient Israel/Palestine was only a receptive one, situated propitiously at the crossroads of the ancient Near East but possessing "no civilization of its own" (Sendrey, 1969b). Recent research, however, has taken a harder look at comparative archaeological materials and found that this musical culture in its own turn exerted considerable influence on

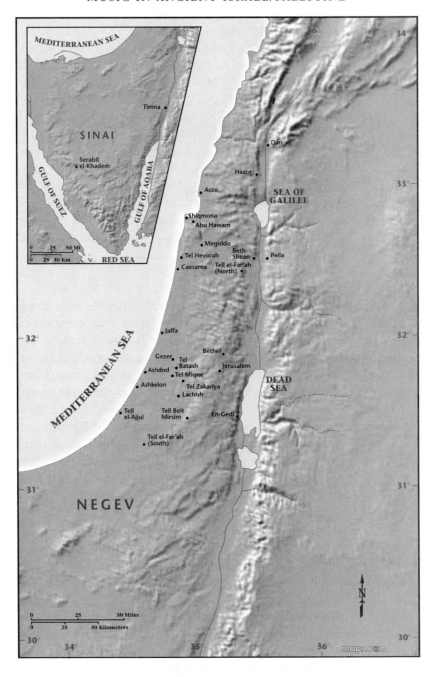

Timna

SINAI

Serabit
el-Khadem

GULF OF SUEZ

GULF OF AQABA

MEDITERRANEAN SEA

0   25   50 Mi
0   25 50 Km

RED SEA

Dan

Hazor

SEA OF
GALILEE

Acco

Shiqmona
Abu Hawam

Megiddo

Beth-
Shean   Pella

Tel Hevorah
Caesarea   Tell el-Far'ah
(North)

Jaffa

Bethel

Gezer   Tel
Batash   Jerusalem
Ashdod
Tel Miqne
Ashkelon
Tel Zakariya
Lachish

DEAD
SEA

Tell
el-Ajjul   Tell Beit
Mirsim   En-Gedi

Tell el-Far'ah
(South)

NEGEV

MEDITERRANEAN SEA

0   25   50 Miles
0   25   50 Kilometers

N

maps.com

68

its surroundings. It is no accident that most written witnesses that mention ancient Israelite/Palestinian music in the neighboring regions of the Near East date to the Bronze Age (see pp. 85-86). Let us mention here only one of the most recently discovered documents from the Manatân corpus of cuneiform tablets to the last king of Mari Simri-Lim (1774-1761 B.C.). This tablet (M5117) contains a letter in Akkadian which informs the king that a delegation from Hazor will arrive at his Mesopotamian residence where, among others, there will be three *lú-nar-mes*, learned, highly professional singers/musicians (instrumental performers) from *mar-tu*, the West (Malamat, 1999).The Mari king kept an impressive group of singers and musicians at his castle, and among them a number from Hazor, which, along with Ugarit, was at this time considered one of the great centers of musical learning. This clearly shows that in the Bronze Age the exchange of musical arts was proceeding in both directions — from the East to the West and from the West to the East.

During recent years the real dimensions and profundity of the many-sided Canaanite, especially Ugarit, influence on later Near Eastern developments have come to light. To show this, Cyrus H. Gordon pointed, along with the Ugarit alphabet and literature, to nothing so much as to music, which "had been cultivated as an art in Canaan for centuries, not only as folk music but also as an academic discipline at centers such as Ugarit" (1996, 2784-85). The biblical Psalms and David, the musician, were the "culmination of a long development of a great tradition that included what has been taught in the academies of Canaan since at least three centuries before his [David's — JB] birth." We may thus maintain that music, like "Ugarit language and literature, including its poetic structures, was taken over by the Hebrews, who built upon a ready-made medium for expressing their original contribution" (idem).

One of the most intriguing aspects of Canaanite musical culture during this period concerns the instruments themselves, the most tangible witnesses to that culture. The Canaanites were familiar with virtually every instrument type already in use in the ancient Near East. At the same time, however, they imprinted upon each of those instruments specifically Canaanite features or altered each in a specifically Canaanite way, affecting such aspects as form, performance, and function. For example, the lyre, already known as the *knr* during the Bronze Age, is attested only in Canaan as a solo instrument. Commensurately, it is played in Canaan in a new position, one more conducive to virtuoso performance in the hands of a soloist. Similarly, the lute seems to have been played in a hitherto unknown way. The features now accompanying its performance suggest a more popular, informal, syncretistic style that combined music together with dance and farce. Prior to this period, the double pipe, a reed instrument, was never portrayed as a solo instrument accompanying erotic dance. The small, round frame drum *(tōp)* appears quite early, at the beginning of the second millennium B.C., on a rock drawing in the Negev as an instrument accompanying a round dance of male figures, attesting thus a Near Eastern tradition thousands of years old. A great many bronze cymbals *(mṣltm)* have been found along the entire length of the Levantine coast from Ashkelon to Ugarit. Independent forms of other idiophones, including especially clay rattles (see chap. III/5), have been found in great numbers in excavations, confirming further the autochthonous nature of the musical culture of ancient Israel/Palestine.

A whole range of historical factors invites us to reassess the musical culture during this period. The understanding of Israel's origins has been revised during the past few years (see Finkelstein/Naaman, 1994). Many scholars no longer believe the country was established by means of conquest, but believe rather that Israel emerged during the eleventh century B.C. as a result of complicated and radical socioeconomic developments accompanying a process of migration which involved the entire Near East during the Late Bronze Age. A dichotomy of highland and lowland cultures developed from the region's demographic dichotomy, which included both nomadic populations and, in greater numbers, sedentary populations. At the same time, the earlier Canaanite city-states were clearly in demise, and the resulting vacuum was filled at least in part by an influx of sea-peoples and other groups, Semitic and non-Semitic alike. The resulting historical situation was characterized by two features that would decisively affect the development of music in the region: the strong Canaanite cultural heritage, and a remarkably heterogeneous local cultural tradition only partially influenced by immigrants.

Even at this time, Canaan possessed a rich indigenous musical tradition. Ugaritic sources from the Late Bronze Age (1400-1300 B.C.) attest the names of numerous instruments *(knr, tp, mṣltm,* also the word *šr,* song) that show up only much later in the Old Testament.

Various comparative attempts have been made to understand the music itself more precisely. One possible bit of evidence in this regard, albeit one that must be approached with caution, is the well-known collection of

Ugaritic cuneiform writings (1500-1300 B.C.), which have generally been understood as representing musical notation (Wulstan, 1971; Kilmer, 1976; Duchesne-Guillemin, 1984; Smith and Kilmer 2000). Scholars have suggested such notation might also apply to contemporaneous Canaanite music as well. Given the similarity between the instrument inventory at least based on the names enumerated in those writings, and the presumed similarity regarding how they were actually played, one might assume that the musical styles and probably the overall results were also similar. Scholars have also compared Ugaritic-Babylonian melodies with Jewish-Babylonian psalms (Duchesne-Guillemin, 1984).

It is also possible, however, that melodies were notated using a different system during this period in Canaan, perhaps even a non-written one. Chironomy is documented in Egypt at least since the 4th Dynasty and has never completely disappeared from musical praxis. It is one of the oldest traditions associated with Israelite liturgical singing, being documented at least since the beginning of the Christian age (*b. Ber.* 62a), and is still in use in some East African congregations.

What we know about the instruments used in Canaan during this period and about musical performance suggests that the resulting music was extremely emotional and perhaps even orgiastic. The large number of rattles and cymbals excavated from this period certainly points in that direction. Similarly, the functional incorporation of aerophones and chordophones into this music would have enhanced such an effect; nor should one forget that certain finds from Iron Age I derive from a Canaanite musical heritage. Moving from one local center of urban culture to the next with their accompanying profusion of deities during the Bronze Age, one would probably find that the musical styles differed primarily with respect to the fullness of sound and the resulting volume, but not significantly with respect to the instruments themselves.

1. Dance with Lyres and Drums

In December 1955, Emmanuel Anati discovered a large number of drawings in the central Negev carved into stone plates with flint or pebble stone (Anati, 1955a-b). The Negev drawings represent a widespread phenomenon of prehistoric art reflecting a style indigenous to the Near and Middle East, extending from southern Syria through the Negev and the wilderness areas of Sinai to northern Arabia, and encompassing an enormous time period, from the Paleolithic to the Byzantine period. The significance of these illustrations is suggested not least by the tenacity with which their tradition has persisted up till the present; even today, nomadic Bedouin tribes still use them to indicate ownership or tribal affiliation. These nomadic peoples were primarily hunters and later livestock herders, and this art form was clearly influenced by their distinctive lifestyle. The desert regions where these stone artists lived and worked, however, does not lend itself to the kind of stratification archaeologists need in order to make decisions regarding dating, and so the chronological classification of this iconography has proven to be extremely problematical. As a result, scholars have suggested an extraordinarily wide range of dates for the Negev drawings (illust. III.1a, b, c) extending from the fourth millennium B.C. (Brentjes, 1968) to the Hellenistic-Roman period (Bayer, 1968c).

The drawings depict two figures with lyres (illust. III.1b). The accentuated hips and the hairstyle (a characteristic Babylonian style from the first half of the second millennium B.C.) identify these figures as nude women, and though they are portrayed as dancing, they are only schematically connected with the instrument, as if the artist was more intent on evoking a conceptual association than on portraying an actual playing situation (as was possibly also the case with the female harpist from Megiddo, illust. II.6a). The animal resembles the jackal from the famous animal chapel of Ur (Rashid, 1984, illust. 8), though it is probably a leopard or a lion. Interestingly, the Semitic origin of the lyre is confirmed by an unexpected witness insofar as the Egyptian hieroglyph for the lyre includes a lion.

One particular feature of this Negev drawing is of interest in this regard. Although animals are among the most widespread topoi appearing in connection with music in Near Eastern iconography, the kind of face-to-face juxtaposition of human being and animal found in this drawing is otherwise virtually unknown. If this scene is depicting a hunting ritual, or perhaps animal worship or even taming, then it might derive from a hunting culture or a culture otherwise engaged in cultivating or domesticating animals as found in Palestine during the first half of the second millennium B.C.

Structurally, the Negev-lyre can be classified within the series of asymmetrical box lyres that migrated from early-dynastic and Akkadian Mesopotamia (illust. III.2a, b, c) through the Negev (illust. III.2d, e, f), and into Egypt's New Kingdom (illust. III.2h, i, j). The oxhead ornamentation dis-

III.1a. Negev rock etchings, *in situ*

appeared quite early in this process (illust. III.2d); the instrument gradually decreased in size from 120-130 cm. to 50-60 cm. and increasingly was played in a more comfortable, horizontal position (illust. III.2f). Indeed, even the Mesopotamian lyres already attest the various playing positions used in the Negev lyres, including both the shorter and longer yoke (illust. III.2b, g). In some examples, animal heads were still discernible within the bulges or curvature of these yoke arms, as also attested in Egyptian lyres (Manniche, 1975). The asymmetrical lyre form has exhibited great tenacity, and the Ethiopian Amharas still use it as a cultic instrument; indeed, Amhara itself lies well within the ambience of the Negev drawings.

To the left and below the lyre players, the artist has portrayed a dance scene (illust. III.1c); the figures have accentuated genitalia and what may be daggers attached to their belts. This dagger-phallus symbolism probably derives from the fertility rite that accompanied the Canaanite Baal cult. Each of the three figures performing a round dance holds one hand up in the air and the other at his side. One of the dancers seems to be waving a kerchief of some sort above his head, and some other object also seems to

III.1b, c. Rock etchings, fragments with lyre players, dancers, and drummer

be hovering above the head of the second. Although the round dance as such is attested in the glyptic of ancient Israel/Palestine at least since the second half of the fourth millennium B.C., this particular type, possibly cultic in nature, derives not from Palestine, but from northern Syria, or, more exactly, from ancient Mesopotamia (Ben-Tor, 1977), confirming once again the Mesopotamian origin both of the drawing as a whole and

III.1d. Modern round dancers, Israel (from Bahat 1970)

of the female lyre players. Virtually all Semitic male round dances today still include this type of dance in which kerchiefs or daggers are swung above the head (illust. III.1d; cf. 1980, Qassim plate 3).

The figure dancing to the left seems to be shaking two basket-, fruit-, or terra-cotta rattles. The man to the right is either dancing or squatting, and is playing the small round drum so familiar from Near Eastern iconography (diameter ca. 30-50 cm.), in this case with his arms outstretched in front. This position, however, although not attested later in ancient Israel/Palestine proper, is familiar from the early second-millennium Babylonian tradition (Rashid, 1984) as well as from later Egyptian performances from the 18th and 19th Dynasties (Hickmann, 1961). Still, even though the two witnesses from these neighboring cultures show the drum being used to accompany dancing as in the Negev drawing, the Old Babylonian drum is probably more closely related to the instrument used in ancient Israel/Palestine as far as both chronology and the gender of the musician are concerned. It was the earlier tradition that took the familiar east-west route through ancient Israel/Palestine.

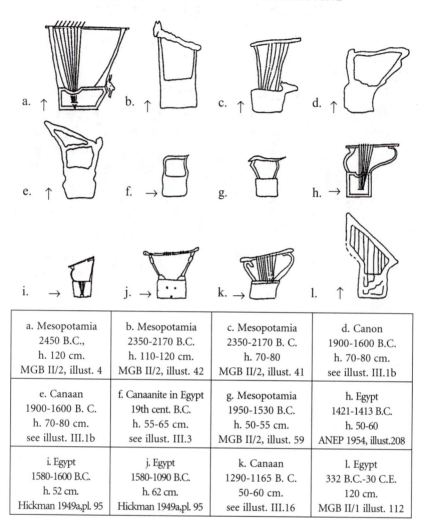

a. Mesopotamia 2450 B.C., h. 120 cm. MGB II/2, illust. 4	b. Mesopotamia 2350-2170 B.C. h. 110-120 cm. MGB II/2, illust. 42	c. Mesopotamia 2350-2170 B. C. h. 70-80 MGB II/2, illust. 41	d. Canon 1900-1600 B.C. h. 70-80 cm. see illust. III.1b
e. Canaan 1900-1600 B. C. h. 70-80 cm. see illust. III.1b	f. Canaanite in Egypt 19th cent. B.C. h. 55-65 cm. see illust. III.3	g. Mesopotamia 1950-1530 B.C. h. 50-55 cm. MGB II/2, illust. 59	h. Egypt 1421-1413 B.C. h. 50-60 ANEP 1954, illust.208
i. Egypt 1580-1600 B.C. h. 52 cm. Hickman 1949a,pl. 95	j. Egypt 1580-1090 B.C. h. 62 cm. Hickman 1949a,pl. 95	k. Canaan 1290-1165 B. C. 50-60 cm. see illust. III.16	l. Egypt 332 B.C.-30 C.E. 120 cm. MGB II/1 illust. 112

III.2a-l. Mesopotamian, Egyptian, and Canaanite lyre shapes

We cannot help but notice that one significant characteristic of Old Babylonian musical culture recurs in these Negev drawings, namely, the association of rhythm instruments (drum, rattles) and chordophones (lyre) with dancing (Rashid 1984, 76), an ensemble also associated with the Dumuzi cult discussed earlier. Dancing and music, including drummers and lyre players, were an indispensable part of the celebrations accompanying fertility rites, the "sacred wedding" of the prince/priest with the high priestess symbolizing the deities Inanna and Dumuzi.

To what extent, however, did this tradition or some form of it continue on in ancient Israel/Palestine? The Negev drawings clearly attest that the Sumerian or, more properly, the Old Babylonian cult was not cultivated here in its earlier imperial form. During the Middle Bronze Period, the strictly canonized form of the Tammuz cult was relaxed in ancient Israel/Palestine, especially in those parts of the Negev Desert still characterized more by the earlier nomadic culture. These changes doubtless also had an effect on the music associated with the cult. Whereas Old Babylonian terra-cotta reliefs depict the nude female musicians in static positions, these musicians are dancing in the Negev drawings. Moreover, whereas both sources portray men dancing (or squatting) in sparse clothing and with drums, the Negev drawings depict them in slightly different clothing and participating in a group dance. It may be that the Old Babylonian materials are portraying professional musicians, whereas the Negev drawings reflect their surrounding culture in portraying local shepherds or warriors. The chordophones are likewise different. In the Old Babylonian sources, the smaller, portable stringed instruments are already making an appearance (lyres and lutes held horizontally), while in the Negev the older, more cumbersome lyres are still portrayed, rather primitive and crude imitations of the original imperial instruments (illust. III.1b).

Our findings so far, however, do not exhaust what we can know about musical performance in Canaan during the early second millennium B.C. At least as far as stringed instruments are concerned, a great deal can be learned from the well-known fresco unearthed in Beni-hasan in Egypt (illust. III.3, III.2f), one of the rare instances in which iconography from outside ancient Israel/Palestine in the stricter sense can be used to teach us more about the musical history of Canaan itself. The Beni-hasan fresco has been dated to approximately 1900 B.C. (12th Dynasty), and has since the nineteenth century been adduced and voluminously discussed as a witness to the culture and musical activity cultivated by the nomadic tribes in the Sinai and its vicinity. Indeed, more popular writings have even used it to illustrate Abraham's journey to Egypt. Thomas Staubli has presented the most thorough criticism and analysis to date of this illustration (Staubli, 1991).

III.3. Grave mural, Beni-hasan, tomb of Khnumhotep II, fragment of the northern wall, by Newberry, 1893, pl. XXXI

The group portrayed on this mural seems to have consisted of thirty-seven men, women, and children. They have arrived with weapons, asses, and wild animals (ibex and gazelle) and have been introduced to the master of the grave, the overseer of hunters Khnumhotep. A superscription tells us that the leader of the group is a certain Abî-shar, "the ruler of a foreign country," who brings stibium, a black eye cosmetic valued by the Egyptians. Staubli believes these people actually represent a group familiar with the desert whom the Egyptians have hired to find the raw material necessary to make the eye cosmetic. Yet neither this suggestion nor Staubli's identification of this nomadic group as desert gypsies is entirely convincing. The group's possible relationship with Israelites also remains unresolved. These uncertainties notwithstanding, however, it seems clear enough that the group represents Semitic nomads, tent-dwellers whose leader bears the Canaanite name Abî-shar. These nomads were not only hunters, however, but also apparently engaged in smithing, and at least part of their musical activity included the use of lyres. In this context, the parallel with Gen. 4:20-22 is indeed amazing.

One of the nomads is holding a completely new instrument. Unlike the older, larger, rather cumbersome lyre, which was held vertically, this instrument was smaller (ca. 50x30 cm.), portable, and almost symmetrical in form. It was held horizontally so that it could even be played comfortably while walking, as is the case in the representation here, while simultaneously allowing the musician to breathe more easily while singing. This particular instrument, portrayed here in the hands of distinctly Semitic nomads and yet far to the southwest of Canaan proper, is richly attested and doubtless represents an early example of the horizontal lyre, a logical development for musicians who, as part of a nomadic group such as this one, were constantly in motion and thus needed a more portable instrument. Present evidence does not yet allow an unequivocal answer to the question whether this nomadic instrument migrated to the east, to Mesopotamia, or in the opposite direction, to the west.

One thing does seem certain. During the Middle Bronze Period, the inventory of musical instruments in the larger sense, their mode of performance (particularly the way the drum was held), and the artistic context in general suggest that such activity in ancient Israel/Palestine was still closely associated with the Old Babylonian culture despite the dominant presence of Egyptian influence in virtually every other area of both material and intellectual culture.

The stone drawings under discussion here were found near Kadesh-Barnea. During the middle Canaanite period, often called the patriarchal age, this area was an important center of nomadic Israelite tribes, who used it as a stopover during their migrations from Mesopotamia to Egypt. The patina color of these drawings is much darker than that of the later groups (Anati, 1963). Moreover, because later contour drawings were also more static, the more dynamic movements and more profuse compositional style as well as the deep-notch technique of these illustrations seem more closely related to the style obtaining at the beginning of the second millennium. Considerations of both the lyre players and the dance group thus date these illustrations to the early second millennium B.C. and suggest Mesopotamian provenance.

Our source materials do not yet permit us to determine with any certainty the actual names of the instruments familiar during the Bronze Age which we have identified here as the lyre and drum. Modern musical instrument scholarship concurs that the lyres used in ancient Israel/Palestine were designated by the biblical words *kinnôr* and *nēḇel*. If we take this as our point of departure in this context as well, then the type of lyre portrayed in the Negev drawings moved from the Babylonian-Syrian region toward the west at about the same time the word *kinnôr* itself first appears in written sources, or perhaps even earlier, when cultural exchange was becoming especially active in the Near East. The small round frame drum also identified in these drawings did not really undergo any significant change in form in ancient Israel/Palestine from this time on, and may already have been called a *tōp* during this period as well.

These findings suggest that in ancient Israel/Palestine, too, the organological-acoustic revolution reached a high point. The full power of that revolution is attested not only in the instrumental timbral innovations of the harp, lyre, and a bit later also the lute (see below), but also in the sheer profusion and variety it produced and in the new modes of performance these new instruments themselves prompted.

2. The Lute

As trading increased with partners from the Early Bronze Period such as the older Babylonian dynasties, and as new contacts were made with the emergent Egyptian New Kingdom, the attendant cultural exchange also introduced into ancient Israel/Palestine new musical traditions, new modes of performance, and even new musical instruments. The result was a clearly discernible change in the region's musical life manifested not least in a changed inventory of musical instruments.

The lute, an instrument with completely new possibilities and new performance principles, had for at least eight hundred years already been a standard musical instrument in the Babylonian Kingdom before finally appearing in ancient Israel/Palestine during the first half of the sixteenth century B.C. Interestingly, it appears concurrently, or perhaps one or two centuries later, in Egyptian iconography. A peculiar situation now arises insofar as from the early sixteenth to the thirteenth century B.C. — a relatively short period — the lute and music based on it seems to have experienced a unique golden age in the Canaanite settlements of the Late Bronze Age; then, however, it disappears completely before reappearing during the Hellenistic period.

The terra-cotta figurine from Tell el-ʿAjjûl (possibly ancient Sharuhen, ca. 12 km. south of Gaza) (illust. III.4) dates to the first half of the sixteenth century B.C. and can thus be viewed as deriving from the Hyksos

III.4. Lute player,
terra cotta, Tell el-ʿAjjûl,
IAA 33.1567

culture (Petrie, 1933). The Hyksos (1650-1550 B.C.) are generally identified as western Semites coming originally from the Syrian-Canaanite region. During the 13th Dynasty, they penetrated into Egypt, and by the 15th
Dynasty had come to power in lower Egypt and were ultimately expelled
from Egypt around 1550 by forces from upper Egypt.

Enduring Hyksos innovations in Egypt included lute playing. The
small terra-cotta figurine from Tell el-ʿAjjûl, about 9.5 cm. tall, is probably
an object left in transit; it clearly resembles a lute player from the Old Babylonian period now in the Iraq Museum (Rashid, 1984, illust. 81). In both
instances, the instrument itself is actually a lute-shaped block, indicating
perhaps that the artists did not have a clear understanding or image of the
new instrument. The head covering is also similar in both examples. More
importantly, however, the lute player from Tell el-ʿAjjûl is holding the instrument not horizontally, but in a more modern position, with the neck
held up at an angle, suggesting that a change took place when the instrument migrated from Mesopotamia to ancient Israel/Palestine.

The terra-cotta relief from Dan (Lachish, at the foot of Mt. Hermon), known as the "Dan dancer" (illust. III.5), dates to the fifteenth century and is one of the most remarkable representations of lute players we have. The biblical city of Dan was occupied from about the fifth millennium onward, and during Middle and Late Bronze periods was actively engaged in trade with middle and northern Syria, especially with Mari. The instrument's

III.5. Lute player, terra cotta, Dan, HUC 23.095

long neck, almost rectangular resonance body, and upright position suggest Cassite influence. Biran (1986) thinks the figure's clothing exhibits Hittite characteristics, but one also finds such features among the Shosu nomads who lived much farther south in southern Transjordan (Giveon, 1971, plate XVIc:1), suggesting the figure from Dan may also be an itinerant guild musician from the Canaanite period. Several features support the interpretation of the "Spielmann-Natur" of the musician: the player holding his left arm in a highly unusual position, with the resonator body tucked behind the arm; the hand above the instrument with its elevated elbow, and the plucking technique almost in the middle of the fingerboard — everything suggests that this figure is a folk musician. The dance position with a raised leg is also unusual, while the expressionless face might represent a mask worn during performance. Although masks appear in ancient Israel/Palestine as early as the seventh millennium B.C. as well as during the Bronze Age, this is the only archaeological evidence we have of a person actually wearing a mask.

None of these characteristics has any Near Eastern parallel from this period, and the combination of instrumental music, dance, and theater in the Dan figurine suggests that a highly professional group of entertainers had developed whose activity was quite separate from the cult. This particular relief was found on a paving stone in an interior courtyard where such performances were perhaps conducted, suggesting that the terra-cotta tablet is actually a representative symbol or even the identifying icon of a particular artists' guild (Biran, 1986).

The third witness to the lute, dating between the Late Bronze Age and the Hellenistic period (James, 1966) and unearthed in Beth-shean, is the bronze figure, about 15.6 cm. tall, of a nude woman wearing a headpiece (a crown?) and jewelry on her neck, arms, and feet (illust. III.6a). Although the figure is still intact in the first published photograph (Fitzgerald, 1931, plate XXVI:2; here illust. III.6a), the neck of the lute has already been broken off in the IAA photograph of 1944 (see also *ISBE*, I, 476). In the original photograph, the instrument seems to have two strings. Its structure exhibits clear Egyptian influence insofar as the neck penetrates through the resonator's leather covering (perhaps a turtle or tortoise shell) in two places, and the instrument itself is about 60-70 cm. long; these features correspond exactly to the smaller form of the long-necked Egyptian lutes of the 18th Dynasty. Indeed, this nude female figurine resembles the ivory figurine of Megiddo, which Barnett has called an "Egyptian-Canaanite hy-

(a)   (b)

III.6. Female lute player, bronze, IAA M969:
(a) original, 1931; (b) present state

brid" dating from the thirteenth-twelfth century B.C. This figure, however,
rather than depicting a slave girl, now allegedly portrays a sacred prostitute, the qᵉdēšâ (Barnett, 1982), suggesting that these Canaanite prostitutes
adopted the lute as their own, changing what was earlier an instrument re-
served for men in the Babylonian culture into one for women. In sexual
terms, this figurine's association with the lute betrays her profession as a
(sacred) prostitute, a function maintained even as late as the Baroque period. It is perhaps worth noting that Egyptian grave murals from the fif-
teenth-fourth centuries B.C. portray lute players nude, in marked contrast
to the depictions of female lyre or harp players.

We are still unsure what the lute was called in Canaan, although various suggestions have been put forth drawing on names used in the Bible: *šālîšîm* (Kolari, 1947); *kinnôr* (Stainer, 1914); *minnîm* (Bayer, 1968a); *nēḇel* (Benzinger, 1927), and *sabbᵉkā'* (Engel, 1864). The word *šālîšîm* is the plural of *šlš* and derives from Akk. *schalaschtu*, Heb. *šalōš*, meaning three. Though mentioned only once in the Old Testament (1 S. 18:6), here, too, *šālîšîm* refers to an instrument associated with women and pleasure. Similarly, after a brief period of popularity, the lute does not appear again in any Palestinian iconography. In any event, the ensemble consisting of lute and drum is a characteristic of ancient Near Eastern iconography (see Rashid, 1984, illust. 58), and in the Old Testament, too, the *šālîšîm* appears together with drums ("*bᵉtupîm* [with drums], *bᵉšimḥâ* [with joy], *ûḇšālîšîm* [and with *šālîšîm*])" (on the etymology of the biblical term *šālîšîm* see chap. I, pp. 41-42).

The origin of the lute has been the topic of much recent discussion. Rashid (1984) has shown that it probably can be traced back to Akkadian culture (see also Eichmann, 2000). Canaanite examples suggest that the lute went through a transformation during this period. Whereas it was originally associated with men and was used primarily in connection with gods, the cult, and pastoral contexts, it ultimately became an instrument used by women in contexts with sexual and other secular connotations. Perhaps this instrument did indeed migrate from the Near East to Egypt, after which its function and playing position changed and went back in the opposite direction; Canaan itself may have been the actual center of change.

3. Egyptian-Canaanite Music — Gods and Musicians

In one of the Amarna Letters from the fourteenth century, written in Akkadian, we read: "To Milkilu, prince of Gezer. Thus the king. Now I have sent thee this tablet to say to thee: Behold, I am sending to thee Hanya, the commissioner of the archers, together with goods, in order to procure fine concubines: silver, gold, garments, turquoise, all sorts of precious stones, chairs of ebony, as well as every good thing. Total: 40 concubines: the price of each concubine is 40 (shekels) of silver. So send very fine concubines in whom there is no blemish" (ANET, 487; Amarna-Letter RA, xxxi). The Canaanite slave girls at issue in this letter were also dancers and musicians, and were a highly valued commodity in the 18th and 19th Egyptian Dynasties. The singers of the local Canaanite aristocracy, however, were even more popular. In the fifteenth century B.C., an Egyptian governor in Canaan wrote to Rewashsha, prince of Taanach near Megiddo, concerning the latter's daughter: "As for your daughter who is in the town of Rubutu, let me know concerning her welfare; and if she grows up you shall give her to become a singer, or to a husband" (Albright, 1944; ANET, 490). That is, a daughter from the aristocracy is to become a singer in the temple of Amon and then take a vow of chastity. One of these singers in Canaan was Kerker (Kurkur, Kulkul), the cult servant and minstrel of the Memphis deity Ptah, who also had a shrine in Ashkelon. Four famous ivory tablets from Megiddo (fourteenth-thirteenth century B.C.) mention both Ptah and Kerker together: "Servant of her Mistress every day, the Singer of Ptah, Lord of the Life of the Two Lands, and Great Prince of Ashkelon, Kerker" (Loud, 1939; ANET, 263). Barnett believes that the singer Kerker was also the owner of the legendary Megiddo ivory collection, consisting of approximately four hundred precious items (Barnett, 1982); such ownership would certainly be commensurate with both the status and the wealth of the singers of Amon. Albright believes the figure of Kerker/Kulkul goes back to the biblical Calcol, whom 1 Ch. 2:6 mentions together with the musicians Heman and Ethan, possibly documenting the emergence of musicians' guilds and as such a Canaanite origin of Judean temple music (Albright, 1956).

The alternating male-female semantic elements of deities in the ancient world is well known, and recurs here in the figure of the male/female Amon singer "Night." One basalt stela (44 × 39 × 13 cm.) from a temple in Beth-shean dates to the period of Ramses II (illust. III.7) and depicts the goddess of war, Ashtoreth, Anath, "Queen of Heaven, Mistress (Beloved of all the Gods)." In her left hand she holds the w3s-scepter, the symbol of power, and in the right the *ankh*-symbol, which means "life." The "Singer Night" stands opposite her with hands raised in an honorific gesture. The inscription reads: "For Antit, that she may give life, wealth, and health to the image of the Singer Night." Although neither the text nor even the gender of the singer is entirely clear, it is of enormous significance that the singer Night does indeed appear during this period in a Canaanite cultural context. The "Singer Night" mentioned here on the Antit-stela is an Amon singer, and since other stelae were found nearby depicting the God Amon-Re, whom the Amon singers venerated, the presence of the Antit-stela comes as no surprise. Sources in Egypt from

III.7. Antit basalt stela, Beth-shean, IAA 36.920

the time of Ramses II also mention both a female and a male singer "Night" (Hickmann, 1961a).

Several other, similar basalt stelae have been found in ancient Israel/ Palestine, primarily in Beth-shean, which, significantly, was under Egyptian rule (Keel/Uehlinger, 1992). All reflect the genre of monumental art, their main topoi being gods and goddesses, kings, and high cultic and state functionaries. Precisely because these artworks were so highly politicized, permeated as they were by the Egyptian ideology of kingship, which in its own turn was closely related with musical performance and made extensive use of it, they exerted a formidable influence on the development of Canaan's indigenous musical culture. Because such music functioned as a status symbol in the presence of those in power, it acquired an increasingly more stable position within the local culture, with vocal performance as its apparent focus.

At the other end of the institutionalized musical spectrum we have instruments whose capabilities were quite the opposite of those of the human voice. These simple instruments or noisemakers, largely idiophones, were unable to play a definite pitch, unable to sustain the sounds they did make, and were of extremely limited dynamic amplitude. Here we find the widely attested sistra and clappers associated with the Canaanite Hathor cult, instruments already in use in pre-dynastic Egypt which then attained their classic form as attributes of the Hathor cult in the third millennium B.C. Several stone etchings from the temple at Serābît el-Khâdim in the Sinai illustrate nicely the migratory route from Egypt to Canaan taken by the more advanced form of the sistra from the 19th-20th Dynasties. This particular locale functioned as a meeting place for two cultures, the Egyptian and Canaanite, and the temple located there contains at least ten reliefs depicting the sistrum (illust. III.8). Because Egypt and accordingly also Egyptian culture exerted such an enormous influence on the region, it is not surprising to find that the Hathor cult, a cult in which the sistrum played such a central role, was a fixed part of the Late Bronze Age culture in ancient Israel/Palestine.

The bone sistrum handle (illust. III.9) was found in Bethel in one of the most beautiful stone buildings in Canaan, a building probably to be identified as a temple. Both it and the curved ivory clapper from Shiqmona, about 37 cm. long (illust. III.10), were associated with the Hathor cult, and both can be considered as witnesses to the Egyptian-Canaanite cultural period that around 1200 B.C. was entering its final stage. A bronze sistrum from Beth-shean also belonged to this cult (PAN, 26-9-217). It should be pointed out, however, that the Hathor cult itself or at least its accoutrements and attributes exhibit great staying power in Palestine, apparently persisting well into the Iron Age or even into the Roman period. A bronze figure about 7.9 cm. tall and dating to the Persian period was found in Ashkelon; it depicts the cat goddess Bastet, who was also as-

III.8. Sinai Serabîṭ el-Khâdim temple, sistrum illlustration, *in situ*

III.9. Sistrum handle, Bethel, IAA 35.444

sociated with the Hathor cult and here is carrying a sistrum over its shoulder (illust. III.11). Finally, a bronze sistrum about 15 cm. tall and exhibiting a rather peculiar shape was found in Beth-shean grave no. 201, dating probably to the Roman period (PAM 26-9-217).

One of the characteristic features exhibited by virtually all the sistra and clappers associated with the Hathor cult is the image of the goddess herself with her long hair flowing down over her shoulders, exaggerated

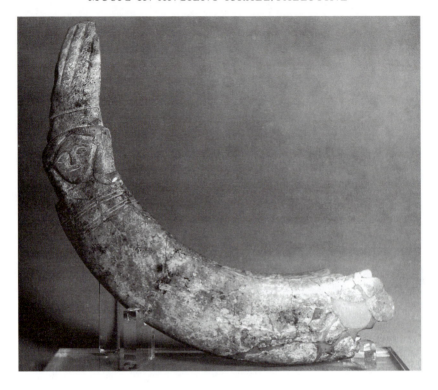

III.10. Ivory clapper, Tell Shiqmona, IAA 81.248

ears, and sistrum-shaped crown (e.g., the fourteenth-century B.C. golden pendants of Tel el-ʿAjjûl, illust. III.12). The significance of these noisemakers, and especially of the sistrum [[*šešet*]] with the Hathor-image, is complex insofar as they not only *symbolize* the goddess of beauty, love, and music, but also represent or portray the goddess herself.

Some important conclusions can be drawn based on the workmanship and materials of these sistra and clappers. The Canaanite examples associated with the Hathor cult, including the sistrum handle and clapper, are made of bone, and the carving is rather primitive and crude in comparison with the many masterfully shaped ivory clappers familiar from Egypt. Given this difference, the Canaanite finds were probably produced locally in Canaan itself. On the other hand, not many of these Hathor accoutrements have been found, suggesting that they were not widespread among the population at large and belonged rather to the higher, probably

III.11. Bastet bronze
figurine, Ashkelon,
IAA 33.2771

III.12. Hathor gold pendant,
Tell el-ʿAjjûl, copy by
McGovern, 1980, pl. 6:14

local, Egyptian-influenced priestly class among the population. The precious golden pendants from Tell el-ʿAjjûl certainly also suggest that these artifacts were not possessions of the non-ruling or non-priestly classes.

The Egyptian-oriented elite of Canaan were in need of music not only for their cult ceremonies, symposia, and social gatherings (see chap. III/4); music also served to herald and promulgate the will and power of the ruling class, and for this there was no better instrument than the metal trumpet, of which we now have archaeological evidence. Professor Amihai Mazar recently excavated in Beth-shean, at that time a center and headquarters of Egyptian rule in Canaan, and the dwelling quarters of soldiers of the Egyptian garrison (Mazar, 1997). In the strata of the eighteenth dynasty (fourteenth century B.C.) a painted pottery sherd was found with a painting of a human figure holding an object, which we may identify as a trumpet (illust. III.13). Although the upper part of the drawing on the

III.13. Pottery shard with drawing of a trumpetist, HUIA, photo by G. Laron

shard is broken, we believe that the trumpet is some 60 cm. long and has a cylindrical or slightly conical tube (length ca. 50 cm., diameter 2-3 cm.) that gradually splays out into a bell with a diameter of some 7 cm. This corresponds almost exactly to the type of instrument and measurements of the silver trumpet found in Tutankhamen's tomb (second half of fourteenth century B.C.). The trumpeter holds the instrument with his left hand, which in ancient Egypt was the usual way to carry the instrument when not blown (cf. Hickmann, 1961a, fig. 89; Manniche, 1991, fig. 48). At the mouth end this type of trumpet has a sort of mouthpiece. A mouthpiece of this type (length 5.2 cm.), somewhat damaged, was discovered by Alan Rowe (1940, x, plate LXIXA, 6) at his 1925/26 Beth-shean excavations and classified as a pre–Amenophis III find (i.e., end of the fifteenth century B.C.). This shows that trumpets in Beth-shean were not only depicted but also used.

The trumpet, known in Egypt and in a less developed form in Mesopotamia from the middle of the third millennium (Hickmann, 1961a, 40-43; Rashid, 1984, 60, fig. 37), served in both countries as a sound instrument in cultic, martial, work, and ceremonial activities. It could produce not more than one or two sounds of exact pitch and served mainly as an instrument of communication by producing rhythmical signals. Until now the earliest archaeological evidence in ancient Israel on the use of trumpets could be dated only to the third century B.C. The biblical text does not confirm unequivocally the use of trumpets in pre-exilic times (cf. 2 K. 12:14). The Beth-shean trumpet finds show that at this center of Egyptian influence, ceremonial, martial, and building activities accompanied by trumpet signals took place. It remains to be proven that this fourteenth-century-B.C. find confirms the theories of the penetration of the trumpet into Israel's cultural life from Egypt and that this was the time when the trumpet was acculturated in ancient Israel/Palestine.

It may be that the elite classes of Canaanite society were the only ones versed in certain musical arts. Members of these classes may have been versed in the art of playing the sistrum and in pursuing other aspects of Bronze Age musical life such as virtuoso lyre playing or the more sophisticated dance styles accompanied by double-reed instruments. Though the number of such persons engaged in these arts was rather small considering the sparse archaeological evidence, still they left behind an enduring tradition in ancient Israel/Palestine that ultimately became an integral part of the indigenous music scene.

Cultic utensils appearing during the Late Bronze Age or on the cusp of the Iron Age include the relatively rare primitive scraper from Tel Miqne/Ekron (twelfth-eleventh century B.C.; illust. III.14). Such bone-scrapers are widely attested from the Paleolithic Age on into the present, and have always been associated with cults characterized by totemistic thinking, fertility rites, and various other magical notions. Noisemakers associated with shaman practices such as these, produced by rather crude methods from unworked bones *(scapulae),* have also been found in Cyprus (Webb, 1986). Such bones were generally notched along the surface and then scraped against some other object to produce the characteristic sound. It is difficult to determine the context, musical or otherwise, in which the Tell Miqne scraper was used (for more on these sound tools see chap. IV/4).

III.14. Scapula, Tel Miqne, Albright Institute of Archaeology, Jerusalem and HUIA, Obj. No. 157

4. Music in the Symposium

Two ivory engravings dating to the late Canaanite/Late Bronze Age are of great interest with regard to the actual instruments used in connection with symposia, and have generated a great deal of scholarly discussion. One of these engravings depicts a double pipe, the other a lyre, and because they both portray the same setting, namely, a victory celebration or symposium, they are particularly well suited to illustrate a bit of the *Zeitgeist* of the period.

The first ivory tablet was found in Tell el-Farʿa (Sharuhen, ca. 24 km. from Gaza) and depicts a symposium scene accompanied by dance and a female double-reed player (illust. III.15). The scene might be taking place in the residence of the local Egyptian governor (Petrie, 1930) since the tablet was found in one of the rooms of the el-Farʿa residence itself, which dates to the early 19th Dynasty. This particular tablet is one of three decorative portions of a wooden box, and, on the basis of stylistic considerations, can be dated reliably to the time of an Egyptian official during the 18th Dynasty, Nefer-hotep (1352-1349 B.C.; Liebowitz, 1980, 168).

The scene on this tablet reflects a common Egyptian topos. A resident prince in Canaan holds a bowl as the symbol of power. A subject offers him a drink, and a female dancer presents her own artistry accompanied by a double-oboe player. Scholars generally agree that both the artisanship of the tablet and its artistic style betray its local, that is, Canaanite-Syrian provenance, and that a local artist produced the tablet for the Egyptian governor himself (Barnett, 1982). An interesting observation, however, emerges when this tablet is viewed in a larger context. The scene itself reproduces various details of Nefer-hotep's court and is part of the familiar sequence of war and victory in Canaan. What is actually portrayed in the scene, however, does not quite accord with the tenor of that topos. The lascivious atmosphere in which a nude female dancer performs an erotic dance seems to express more a milieu characterized by decadence, skepticism, melancholy, and pessimism. This atmosphere in its own turn seems more appropriate to the crisis experienced both by the solar cult of

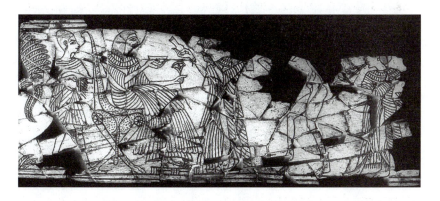

III.15. Ivory tablet, Tell el-Farʿa, dance with female pipe player, IAA 33.2537

Akhenaten and by Canaan itself, a crisis ultimately bringing to an end that very culture. Even the love songs of this period reflect this melancholy atmosphere, including one sung by a harpist from the grave of Nefer-hotep: "You climb not to the cemetery to see the sun, so listen to me! Follow the beauteous day and forget care; How weary is this Great One" (Schott, 1950).

The autochthonous, specifically Canaanite character of this scene is fairly evident, since these details occur in neither Egyptian nor Babylonian contexts. Lise Manniche, who has described the erotic function of the Egyptian double oboe, does not mention any dancing scene in which that oboe plays a role, nor does she mention solo dancing to the accompaniment of the oboe in her discussions of scenes portraying symposia (Manniche, 1987, 1988). Nor does this particular topos appear in any Babylonian-Syrian contexts. Only a thousand years later does anything similar occur, and then only in classical Greek painting (Buchner, 1956).

The double oboe from Tell el-Far'a is the Egyptian version, about 40-50 cm. long and extremely slender. Here, however, the player is holding it a bit more vertically than is the case in the Theban grave murals, in a more forward position, and more widely apart, as was the custom during the Hellenistic period. It is not until the ninth-eighth century B.C. that this position appears in the Babylonian context. The Egyptian cultural context certainly suggests we are dealing here with an oboe-type instrument. Of even more significance, however, is that both the playing position and the overall topos portrayed by the el-Far'a ivories seem to anticipate later developments.

Yet another ivory tablet from Megiddo (illust. III.16) has also been reproduced a great number of times. Dating to the time of the Ramses (1290-1165 B.C.; Liebowitz, 1967), its style has been described as "Canaanite proper" (Kantor, 1956) and thus as indigenous, and its content

III.16. Ivory tablet, Megiddo, female lyre player, IAA 38.780

as typically Canaanite (Barnett, 1986). Most scholars consider this tablet to be depicting an abbreviated version of the war and victory cycle.

To the right, a deified prince (the ruler of Megiddo?), blessed by the winged sun disk, accompanies his naked, bound, and humiliated prisoners (Shasu bedouins) back home. To the left, the same prince sits on a Cherub throne with the biblical symbol of power, a bowl, in his right hand. With his left hand, he receives a lotus flower as a symbol of grace from his queen or priestess (perhaps the Amon singer Kerker?), who wears Canaanite clothing. The priestess/queen is in turn accompanied by a similarly but more simply clad female lyre player. The latter, however, also seems to belong to a higher social class, since her own clothing resembles more that of the ruler and those around him than that of the servant standing behind the throne. The three birds are of particular interest with regard to the musical context, since they might well be part of some symbolism involving the ruler, birds, and music (see Aign, 1963). In any event, the scene does clearly underscore the enormous significance music had in Canaanite cultural life. Although the exact meaning of the symbolism is not clear, it may be portraying an epiphany in which the deity appears as a bird (Astarte/ Anath/Asherah?) and at which the ruler and music also play a role. By way of the symbolism of fertility and sexual life often associated with victory celebrations (festival — sex — music), the scene may be reproducing elements of the *marzēaḥ* cult familiar within the Phoenician, Punic, and Israelite-Judean milieu, one whose ritual Greenfeld (1974) has suggested Amos 6:4-7 may in turn be describing; this cult attained its classic form during the reign of Ashurbanipal.

The instrument on this tablet is an asymmetrical lyre with nine strings; although it has been extensively discussed, questions certainly remain. Kilmar (1976) and several other scholars have proposed a reconstruction that, in reality, is quite impossible. On that view, the strings allegedly rise directly up from the resonator, as in the illustration, rendering the instrument itself, however, non-functional. This lyre player, however, is depicted from the left side such that the back rather than the front of the instrument is facing the viewer; that is, one cannot actually see the strings that are drawn from the bridge over the resonator. Because one sees the player's left hand damping the strings, naturally no plectrum is visible; Stauder (1961a) describes this mode of playing, namely, without a plectrum, as a peculiarity. But Stauder indeed drew attention to an unprecedented feature in the illustration; the most interesting feature is not the instrument itself, for which in any case many parallels can be adduced from Theban grave murals, but the new position in which the instrument is held, a position that may well be of Canaanite origin. The player is holding the resonator under her left arm, a position not found in Egyptian representations, and one not appearing in Mesopotamia until four or five hundred years later, toward the end of the New Assyrian Empire or at the beginning of the New Babylonian period (Rashid, 1984). Most interesting of all, even the earliest witness in that context is Sennacherib's alabaster relief from Nineveh depicting three Judean lyre players from Lachish (illust. IV.22). This particular playing position could easily have migrated to the north through precisely such contact, suggesting that it probably did not originate in Mesopotamia. The Megiddo scene seems to attest yet another specifically Canaanite feature. Nowhere else did a priestess-singer use the lyre as her solo or accompanying instrument; up to this time in Egypt and even later in Assyria, the lyre was used only within the context of an instrumental ensemble.

The artistic quality of these ivory engravings is clearly quite high, and there can be little doubt they represent products of the more elite artistic community of the time. Both portray the Egyptian-influenced upper class of Canaanite society, and both were at home both thematically and functionally in precisely that class. The musical contexts portrayed here, including the musicians and musical instruments, are also at home in the socioaesthetic context attaching to this class. The scope of the two, clearly different contexts extends from a sexual cult still bound to nature on the one hand and to an institutionalized ruler cult on the other. The function of music within the daily life of the aristocracy exhibits a movement parallel to the iconographic movement from the "nude goddess" in the first scene to the reigning or warrior male deity in the second scene (see Keel/Uehlinger, 1992), moving from a context bound to nature and the cult to one associated with institutionalized ceremonies involving the ruler.

5. Clay Rattles: Mass Music —
Mass Cults — Mass Culture

The most enduring musical tradition in the Near East and perhaps even the world may well be the use of idiophonic noisemakers within cultic contexts. From the Neolithic period in ancient Israel/Palestine through the Bronze Age and even into the present in various parts of the world, including Israel (cf. the Ethiopian sistrum, the [[ṣanaṣel]]), these instruments or noisemakers were clearly the most widespread devices used exclusively in such contexts (see illust. III.17). Two features exhibited by this sistrum might be noted. First, its u-shape resembles the Sumerian sistrum but differs from the Egyptian. Second, the name itself, [[ṣanaṣel,]] derives from the Hebrew (ṣlṣl, sound; to sound, to ring). Such idiophones represent an ongoing example of what we earlier called "non-simultaneity within simultaneity" during the Bronze and Iron Ages in ancient Israel/Palestine, clearly functioning within tradition as a kind of "bridge" of continuity between the two periods. Today we can hardly imagine the enormous diversity of instruments encompassed by these idiophones, though we can certainly see how tenaciously both their form and their function endured throughout their history. Just as was earlier the case, many objects used as jewelry also functioned as noisemakers. On the other hand, a new "singing stone" appears, a lithophone recently discovered by Anati in the Negev and dating to the Middle Bronze Age (Anati, 1986); striking these stones on a specific place produces a sound similar to that of a bell.

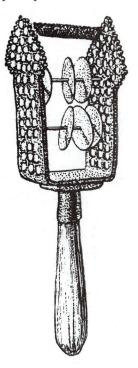

III.17. Ethiopian sistrum, Jerusalem, 1996, Ethiopian Church, copy

99

Archaeological efforts have been richly rewarded with regard to clay rattles, that is, vessel-shaped rattles molded either by hand or on a potter's wheel. We have over seventy intact examples of reliable provenance spanning a period of more than fifteen hundred years, from the early third millennium B.C. to the mid-first century B.C. Rattles from the region encompassed by ancient Israel/Palestine exhibit largely geometric shapes, with the spool shape dominating (illust. III.18, 6-11 cm. long, 4-7 cm. in diameter). Other shapes include integrated handgrips (illust. III.20) or an eyelet at one end (illust. III.19), probably used for hanging the vessel in some manner. Isolated examples of animal- and human-shaped rattles (illust. III.21; III.22) have also been found.

Rattles with identical forms have been found spanning considerable time periods. Still, those with handgrips consistently date to the Bronze Age, while the spool form seems to have established itself throughout the countryside only during the Iron Age. The bird form (illust. III.23a, b) or female form (illust. III.22) seem to have come from local workshops with limited distribution.

Several rather crudely made animal forms (illust. III.21) probably date to the Late Bronze Age. Only a relatively few examples — and not even the oldest ones at that — exhibit the fruit-shaped forms which, according to Sachs (1965), betray how the rattles were originally made, namely from dried fruit, e.g., gourds (illust. III.24).

Although only rarely attested by archaeological evidence, the bell form still represents one of the most significant shapes among rattles. A clay rattle shaped like a bell was found in the Iron Age II stratum at Hazor (illust. III.25a, b), and clearly attests the continuity of the bell shape in the transition from clay rattles on the one hand to idiophones made of metal on the other. Clay rattles disappear toward the end of the Iron Age, with metal bells and ringers now usurping at least part of their function from the seventh-sixth century B.C. onward.

Because the overwhelming number of rattles has been found in cultic sites and grave sites, scholars generally agree that these rattles functioned largely in cultic contexts in ancient Israel/Palestine (May, 1935; McCown, 1947; Albright, 1943; Hickmann, 1963; Rashid, 1984). A reciprocal argument in this regard is the rattle shape exhibited by many cultic objects and accoutrements in their own turn. Perhaps the best demonstration of the clearly cultic function rattles maintained even into the Late Iron Age is the rattle-shaped vessel on the head of a unique terra-cotta idol excavated by

III.18. Clay rattle,
spool form,
Hazor, IAA
67.1160

III.19. Clay rattle, spool
form with perforated eyelet,
Gezer, IAA P219

III.20. Clay rattle,
with handgrip,
Gezer, IAA 74.262

III.21. Clay rattle,
zoomorphic form,
PU, IAA P220

III.22. *(left)* Clay rattle, female
anthropomorphic form,
Tell el-Farʿa-South, IAA I6936

III.23. *(below)* Clay
rattle, bird form:
(a) Tell el-Hasi, EIM MHP62460,
(b) Ashdod, IAA 60.103

(a)

(b)

III.24. Clay rattle, fruit form,
Megiddo, OI A18362

III.25. Clay rattle, bell form,
Hazor, HUIA 9245:
(a) natural form (above);
(b) x-ray (right)

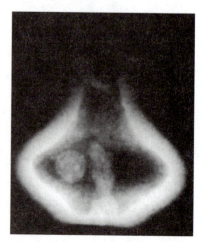

Itzhaq Beit-Arieh (Beit-Arieh, 1987) in the Edomite cultic site Qitmit in the Negev (illust. III.26) and dating to the seventh century B.C. The vessel exhibits the spool form characteristic of ancient Israel/Palestine, while the head itself has three horns, strikingly accentuated eyes and nose, curly hair, and a mysterious smile. Indeed, because the head is hollow and has what might be part of a handgrip on its neck, it may have been part of a rattle itself. The most obvious comparison is that with the Hathor figures and sistra, which also have the idiomatic noisemaker on top of the head and whose symbolism consists precisely in the musical instrument itself.

There is little doubt that the clay rattles in ancient Israel/Palestine represent an artistically autochthonous musical device, differing noticeably

III.26. Terra-cotta figurine, idol with rattle on his head, Qitmit, IAA 87.117

from all other known types of rattles, including those from the neighboring cultures of Egypt, Babylon, Syria, and Cyprus. The indigenous spool-form mentioned above is of particular importance insofar as toward the end of the Iron Age it spread in stages throughout the country, becoming thereby the most common form of clay rattle. Of seventy-one clay rattles that have been excavated, forty-six exhibit the spool form. This particular form may have become so widespread because of its mode of manufacture. Whereas all other forms require at least a certain measure of hands-on craftsmanship, the clay spool could be produced mechanically on the potter's wheel. One direct result of this nascent "industrialization" was that this form became increasingly more common, a situation certainly also commensurate with its mass function during the period of the emergent Israelite/Judean state.

The enormous number of clay rattles already excavated as well as the more or less even distribution of these finds over the entire area encompassing ancient Israel/Palestine derives not only from the durability of the actual material out of which these rattles were produced, but also from the fact that they were used literally by the masses: they were among the most popular artistic and cultic objects. Because they were small and relatively easy to produce, they were both cheap and readily accessible to an enormous number of people; as such, they became one of the objects mass production made available to the people at large for use in its musical, cultic, and cultural life.

During the Bronze and Iron Ages, the clay rattle was clearly a syncretistic or pluralistic cultic phenomenon, and as the sheer quantity of rattles shows, it also occupied an important position within the cult of Israel and Judah. Because these devices were so widespread and were produced in such great numbers, asking about their ethnic or religious affiliation actually misses the point.* The mere quantity of excavated rattles, however, does not necessarily mean they encountered no resistance from the religious establishment in Israel and Judah. In fact, quite the opposite was the case, and decisively so. Rattles are designated by a single Hebrew word, $m^e na'an\hat{i}m$ (2 S. 6:5), from nw', "to quiver, shake," a term also used to refer

---

* My latest research, concluded while this book was already in print, made me change my mind. From a poly-ethnic sound tool in the Bronze Age the clay rattle changed its ethnic affiliation to a definite Judean sound tool in the Kingdom of Judah of Iron Age II (paper presented at the ICTM Congress, Rio de Janeiro, June 2001).

to the sistrum. E. Werner (1980) believes this word was actually applied to any shaken or rattled idiophone. Given the superabundance of archaeological evidence for such rattles, however, it comes as somewhat of a shock that the Old Testament mentions the *m^ena'an'im* in but a single passage (see p. 19). Does not this incommensurability between the omnipresence of rattles in ancient Israel/Palestine and the Old Testament's apparent disinclination to mention it perhaps also betray the Israelite/Judean religious establishment's disinclination to have anything to do with these clearly Canaanite musical devices?

The context of 2 S. 6:5 lends a certain element of ambivalence to the term. "David and all the house of Israel" do not really dance "with all their might in dances to songs," as many translations suggest, but rather *m^esaḥ^aqîm*. Although this word is generally translated as "to play," it is quite ambiguous and can refer to concrete "playing" in the more direct sense associated with singing, dancing, instrumental music, mime, and costume procession, yet not without undertones of all sorts of eroticism and intoxication; in other languages, too, the word "play" can evoke erotic associations. The shamanistic-orgiastic, intoxicating undertone of the passage is enhanced by the other instruments mentioned, all of which evoke such associations. In addition to the *kinnôr* and the *nēḇel*, the writer tellingly mentions the *'aṣê ḇ^erôšîm* (clappers?), *tūpîm* (drums), *m^ena'an'im* (shaken idiophones), and *ṣelṣ^elîm* (cymbals?). Indeed, the *ṣelṣ^elîm* mentioned here reveal a significant feature about this passage. The much later parallel passage, 1 Ch. 13:8, *replaces* them with *m^esiltayîm*, and excludes any clappers and shaken idiophones, thereby effectively extinguishing from that earlier scene elements evoking pagan intoxication. In the later scene, the dancers (*m^esaḥ^aqîm*) are accompanied by chordophones and by song (*šîrîm*), drums (*tūpîm*), cymbals (*m^esiltayîm*), and trumpets (*h^aṣōṣ^erôt*). An organized, solemn liturgical ceremony of consecration has replaced the orgiastic procession.

6. The Priests' Bronze Cymbals

Alongside clay rattles, bronze cymbals are the most common musical instrument found at archaeological sites relating to ancient Israel/Palestine, with at least twenty-eight (either individual cymbals or pairs) having been found at fourteen different sites. Like the clay rattle, the bronze cymbal was also an instrument bridging the transition between the Canaanite and Is-raelite culture; indeed, the continuity exhibited by this instrument within tradition extends down even into the Hellenistic period. Archaeological evidence, however, confronts us with a puzzling situation insofar as not a single example has been found that dates reliably to the Babylonian/Persian period. Even the five pairs associated with the Iron Age actually date to the earliest stage of this period, namely, the twelfth-eleventh century B.C., and come from areas that were incorporated into the kingdom of Israel only at a later stage (Megiddo). How is this evidence, or lack thereof, to be explained? Most scholars have thought these cymbals were the pri-mary instrument used in worship during the time of the first temple (Sachs, 1940; Sendrey, 1969b; Keel, 1972). Does the peculiar lack of evi-dence now cast doubt on this assumption?

The customary designation for cymbals, *m*^{e}*ṣiltayîm*, stems from an onomatopoeic dual form of *ṣlṣl*, the Hebrew and Arabic word for "to ring, clink." Although the term *msltm* does already appear in Ugaritic texts of the fourteenth century B.C. (see below), the word *m*^{e}*ṣiltayîm* significantly does not appear in Old Testament texts until the Persian-Hellenistic pe-riod, its first appearance coming in Ezra 3:10, thereafter twelve additional times. These passages associate it with the loftiest cultic events, and as such it ranks as one of the most important instruments associated with the cult, the instrument of Levites, of the Davidic musicians, and especially of the Asaphites (Ezra 3:10; 1 Ch. 16:5); it was never played by women. In texts antedating the Hellenistic period, another term with a similar root, *ṣelṣ*^{e}*lîm*, appears, now in plural form. Used only twice in the Bible (2 S. 6:5; Ps. 150:5), it probably belongs to an early period of Judean monotheism.

1 Chronicles 13:8, the parallel passage reiterating the events of 2 S. 6:5, was subjected to revealing redactional alterations insofar as we now read *m*^{e}*ṣiltayîm* instead of *ṣelṣ*^{e}*lîm*. Apparently the authors writing during the Persian-Hellenistic period wanted to avoid any mention of the *ṣelṣ*^{e}*lîm*, which was traditionally associated with the pagan Canaanite cult. It was not until the Hellenistic period, when the legend of the first temple was canonized, that the *m*^{e}*ṣiltayîm* underwent a certain process of mytholo-gization and were incorporated into the text to reflect an idealized golden age of the first temple. Of course, it may also be simply that the authors in-corporated the *m*^{e}*ṣiltayîm* into the description of worship in the first tem-ple without having any accurate understanding of the reality of that wor-ship service in the first place.

A consideration of the rather complicated production requirements and of the expensive material out of which these cymbals were made precludes any possibility that they were simple mass instruments of the people. It is thus impossible to interpret them (whether as *ṣelṣᵉlîm* or as *mᵉṣiltayîm*) as such within the context of 2 S. 6:5 as well. The events described in 2 S. 6:5 were doubtless of a cultic nature even if not in the sense the authors of Chronicles would have understood as in their own canonized Jewish faith.

In the second temple, there was allegedly only a single cymbal (*m. Tamid* 6:3), and it was used as a signal instrument. The Israelites had no notion of how to make or repair the cymbal (*b. ʿArak.* 10b).

Cymbals have been found in two different sizes but identical in form, one larger (illust. III.27), with a diameter of 8-12 cm., and one smaller, with a diameter of 3-6 cm. (illust. III.28). Sachs (1940) thinks that Ps. 150:5 is referring to the two different sizes with the expressions *ṣilṣᵉlê-šāmaʿ* and *ṣilṣᵉlê-tᵉrûʿâ*. The form of these cymbals did not change much over time. A round disk was cupped in the middle to varying degrees and perforated at the center to facilitate a metal pin to which a leather or cloth handle could be attached. Even at this early stage, the smaller cymbals were apparently attached to one's fingers. These cymbals from the Bronze Age had an extremely bright, clear sound, and even today the well-preserved and restored cymbals can produce a brightly ringing tone.

Isolated cymbals of Canaanite provenance (Caubet, 1987), dating to the same period as most of the Palestinian finds or slightly later have been found at Ugarit. Prior to this period, cymbals are attested only in Mesopotamian iconography, and then only in extremely small numbers (Rashid, 1984); moreover, they seem to be of a different type and are con-

III.27. Large cymbals, Megiddo, IAA 36.1986

III.28. Small cymbals, Acco, IAA 71.962

siderably larger, measuring approximately 20-25 cm. across. The indigenous examples of the Late Bronze Age cymbals probably thus represent the earliest preserved plate cymbals in the Near East, appearing then in Mesopotamia in the ninth-eighth century, and in Egypt in the eighth century B.C.; Hickmann, 1961a). Significantly, it is precisely during the period in which these Canaanite cymbals appear that we find the earliest witness to the word m^eṣiltayîm (mṣltm) in a paramythological Ugaritic text. That text describes the singing and playing of Rapihu, King of Eternity, in a hymn similar to Ps. 150, mentioning these cymbals together with the kinnôr, tōp, and other instruments (Caubet, 1987).

7. The Megiddo Flute

While excavating the floor of a building in Megiddo from the third millennium B.C., archaeologists found a flute capable of producing one or two tones and probably used for communication or for issuing a call (Loud, 1948). Pipes of this sort are attested in ancient Israel/Palestine over a period of more than two thousand years. They are generally made of bird or goat bones, are 7-12 cm. long and .8–1.5 cm. in diameter, and have a single hole more or less in the center of the instrument. Unlike later pipes, these examples are not decorated in any way, though they are finely polished.

When actually played, even now they produce shrill tones. When blown at the end with an open hole, they produce a d'''', and when blown with the hole covered, an a''''; they are also capable of producing a rapid fourth trill. When blown as a cross flute, they produce a d''''. This Megiddo pipe certainly represents one of the earliest intact, archaeologically attested wind instruments in the entire Near East (illust. III.29).

Among the eleven pipes like the one in Megiddo that have been found in the region encompassed by ancient Israel/Palestine, the most recent is the En-Gedi pipe dating to the seventh-sixth century B.C. (illust. III.30), the waning years of the Judean monarchy. It derives from the same Canaanite tradition as the Megiddo pipe, and is of the same type. When blown from the end, it produced an a''', when blown as a cross flute, a b'''. It was found in a precinct in which the perfume Opal Balsam was produced, a line of work quite famous in ancient Judea and performed largely by women. For centuries, these instruments were almost always decorated with this characteristic ornament, and the En-Gedi pipe is no exception in this regard; indeed, it constitutes an exquisite example of this ornament. Local tradition offers no unequivocal information about just how this type of pipe was used, but during this particular period it probably functioned as a children's pipe or amulet.

The only biblical term that seems appropriate for this type of flute is the word *mašrôqîṭāʾ* found only in Dnl. 3:5, 7, 10, 15, from *šᵉrîqâ*, referring

III.29. Two-tone flute, Megiddo, IAA 39.680

III.30. Megiddo-type flute, En-Gedi, IAA 67.487

111

to a whistling sound or shrill tone. The context in Daniel strongly suggests this flute type represented an instrument quite alien to the Israelites. The Talmud associates this term with the Akkadian word [[šarkukita]], explaining that the reference is to a hollow instrument used by shepherds for herding their animals together (*y. Qidd.* 1:4). Samuel Krauss is persuaded that the reference is to a flute or syrinx (1910/12, II, 527; III, 88), a view supported at least in part by the expression found in Jgs. 5:16, *šᵉriqôt ᶜᵃḏārîm,* "flute playing, the piping of the flocks." This type of pipe is not without its comparative ethnic parallel even today, since fishermen and hunters still use such pipes in Scandinavia.

The Megiddo flute attests examples about 7-12 cm. long with the hole close to the middle of the body, which has no core and is blown either from the end or on the side. Peculiarly, traditional organological studies do not mention this flute-type at all, or do so only peripherally in connection with falange-pipes (Megaw, 1960).

Some scholars have suggested the bone-pipe may actually have originated in the Cyclades (Prausnitz, 1955). Considering the possible contacts between ancient Israel/Palestine and the Cyclades, this hypothesis seems quite plausible. In precisely this regard we may recall the Megiddo and Cycladic harps already discussed earlier (chap. II/2B).

Before closing this discussion of the Megiddo flute, several additional points should be noted. First, various pieces of evidence suggest that this particular flute-type was extremely widespread in ancient Israel/Palestine. Its form and even its ornamentation endured with surprising tenacity not just over centuries, but over millennia. In addition, a relatively large number of these flutes have been uncovered (ten), and yet not a single example of any other type of aerophone made from bone, either from the Stone Age or from the Bronze Age. As already mentioned, ornamentation was characteristic of this flute-type; significantly, it did not appear until the Iron Age, after which it never changed again. What all these considerations suggest is that the cultural tradition associated with this flute in ancient Israel/Palestine was both indigenous and quite tenacious, and that the flute itself likely had a variety of functions ranging from "piping the flocks" to communication to amulets to children's toys. The organological tradition in ancient Israel/Palestine was in many instances quite linear, exhibiting elements of continuity extending over several different historical periods and deriving from a clearly indigenous cultural impetus; the Megiddo flute-type represents yet another example of that continuity.

CHAPTER IV

THE IRON AGE

(1200-587 B.C.)

The balance of power shifted dramatically in ancient Israel/Palestine in the thirteenth-twelfth centuries B.C. The golden age of the Egyptians and the Hittites came to an end, and peripheral tribes penetrated into Egypt and the Levant to fill the vacuum these two great powers left behind. This was also the time of the emergent "sea peoples," the Philistines in the south and the Phoenicians in the north, who created not only a progressive, technologically mobile culture in the larger sense, but also an extraordinarily rich artistic tradition. Unfortunately, the history of these cultures still "remains to be written" (Muhly, 1985). A similar situation applies to the emergent kingdoms of the Edomites, Moabites, and Ammonites in Transjordan, whose cultural tradition in many respects was quite independent and about which still "little is known" (Beit-Arieh, 1987). Only recently have the material and musical cultures of this group come under more detailed study, a situation all the more regrettable because they quite possibly represent one of the most striking examples of the aforementioned "heterogeneity within homogeneity" within the region. Easily the most important development during this period was the gradual emergence of monotheism, which the Hebrew tribes cultivated until it finally established an enduring position for itself in Judea toward the end of this period. The first entities within which the Hebrew tribes finally consolidated themselves politically were the kingdom of Israel in the Judean-Israelite mountains (ca. 1020-928

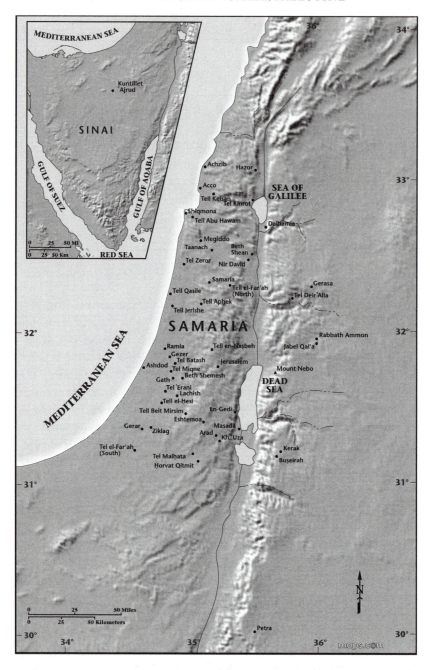

B.C.) and then later the divided kingdoms of Israel (until 721 B.C.) and Judah (until 587 B.C.).

This emergence of national political entities in the form of territorial states was the dominant characteristic of Iron Age Israel/Palestine. While the units of city-state cultures continued to exist within this context, a whole series of sometimes larger, sometimes smaller ethnic entities emerged, some lasting longer than others, but all involved in one way or another with this new phenomenon of statehood and national identity. Not surprisingly, this political consolidation in its own turn profoundly affected the development of the region's musical culture.

Considering what the Old Testament says about music among the various peoples in ancient Israel/Palestine, we find that music during this period played a significant part in a wide variety of situations within the life of these nations. Music was engaged in connection with cultic activities, victory celebrations, secular rejoicing, communication, situations involving ecstasy and rapture, and mourning or grief. In a more abstract sense, music or the musical instruments themselves could even be used symbolically.

The Old Testament offers a plethora of examples demonstrating not only how music functioned in society, but also how it was understood or perceived. The sound of the *šôpār* was so powerful that it was perceived as being supernatural (Ex. 19:13; Josh. 6:4-9). The famous scene in which David plays for Saul shows how the *kinnôr* was also engaged for its therapeutic effects (1 S. 16:16). Certain kinds of music or musical instruments were perceived to be so powerful that they were used to stimulate or enhance moods of ecstasy or prophecy (1 S. 10:5; 2 K. 3:15). Indeed, the importance of certain instruments derived from their association with God himself, such as the two silver trumpets he ordered Moses to make in the wilderness (Nu. 10:1-10). The Old Testament offers especially detailed information about the significance of music during the waning years of David's rule (1 Ch. 23–25), and later in connection with the central rite of worship in the temple, namely, the sacrifice (2 Ch. 5:6-14) and burnt offering, "according to the commandment of David" (2 Ch. 29:25), during the reign of King Hezekiah of Judah (2 Ch. 20–30). But is this merely wishful thinking? As is well known, tradition has it that King David himself organized the musical liturgy to be used in worship, and that this music played an especially important role in connection with the burnt offering. Peculiarly, however, neither of the original descriptions of the Davidic liturgy and sacrificial ritual, that is, neither 2 S. 20–24 nor 1 K. 8:62-64, mentions this musical liturgy at all. It is only much later, in the parallel verses from Chronicles, that such a liturgy appears in this connection. This situation may reflect the imposition of an idealized notion onto later texts.

If we are to believe the Old Testament evidence, music accompanied a remarkable number of activities in secular daily life. Such occasions included honorific farewell ceremonies (Gen. 31:27), homecoming after military victories (2 Ch. 20:28), or simple celebrations of rejoicing (Isa. 30:29; Job 21:12).

The oldest parts of the Old Testament contain various texts that were sung or that themselves mention different song forms performed in connection with victory, rejoicing, praise, veneration of heroes, or even lament (Ex. 15:1-19; Nu. 21:16-18; Dt. 32:1-43; 1 S. 18:6-7; 28:3; 2 S. 1:17-27; Jgs. 5; 1 K. 13:30). Structural or rhythmic forms can often be discerned in these song texts, including refrains (e.g., Ex. 15:2, 21; 2 S. 1:19, 25, 27), or the familiar device *parallelismus membrorum,* in which a poetic motif is repeated two or more times in varying forms, e.g., "Tell it not in Gath, proclaim it not in the streets of Ashkelon; or the daughters of the Philistines will rejoice, the daughters of the uncircumcised will exult" (2 S. 1:20), or "Oh, may your breasts be like clusters of the vine, and the scent of your breath like apples" (Cant. 7:9). Such structural features within the texts themselves probably reflect parallel, slightly varying musical structures that cannot now be reconstructed, given the present status of scholarship.

Unfortunately, no iconographic evidence has come to light corresponding to these cultic and secular musical performances in the Old Testament. One might perhaps adduce the grave mural from Beni-hasan as an indirect allusion to the original myth of the three initial and most important activities, namely, shepherding, metallurgy, and music (Gen. 4:19-23; see illust. III.3). The absence of any significant archaeological correlation for the biblical texts makes it all the more difficult to derive more from Old Testament musical texts as historical documents.

Ultimately, the effect of Canaan's musical culture is essentially the same as that of its mythology, namely, "both where the Old Testament incorporates it, and where the Old Testament reacts against it, Canaan continues to exert its impact upon us through the Bible" (Gordon, 1961). It is not just the Ugaritic texts that exhibit a relationship with the later biblical books; elements of the Canaanite musical tradition are also discernible in the Old Testament. One need only compare the two parallel verses 2 S. 6:5

and 1 Ch. 13:8, both of which describe a cultic act that for the first time is also accompanied by music. The second, later text clearly has repressed elements of the older Canaanite tradition. The first text describes a loud, orgiastic orchestra consisting largely of idiophones and membranophones, including the *ʿᵃṣê bᵉrôšîm, tūpîm, mᵉnaʿanʿîm, ṣelṣᵉlîm, kinnôrôt*, and *nᵉbālîm* (see chap. I/3 above). The second, later text, after being subjected to revision and even possibly after the musical ritual itself had undergone some change, describes a well-organized ritual featuring liturgical, vocal-instrumental music that includes *šîrîm* (singing), as well as the *kinnôrôt, nᵉbālîm, tūpîm, mᵉṣiltayim*, and *hᵃṣōṣᵉrôt*.

During the late Canaanite period, local female musicians were admired throughout the entire Near East. Nor did this change during the reign of the Judean king Hezekiah (ca. 727-698 B.C.); indeed, the lyre players and female Judean minstrels were viewed as the highest tribute for the Assyrian king Sennacherib (see the Sennacherib reliefs, ca. 701 B.C.; 2 K. 18:14-16 and chap. IV/3A).

Although many elements of tradition did indeed continue during the Iron Age, distinct changes become discernible which were probably part of a lengthy cyclical process. On the one hand, many instruments and noise-makers clung tenaciously to their previous forms and functions. Mass devices such as clay rattles (see chap. III/5) continued to be used, and indeed it was not until the Babylonian-Persian period that iron bells replaced them for good. Similarly, drums changed only slightly during this period and, like the rattles, became to a certain extent a mass fetish instrument. On the other hand, several instruments either disappeared entirely or underwent changes. Archaeological evidence disappears entirely during this period for certain idiophones such as cymbals, instruments originally used only by the upper classes or by those familiar or involved with the cult. These particular instruments do not reappear until much later, during the Roman period. The lyre, originally in use among a wide variety of population groups, especially among priests, remained the most commonly played instrument, but now acquired a more convenient, simplified form. These structural changes in the lyre resulted from a reduction in the number of strings and accordingly from a change in the music itself (see chap. IV/3). The lute and the harp disappeared entirely from musical life in ancient Israel/Palestine during this period, and did not reappear before the late Hellenistic period. Still other instruments continued to be as popular as ever, such as the double pipes, which maintained their dominant status

117

and yet in certain areas, such as Edom, underwent revolutionary changes, metamorphizing into the conical Edomite mono- and double pipe of the *zmra*-type.

1. Female Drummers in the Israelite-Judean Kingdom and Surroundings

Archaeological evidence for drums dating to earlier periods invariably leaves unanswered questions; finds (rock etchings) are often difficult to date or interpret, and the particulars of their history or status within a region are difficult to assess. For the Iron Age as well, we have access to precious little hard evidence regarding the actual instruments themselves. The only potential evidence involves clay rings about 15-30 cm. across attested continuously from the Bronze Age forward. Archaeologists generally interpret these rings as supports for storage jars (Lamon/Shipton, 1939), though they might easily have been used as frames for drums. Another find that might possibly indicate a drum is a small cylindrical clay fragment from Abu Hawam (see Braun, 1999, illust. IV.1) found in a temple. The perforations along the upper and lower edges of the clay frame would certainly suffice for securing a stretched skin, suggesting the device might be a double drum; given the small dimensions of the frame (h. 13 cm.), however, interpretive caution is probably well advised.

During the Iron Age, however, terra-cotta figurines and reliefs depicting a female figure with a round frame drum begin appearing in iconographic materials. This new topos of the female drummer appears with striking, even extraordinary frequency in Israel/Palestine and is of equally extraordinary significance for the musical culture of the region, attesting as it does a new function for the instrument as well as its new status and the symbolic understanding it acquired within society.

The nearly sixty terra-cotta figurines depicting this motif (or interpreted as depicting it) can be classified according to two quantitatively unequal groups: a. bell-shaped figurines, and b. relief terra cottas.

A. The fourteen hollow, bell-shaped figures portrayed with longer garments, without any of the traditional adornment associated with women, and with the drum itself held perpendicular to the breast constitute only a very small portion of the more than seven-hundred terra-cotta female figurines, approximately 15-25 cm. tall. The mode of manufacture of these figurines, and their styles, vary greatly. Most portray a female figure of the *dea nutrix,* the mother-goddess, or Astarte, with both hands supporting voluptuous breasts. Others portray a pregnant woman in a sitting position, or a woman holding either a child or a bird. The hollow type is found primarily in coastal areas, and according to Holland (1977) indicates "some peripheral cultural influence involving a non-Israelite group." The fact that at least some of the examples from this group were also found in Transjordan, Holland continues, "is not easy to explain . . . except via trade or independent development." The disposition of the female drummers accords perfectly with this explanation. The five examples from Achzib (illust. IV.1) and one from Shiqmona (illust. IV.2) that have been reliably dated, and apparently also the figure of unknown provenance (illust. IV.3) all belong to the Phoenician coastal cultural sphere of ancient Israel/Palestine. By contrast, the three figurines from the Nebo and Samaria (illust. IV.4a; IV.4b) all deviate from the classic Achzib-Shiqmona type. The upper torsos on the earliest figurines from Nebo are nude, and thus resemble more the mass of bell-shaped figures with the typical Judean topos of the woman supporting her breasts with her hands (Engle, 1979), offering thus a fine example of the local Phoenician-Moabite-Judean process of acculturation. All this clearly allows us to assume a local independent development for the drummer figurines (as suggested above by Holland).

Although some scholars are inclined to assign this entire initial group of bell-shaped figurines exclusively to Phoenician provenance, it seems a gross exaggeration to assert that "the origin of the entire group can be found in a single Phoenician workshop" (Weippert, 1988). The suspected similarity might involve a genuine relationship between at most only a few artifacts. That said, the similarity between the Shiqmona figurine on the one hand and the figurine from Amathus (eighth century B.C.) in the Limassol (Cyprus) District Museum (T. 276/253) is certainly striking. The most important characteristics of the Limassol female drummer include its bell-shaped form, its hairstyle, the shape of the drum itself, the position in which she is holding it, and her hand position; typological analysis of precisely these features suggests that this figure indeed belongs to the Shiqmona-Achzib group (see illust. IV.1), and that it is fundamentally different from all the other Cypriot statuettes with discus (see illust. IV.5). The latter hold the instrument more rigidly or stiffly than is the case in ancient Israel/Palestine, with the instrument in a strictly vertical position and the hands generally positioned symmetrically to both sides in the middle

IV.1. Bell-shaped terra-cotta figurine, female drummer, Achzib, IAA 44.54

IV.2. Bell-shaped terra-cotta figurine, female drummer, Shiqmona, IAA 81.246

IV.3. Bell-shaped terra-cotta figurine, female drummer, PU, IMJ 82.2.7

(a)

IV.4. Bell-shaped terra-cotta
figurine, female drummer:
(a) Nebo, SBF M1072;
(b) Samaria, copy by Crowfort/
Kenyon, 1957, pl. XI:8

(b)

IV.5. Bell-shaped terra-cotta figurine, PU, Louvre AO25947

of the membrane, making it virtually impossible actually to play as a drum (cf. Proceedings, 1997, 154:7). This leads us to believe that the artists frequently intended to depict cymbals here.

Chronological considerations, although not always precise, also suggest that the female drummers from ancient Israel/Palestine were the first to appear; the first of these date to the eleventh-tenth century B.C. (Mt. Nebo), while the Phoenician examples do not appear until the eighth-seventh century B.C. Because the Cypriot figurines replicating the way the drum is held in the Achzib-Shiqmona finds date to a much later period (e.g., the Kamelarga figurine from the 6th century B.C., Caubet, 1986, fig. 3a), the more appropriate conclusion is that the northwestern Phoenician group adopted the topos of this initial group from ancient Israel/Palestine's central and eastern areas and perfected its artistic embodiment. The typical North Phoenician examples of female figures exhibit superb technical craftsmanship, striking attention to detail, refined facial features, often including a wry or concealed smile, and a sophisticated rendering of the body (illust. IV.5). None of these features are found in the much more primitive and relatively crude figures from other areas of ancient Israel/Palestine. The migration of the topos itself seems to have occurred in a westerly rather than an easterly direction.

One of the figures from Samaria I (illust. IV.4b) is wearing some sort of adornment on her forehead, probably a phylactery, as well as makeup, recalling the popular topos of the "woman at a window" associated with the Astarte cult, "the symbol of religious sacrifice of virginity" whose priestesses "were mortal women whose duty was to grant the fruits of their love" (Barnett, 1975). This forehead adornment may well be what Jeremiah was referring to when he castigated Judah with the words, "you have the forehead of a whore" (Jer. 3:3).

These figurines are generally and characteristically associated with symbols of fertility and sexuality, and in every instance the drum contributes to that symbolism. In addition, the Achzib-Shiqmona figurines exhibit various features possibly reflecting Egyptian influence that enhance that symbolism. Some of the hairstyles seem more like a wig or some other artificial head covering than natural hair (e.g., illust. IV.4), and the clothing seems to imitate schematically the transparent Egyptian garments typically worn by female Egyptian minstrels (Hickmann, 1961a). The overall symbolism here may be that of a half-sacred, half-secular love priestess.

The synthesis between the sacred and the profane in these figures is quite commensurate with the unified relationship these two aspects enjoyed within life at large in the ancient world. That is, these figures are not deities; they are domestic icons or objects with some other sacral-secular and perhaps aesthetic significance reflecting more or less accurately the Israelites' own understanding and perception of the female minstrel, "the human rather than divine identity of the woman" (MeyersC, 1987). These women performed at a variety of functions. They drummed at festivals of rejoicing, for women's dances (Jgs. 11:34), along with the entire people (Gen. 31:27), in connection with the "song of victory" (Ex. 15:20; 1 S. 18:6), and at the front of the procession of both male and female instrumentalists (Ps. 68:26). Indeed, the "song of victory" performed by women and accompanied by drumming and dancing became a characteristic genre within the Hebrew tradition. In this light, Bayer's assertion (1982a) that these figurines represent "not an earthly player but a goddess" is wholly unpersuasive.

Our drummers hold the instrument at a right angle in front, usually at a bit of an angle, close to the body and at about breast-height. This particular playing position is characteristic of the Near East and is still used even today in some areas (Buchner, 1968; Karamatov, 1983). The player strikes the drum with an almost completely flat hand close to the center of the head, producing the stronger, deeper tones. The other hand holds the instrument and strikes the head only at the edge and only with the fingertips, producing quieter, higher tones. In this context, the player can perform using either a right-handed or a left-handed style, and can sometimes change positions during a single performance (interview with Abu Aran, Jerusalem, Feb. 1987). In ancient iconography, players almost always hold the drum with their left hands (Rashid, 1984; Wegner, 1963; Fleischhauer, 1966).

One peculiarity of the actual drum construction attested by almost all these figures, and especially by those exhibiting more sophisticated craftsmanship, is the recessed drumhead, suggesting that these drums might have had but a single head and casting doubt on the widespread assertion that Near Eastern frame drums had two heads (Nixdorff, 1971). These drums quite possibly could have been struck from the interior rather than from the exterior, and the frame itself may even have extended partially above the head as is common even today in several drum types (Wegner, 1963).

B. Terra-cotta relief plaques, of which we have more than forty examples, are the second type of artifact employing the topos of the female figure and drum. They portray nude or half-nude, richly adorned female figures usually with some sort of head covering or wig, and with the drum held flat against the left breast. They appeared contemporaneously in ancient Israel/Palestine with the bell-shaped figurines just discussed, namely, between the twelfth and sixth century b.c., but were considerably more popular and widespread.

The female drummers in this group have often been referred as "female figure holding a disk," and are among the most frequently discussed topoi of Palestinian iconography. Pritchard was the first to establish a typology for the group, and believed that the disks themselves could be given various interpretations. One might view them "as a tambourin, as a cake [Old Testament texts such as Jer. 7:16-18; 44:19 attest the cake/bread offering], as a drum, as a rattle in the shape of drums with serrated edges, as a platter" (Pritchard, 1943). Although his suggestion has been well received, most scholars have chosen to view these disks as drums.

This particular group of figures with disks contemporaneous with the bell-shaped figures of female drummers supports the argument that they do indeed represent drummers. One might also add that while the reliefs find a clear thematic parallel in the bell-shaped figures, not a single bell-shaped figure employs the cake/bread theme. Moreover, although these reliefs have been found throughout ancient Israel/Palestine, none have been found in the Phoenician-Philistine coastal regions, that is, none come from precisely that area in which most bell-shaped figures with drums were discovered. Finally, some have suggested that the topos of the nude female drummer may have originated in Egypt, since the largest concentration as well as the oldest examples of such reliefs have been found in areas in which Egyptian influence endured the longest (Megiddo, Beth-shean, Transjordan). A cultic text from the 18th Dynasty provides a lively picture matching the images on our relief plaques: "Consecrate the entire house, and bring two virgins pure of body and with no body hair, with curly wigs on their heads, round frame drums in their hands. . . . Let them sing from the songs of the book," to which the following performance guidelines are then added: "Let the festival priest call four times: A god is coming, O Earth! Let the great mourning woman call four times: Rejoice in heaven and earth! And each time they shall beat the drum!" (Schott, 1950, 158).

Typological analysis differentiates two kinds of disks in this context. The (a) smaller disk (15-20 cm. across) is always held symmetrically with both hands (illust. IV.6, 7); the (b) larger ones (25-40 cm. across) are always held by the left hand at the bottom, while the right hand seems to be striking the drum in the center (illust. IV.8, 9). Most of these disks do indeed seem to be drums, although several in the first group might well be understood as loaves of bread. A closer look at the Taanach figure shows that the disk actually has cross-shaped adornments on it, and even a slightly vaulted or cupped surface, effectively disqualifying it as a (stretched-head) drum (illust. IV.7). The larger disks, however, are clearly frame drums, and even duplicate precisely the position in which the bell-

IV.6. Terra-cotta plaque figurine,
[[Tell ʿIra]], IAA 84.62

IV.7. Terra-cotta plaque figurine,
Taanach, AAM J.7285

IV.8. Terra-cotta plaque figurine,
Tell el-Farʿa South, EB F3426

IV.9. Terra-cotta plaque figurine,
Megiddo IO A18705

shaped figures hold their drums. This typological division may offer a so-
lution to the quite heated discussion regarding the interpretation of the
nature of the disks (see also May, 1935; Keel, 1976; Winter, 1983).

In two terra cottas from this group, the figure is holding her drum in a
different position, and even the drum itself has a different form, recalling
the Arabic darabukka, a form already familiar from the Old Babylonian
period (illust. IV.10). Although the relief form does not lend itself well to
precise identification in this case, still the player is clearly holding the
drum under her left arm. One Megiddo figure is unique insofar as the
player is holding an object in her right hand that could be a bent or curved
drumstick (illust. IV.11), a performance technique still practiced by the
Bedouin tribes on the Arabian peninsula (Buchner, 1968).

IV.10. Terra-cotta plaque
figurine, Beth-shean,
PM29.103.883

IV.11. Terra-cotta plaque figurine,
Beth-shean, IAA 19684

Several considerations suggest that these female-drummer reliefs represent an indigenous topos in ancient Israel/Palestine. Although examples attest both larger and smaller disks being held in the drum position, only the larger disks have ornamentation (Glueck, 1940; Yadin, 1960), ornamentation quite similar to examples dating to the 19th Dynasty in Egypt (see also Manniche, 1973, 1-2; Hickmann, 1961a, illust. 71). The head covering or wigs worn by the nude female drummers possibly also betray Egyptian influence (Osiris cult). On the other hand, no such terra-cotta reliefs of nude female drummers are attested from Egypt. Significantly, however, we do have examples of nude female drummers from Mesopotamia dating to the Old Babylonian period that might have served as models (Rashid, 1984). Artists in ancient Israel/Palestine quite possibly drew from both sources, Egyptian and Babylonian, in a process of acculturation that produced a new, indigenous, and enduring topos in these reliefs.

The idea of a female drummer on terra-cotta reliefs may well have accompanied the immigration of the Israelites' ancestors from Haran (Mesopotamia); one need only recall here the teraphim *(t^{e}rāpîm)*, the small household gods Rachel stole from her father, Laban (Gen. 31:19, 34). Not only is this scene associated with the earliest mention of the drum in the Old Testament (Gen. 31:27), even the chronology of our finds also coincides with astonishing precision with the origin of these Old Testament texts (approx. 900 B.C.). Pritchard (1943) has suggested that "there is no direct evidence connecting the nude female figure represented upon the plaques and figurines of Palestine with any of the prominent goddesses." Although interpretations range from deities to toys (see Winter, 1983), the latter can likely be ruled out given the locales in which many of the figurines have been found, namely, cultic sites and funeral contexts.

The fusion of sacral and profane elements characteristic of this age has generated its own symbolic combination in these reliefs. Nudity symbolizes fertility and sexuality, the adornment symbolizes prostitution, and the wig functions as an attribute of the Osiris cult. Beyond these elements, however, the drum itself underscores this fusion even more emphatically. It is clearly not an instrument of the official cult, and yet a profound symbolism of sexuality and fertility attaches to it. Although it appears in secular life, it also accompanies expressions of praise in religious contexts. The nude female drummer, however, made-up and otherwise adorned, harbors a profound synthetic Middle Eastern symbolism. As a temple servant, she was dedicated to "sacred prostitution," while as a sacralization of sexuality she had a close thematic association with the "sacred marriage." As such, this figure was bound to come into conflict with the official cult of Israel and Judah. Indeed, the broken and damaged drums (illust. IV.12) frequently accompanying these terra cottas may well betray the iconoclastic activity of the new ideologues. In any event, at least at the beginning, these terra-cotta figurines may still have been tolerated as multifunctional amulets or household icons, or may even have represented or been identified with famous female drummers or professional mourners.

The transformation of the contexts in which the *tōp* appears in the Old Testament betrays concealed sexual motifs. In one early text (Jgs. 11:34), Jephthah's daughter assumes the role of drummer as she laments her virginity. Iconographic representations of nude female drummers express a clear erotic element and cater to the habitual needs of rather broad portions of the population, who used these terra cottas as semi-sacred amulets, apparently often with forbidden connotations. After the exile, however, Old Testament writers sublimated this aspect through the metaphor of "virgin Israel." The drum of the "virgin pure of body" and of the "naked priestess," and even the drum of Jephthah's daughter now is associated with "virgin Israel": "O virgin Israel! Again you shall adorn yourself, beat the *tōp*, and go forth in the dance of the merrymakers" (*bimḥôl mᵉśaḥᵃqîm*, Jer. 31:4). Here the ambiguous word *mᵉśaḥᵃqîm*, usually sim-

IV.12. Terra-cotta plaque figurines, Amman,
AAM ATH 66-3 and 66-24 (fragments)

plified in translation as "dance," underscores the erotic undertones of the passage.

These relief figures of female drummers were extremely widespread and popular among broad portions of the population in ancient Israel. Because so many were produced, and because they had a place in virtually every household, one might conclude that they faithfully reproduce both the image of the female drummer in real life and the significance of this topos in ancient Israel/Palestine at large. Indeed, this particular tradition had such deep roots that its traces are still discernible in the songs Yemenite Jewish women sing as dance accompaniment today. Yemenite folk legends also attest the sheer age of these songs that were accompanied by hand-clapping, drumming, and the sound of the [[ṣahan]], a kind of gong about 25-50 cm. in diameter. Here the drum itself not only functions to initiate the motor impulses associated with the dance, but in the hands of the [[mᵉšoreret]], the improvisational poetess who leads the round dance (cf. Ezra 2:65), it also symbolizes the latter's guiding role within the performance. These terracotta figurines confirm that precisely this preeminent significance of the drum derives from the age of the ancient Israelite monarchy.

2. From the Sacred Female Double-Pipe Blowers to Male Double-Pipe Players

Attaining an accurate understanding of the aerophones in use during the monarchies in Israel and Judah has proven to be one of the most difficult tasks facing scholars, and is still one of the unsolved problems in ancient Near Eastern organology. Neither the ergology nor even the precise designations of these instruments have been satisfactorily explained. Archaeological sources are of little use in this regard, since apart from the Megiddo flutes (see chap. III/7) and triton shells (see chap. IV/5), no other intact instruments have been found; moreover, only about ten artifacts in all represent wind instruments. Nor do Old Testament textual studies offer any solutions.

Iconographic sources usually offer only a representation of musicians playing, that is, blowing the instruments; they do not depict in any detail precisely the part of the instrument of crucial interest to us, namely, the upper end itself, which would define or specify which instrument the musician is playing. Hence we cannot determine with any certainty just which instrument is being portrayed, whether a flute, clarinet, or oboe. Nor is this a matter of mere inconsequence, since the timbrel differences between these instruments is enormous, as are their respective performance techniques. All these considerations are of decisive significance for the musical aesthetics and social function associated with music in a certain society. Determining the exact type of aerophone in any given iconographic context is of enormous significance, and mistaken identity can easily mislead us in our attempt to understand the accompanying cultural-historical situation.

Eleven pieces of archaeological evidence contribute to our understanding of double-pipe wind instruments. These examples cover the entire period of the monarchy and suggest that such double pipes were found throughout the country. As one moves from the northwest to the southeast, however, and from the Early Iron Age to the Babylonian-Persian period, changes become discernible in performance technique, construction, social status, and thus also in aesthetic considerations.

These changes in the social status and significance of these instruments, as well as in their construction and performance techniques, are clearly discernible in the three groups into which the artifacts can be classified.

a. The two oldest finds continue the earlier Canaanite-Egyptian tradition and date to a period when the trade and cultural relationships between Israel and Egypt were extremely active. Both artifacts were found in the country's central region, one in Tell el-Farʿa-north, site of the earliest example of the double pipe in ancient Israel/Palestine (illust. IV.15), the other in Megiddo (illust. IV.13a, b), where the Egyptian-Canaanite influence endured most tenaciously in any case. Both statuettes are made of relatively precious materials (bronze, faience), and both portray nude figures with personalized individual features, especially the Megiddo-figurine, which Gressmann (1927) has called a "demoness." Standing on a tripod, this crowned female figurine may represent a deified temple priestess; considering the instrument itself, however, she may also represent one of the undesirable qᵉḏēšôṯ associated with sacred prostitution during the monarchy in Israel (Dt. 23:18). The bronze tripod on which the figure is standing is generally viewed as a typical indigenous product of ancient Israel/Palestine during the twelfth-tenth century B.C. (Catling, 1964). Moreover, this particular female minstrel exhibits a certain relationship with the Beth-shean lute player discussed earlier (illust. III.6). The Faience figurine from Tell el-Farʿa is 5.4 cm. tall. It is a squatting male hamadryad-figure with a

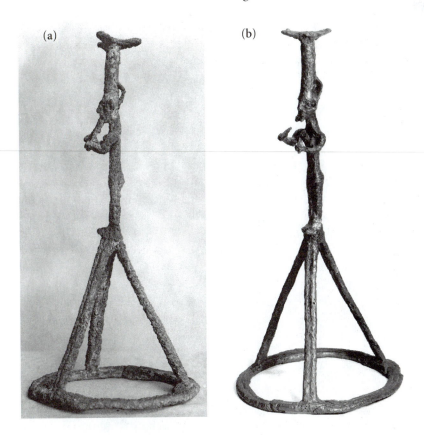

IV.13. Bronze figurine, female double-pipe player:
(a) Megiddo, Berlin VAM-9870, intact; (b) present condition

clearly discernible mane of hair and an erect penis, a clearly Egyptian topos related to the sacred ape and symbolizing erudition, intelligence, and sexual activity. A hole has been drilled into its backside which may have facilitated its use as an amulet. Both the Megiddo-figurine and the hamadryad-figure are deeply rooted in the Canaanite-Egyptian cult, and as such the instrument associated with the figurines is also to be viewed as an accoutrement of the cult.

b. The three terra cottas from Achzib (illust. IV.14), Shiqmona (illust. IV.16), Acco (illust. IV.17), and a figurine of unknown provenance all can

135

IV.14. Bell-shaped terra-cotta figurine, double-pipe player, Achzib, IAA 44.56

IV.15. Faience figurine, double-pipe player, Tell el-Farʿa, EB F-1781

IV.16. Terra-cotta figurine, fragment, double-pipe player, Shiqmona,
IAA 81.1040

IV.17. Terra-cotta figurine, Acco, IAA 86.84

be classified among the bell-shaped figurines already discussed in connection with the female drummers, and even the fragmentary examples can be reliably classified as such according to the Achzib model. Both the female double-reed players and the drummers come from the northwestern part of the country, and although the lack of final excavation reports renders the chronology a bit uncertain, they seem to date to the time of the sea peoples (tenth-seventh century B.C.), when these cities were flourishing culturally. The rather large number of minstrel figurines from this part of the country during the period in question suggests the presence of a local Phoenician tradition that might even be specified more closely as the Achzib/Shiqmona school of musical terra cottas. In its turn, such a school suggests the presence of a relatively high level of terra-cotta art and probably a comparably high level of instrumental music. Three of the figurines show a stylish bobbed haircut, and although the Achzib figure's hair is closely cropped, it still probably does not represent a male, which would be highly unusual given the overall disposition of this group. If by contrast the terra cotta is actually portraying a female figure with closely cropped hair, which would mark this musician as an indecent woman, we may be correct in classifying the double pipe as one of the asacral or even "prostituted" instruments (Isa. 3:17).

c. Four terra cottas come from the eastern and southeastern periphery of the Kingdom of Judah, near the kingdoms of Ammon and Edom. The Beth-shean relief (illust. IV.18) is the only example depicting a female, half-dressed and with a wig, blowing a reed instrument in the widespread artifact group encompassing relief terra-cotta figurines holding the drum in front of their chest. The Qitmit terra cotta (illust. IV.19) is also a singular example from an Edomite outpost or enclave in Judah (Beit-Arieh, 1988). The style of the figurines and the type of instruments suggest that both these artifacts derive from local ethnic folk traditions.

Professor Yitzchak Beit-Arieh of Tel-Aviv University recently found a terra-cotta figure that is of extraordinary significance in this context (illust. IV.20). This bust of a musician blowing a double-pipe with conical tubes was found in a building of unknown function in the Edomite settlement Tel-Malḥata in the Negev and represents one of the most impressive iconographical portrayals of a musician in the entire area of ancient Israel/Palestine. Everything about the figurine, its material, workmanship, style, and so on, betrays a direct relationship with the Edomite art of Qitmit, where the double-pipe player mentioned earlier was also found (illust. IV.19) and the

IV.18. Plaque figure, double-pipe player, Beth-shean, PAN P.29-103-932

IV.19. Terra-cotta figurine, Qitmit, double-pipe player, IAA 87-180

IV.20. Terra-cotta figurine, Tel Malḥata, double-*zurna* player, IAA 94.3394

site of several other noteworthy finds related to music (e.g., illust. III.26). The artist created a richly detailed, animated figure that in all likelihood was drawn from real life. The musician wears a headpiece, which may connect him to clergy or the military, and is playing an instrument with two conical, almost parallel pipes, that is, an aerophone of the *zamr/zurna* type, a wind instrument not unequivocally attested for this period. I believe this to be the first reliable example of this particular group of wind instruments; late, from Hellenistic times on, this instrument appears in many artifacts as a single-pipe instrument (see illust. V.26 and 27) and ultimately it became one of the most popular instruments in the entire Near East. While the horizontal lines discernible on the bottom of each of the pipes may be ornamentation, they may also be mounted hornpieces reflecting a construction technique commonly used on such instruments later on. The pirouette characteristic of these instruments as illustrated by the later Bar Kokhba coins (illust. V.57e, f) does not yet appear in this example. The second Edomite artifact, which I examined in the Israel Museum in Jerusalem, is also a terra cotta of a seated musician playing a conical double-reed instrument; it closely resembles the Tel-Malḥata figure and is of considerable significance insofar as it confirms the widespread distribution of the conical wind instrument in the Edomite sphere and might even suggest that such instruments originated in this area.

The final terra cotta of this corpus was found farther to the east, in Petra, and portrays a covered male head with a double-pipe instrument, possibly depicting a clergyman (preserved at the AI of the London University). It is more closely related to the Hellenistic-Nabataean culture and seems to document once and for all the transformation of the double pipe, at least in the southeastern part of the country, from a women's entertainment instrument to a man's cult/military instrument.

Both the ergological features and the playing techniques differ considerably among the instruments portrayed in these finds. (a) The instruments from the central region are actually made of two strongly diverging pipes of unequal length held in an unshifted, symmetrical position. (b) The instruments from the northwestern region have two pipes of equal length that diverge slightly less than those from the central region, and are held in the same unshifted position. (c) The instruments from the eastern and southeastern periphery are made of two parallel pipes held in the same unshifted position but more closely together. The instrument from Qitmit seems once to have had a horn bell at the end (of the sort found on the Phrygian aulos), though it has apparently been broken off this terra cotta, and the pipes themselves seem to be slightly conical in shape in contrast to the others. Finally, the musician playing the instrument is portrayed with puffed cheeks, suggesting the instrument is actually a double-reed wind instrument. Unfortunately, the lack of sufficient details in these terra cottas prevents us from answering unequivocally the main question regarding the organology of wind instruments in this context, namely, whether all these examples or only some of them represent double-reed instruments.

Double-reed instruments do not appear in ancient Israel/Palestine until approximately one to two centuries after the first reliably dated example of the double oboe in Egypt at the time of the 18th Dynasty. The earliest evidence of such instruments in ancient Israel/Palestine reflects an Egyptian-Canaanite style and appears during a period in which musical instruments in general were undergoing significant change throughout the country. Musicologists believe the most common wind instruments in the ancient Near East were double-pipe, double-reed instruments. At different times and in different parts of the country, the instrument acquired different forms associated with specific locales, and artisans drew from these local Phoenician and Palestinian forms in developing the original Egyptian version into the varied types of aulos characteristic of the later Hellenistic culture. This whole process seems to have moved in successive waves and even in successively alternating directions, first from the northwest to the southeast, then from the southeast to the northwest. In each case, new variations of the original instrument were added to the original inventory of forms associated with this instrument throughout the country, while a local change in both the gender of double-pipe musicians and their social standing becomes apparent.

3. Lyres in Solo and Ensemble Performance

By the beginning of the second millennium, the lyre had established a firm presence in ancient Israel/Palestine. It quickly became the dominant instrument in the region and remained such through the entire Iron Age, enjoying its golden age apparently within the Israelite-Judean monarchy itself as well as in the neighboring areas. A whole array of sources, including especially archaeological evidence, unanimously confirms the preeminent status of the lyre within the musical culture of the Iron Age in a way virtually unparalleled in other areas of music. While evidence for other chordophones is wholly absent for this period, we have at least twelve finds portraying the lyre under actual performance conditions.

These lyre players appear in two drawings on pottery (illust. IV.21; IV.23), in two terra cottas (illust. IV.32a; IV.33), and on each of the ten seals recovered from this period (illust. IV.24 through IV.31). The drawings are clearly individual works of art, while the seals probably belonged to members of the ruling class and were used to indicate possession or other identification. One of the terra cottas is a singular cultic stand depicting a group of priest-musicians. On balance, the social and culture significance of this typology does not emerge with its full impact until we recall that the iconography of membranophones and aerophones is attested largely by terra-cotta figurines, that is, by products of mass culture, while the iconography of the lyre described above confirms the elite role enjoyed by this instrument and by lyre players themselves with regard to cult, power, and high culture.

Written sources confirm this observation insofar as they associate lyres, and especially the *kinnôr*, with the most important cultural-intellectual and social activities of the upper classes of society (see chap. I/3). In their first appearances, the *kinnarātim* (lyres) are associated with the appointment of a sovereign. The root of the word itself, *knr*, appears frequently in divine names such as *kinýras*, [[*kinnaraas, kuthar*]]. Significantly, the Old Testament mentions the *kinnôr* more often than any other instrument except the *šôpār*, associating it with activities such as praise of God, transfer of the ark, national mourning, miraculous healing, and ecstatic prophecy. Only rarely does the Old Testament mention it in connection with any secular or more common activities of the people.

It is quite clear that the lyre and its music acquired and tenaciously maintained a lofty and even dominant position within the cultural and musical life of the country. All the evidence surrounding this instrument seems to confirm the general tendency within this region for national characteristics to attach themselves to the preeminent cultural products of a country while goods produced by mass production, as we saw in the case of the drum and double pipe, generally reflect supra-regional or even pan-Palestinian characteristics (cf. Weippert, 1988, 574).

A. Pottery Drawings

The earliest example of this group is the Megiddo-jar (illust. IV.21a-b), whose procession of animals and single lyre player moving toward a tree-like figure has been the subject of lengthy discussion. The jar was found during the extensive Megiddo excavations and has been dated to 1150-1000 B.C. (Dothan, 1982; Loud, 1948). Prior to its destruction in approximately 1000-950 B.C., Megiddo was an influential Philistine trade and cultural center with its share of wealthy citizens. This particular jar is rather lavishly decorated compared with other specimens of Philistine art, and the large building in which it was found may have belonged to one of those wealthy citizens or even to the Philistine prince of Megiddo himself (MazarB, 1976). The composition of this scene is singular, and was executed by an artist capable of uniting the Philistine tradition with Aegean and local Canaanite elements.

Since its discovery, scholars have associated the scene with Orpheus even though the Orpheus legend originally had nothing to do with music and is not attested iconographically until five hundred years later. A more likely alternative is a scene portraying a topos quite common within the Philistine sphere, namely, worship of the sacred tree (Schoer, 1987). Benjamin Mazar (1976) adduces a thematic relationship with 1 K. 5:12-13 in understanding this scene as the Philistine topos of a singer who accompanies himself on the lyre while reciting his poetry about "animals and birds and reptiles and fish." The four Old Testament persons mentioned in this connection are Ethan, Heman, Calcol, and Darda, who might have been members of a guild of bards or musicians.

The motif of the lyre player in association with animals seems to have been an indigenous development in this area. Although Egyptian and Mesopotamian sources offer many examples portraying animals as musicians or incorporating animal shapes into parts of the instruments themselves (Hickmann, 1961a; Rashid, 1984), they virtually never portray animals, fish, birds, or reptiles together with human musicians in the same scene. Artists in ancient Israel/Palestine, on the other hand, began quite early portraying human musicians together with animals; significantly, the instruments in such scenes are always chordophones (illust. II.5; III.1; IV.33).

The Canaanite-Philistine lyre made a long journey from ancient Israel/Palestine to the Assyrian northwest; we are able to trace this journey in two different documents from a later period, one written and one

(a)

(b)

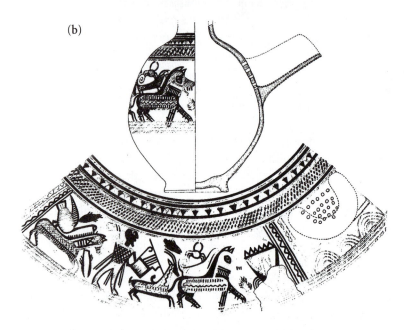

IV.21. Jar with drawing of a lyre player, Megiddo, IAA 36.1921:
(a) natural form; (b) copy

iconographic. King Hezekiah of Judah (727-698 B.C.) introduced a great many economic and cultural reforms during his reign. The Old Testament recounts that he reformed both the liturgical ritual proper and the music associated with it (2 K. 18:4-5), organizing the Levitical musician guilds, their performances, and their instrumental music (cf. 2 Ch. 29:25-26; 31:2); as part of this overall reform, he also incorporated musical instruments, and especially stringed instruments, into cultic singing (2 Ch. 30:21). In these reforms, however, he was evidently providing a point of crystallization for a tradition that had already been developing over a longer period of time. This new musical style might even be called the *ars nova* of the Iron Age, and attracted the keen interest of military conquerors in the region. After taking Jerusalem, the Assyrian king boasts in the Sennacherib tablets (701 B.C.) that "as to Hezekiah, the Jew, he did not submit to my yoke, I laid siege to forty-six of his strong cities, walled forts, and to the countless small villages in their vicinity, and conquered them. . . . I drove out of them 200,150 people, young and old, male and female. . . . Hezekiah himself . . . did send me, later, to Nineveh, my lordly city, together with thirty talents of gold, eight hundred talents of silver . . . all kinds of valuable treasures, his own daughters, concubines, male and female musicians" (Luckenbill, 1924; ANET, 288). The iconographic evidence of this tribute is found on an alabaster relief on the southwestern palace at Nineveh and portrays three captured Jewish lyre players (illust. IV.22). Their lyres are asymmetrical instruments with straight arms and seem to be of a rather simple, unsophisticated design in comparison to the earlier instruments from Megiddo and later ones from Nineveh itself.

Although the whole scene is highly stylized, the three bearded men together with their instruments are still highly informative. The asymmetrical lyres from the Nineveh relief recall the lyre from the Megiddo symposium (illust. III.16) but are much simpler, even primitive, and seem to belong to the type of traditional folk instruments, in contrast to the artistically sophisticated professional lyres. The short, angular yoke arm on the lyre on the Orpheus jar (illust. IV.21) can be understood as a geometrical stylization of a part of the instrument that rises in inconsistent increments to one side, and the instrument itself may be the first appearance of a particular type of lyre one finds two to three centuries later in Nineveh (Rashid, 1984). The Assyrian lyres resulted from a long developmental process that actually began with Canaanite-Phoenician instruments, and the features found on these lyres apparently represent specific characteristics of this genre. We can observe the interim forms of this process on the eighth-century bronze plate

IV.22. Alabaster relief with lyre players, Nineveh, BM 124947

from Idalium (Cyprus), and a bit later on a similar plate from Citium (Aign, 1963, figs. 30, 33). Scholars have tried to ignore the fact that the lyres have only four, obliquely attached strings, though this precise pattern is richly attested on later Aegean, Cypriot, and Assyrian instruments; this feature, too, must be considered peculiar to this particular type.

Earlier instruments may have been rather unwieldy; the large number of strings and the instruments' cumbersome construction or form may have made them more difficult to play or restricted their usefulness to only certain kinds of music. The instruments now under discussion seem to have transcended these cumbersome features and may reflect the emergence of a new, reformed musical style or *ars nova*. It is of considerable iconographic interest in this regard that the jar drawing exhibits certain stylistic and thematic similarities to a later palace relief in Nineveh which also portrays a lyre player and accompanying lion in connection with a tree (Rashid, 1984, illust. 148). All these considerations seem to support the notion that the lyre on the jar does indeed represent a prototype in this sense.

We encounter a completely different type of lyre player on the pottery shards of a large vessel from Kuntillet 'Ajrud (Ḥorvat Teman, northern Sinai) dating to approximately 800 B.C. (illust. IV.23a).

The artist responsible for the drawing of the seated lyre player apparently made two attempts to sketch a symmetrical lyre in various playing positions, one at an angle to the player's body, the other held vertically. Because the artist did not finish the vertical lyre, and the playing position is actually commensurate with that associated with the lyre held at an angle, the artist likely understood the latter to be the valid playing position. The hands are disproportionately large and probably reflect the Egyptian tradition of emphasizing important parts of a drawing. Unless some of the details in the drawing actually represent mere chance strokes on the part of the artist, they present a rather odd situation for the interpreter. The extended cross yoke of the vertical lyre, for example, corresponds precisely to the basalt relief of Harash (Perrot/Chipiez, 1890, II, fig. 281). In any event, both forms of the lyre attested here have very close iconographic parallels from eighth-seventh century B.C. Phoenician and Assyrian monuments, where they are played by both sitting and standing/walking musicians. Stauder (1961a) thinks these simple, small lyres (used by the people at large?) actually represent cultural products of Anatolian mountain dwellers. The Nippur seal is of particular interest in connection with the lyre from Kuntillet 'Ajrud (Rashid, 1984, illust. 120). Parallels can be found for virtually all the details of the seat or throne, the instrument's form, the position in which it is held, the player's clothing and hairstyle, even his mutilated facial features. On the seal, the lyre player is turned toward yet a second musician, a situation that may explain why the player on the shard has his back turned to the other figures in the drawing, especially if one allows that the second musician in the drawing is blurred or vague. The small lyre of Kuntillet 'Ajrud appears yet again in Ptolemaic Egypt in the hands of a Bes-figure (Hickmann, 1961a) and thus seems to confirm the connection between the Kuntillet drawing and Bes which Beck (1982) proposed.

This Kuntillet 'Ajrud drawing was found on one of the pithoi whose sensational discovery in 1975 (Meshel, 1976; 1979) triggered a global discussion (see Beck, 1982; Dever, 1984; Freedman, 1987; Keel/Uehlinger, 1992; *et al.*). Beck subjected these drawings of animals, Bes-figures, processional, lyre players, and tree to exhaustive analysis in 1982. As it turns out, their style reflects a conglomeration of Phoenician, Midianite, Assyrian, Egyptian, and Arabic elements. The drawings themselves are of such enormous importance because they are the only drawings dating to this period in ancient Israel/Palestine that are also accompanied by inscriptions, permitting interpretive proposals regarding just how the texts and drawings relate. The question of greatest interest to scholars is whether the seated musician (male or female?) constitutes a group together with the figures standing behind it, just who the figures are in the first place, and whether the Hebrew inscription above the two figures refers to the entire drawing: "I bless you by Yahweh of Samaria and his Asherah." Is the reference to the goddess Asherah? Does the word "Asherah" refer to the name of the goddess herself or to a cultic object such as a tree, image, stone, or site? Or is the Old Testament understanding of the word as both goddess and cultic object in effect here as well (cf. Jgs. 3:7; 1 K. 15:13; 16:33; 2 K. 17:10)? An interpretation of the male group on the second pithos is fraught with even more difficulty (illust. IV.23b). Does the drawing portray a procession, or is it a choral group whose members are holding their hands aloft as is customary when singing their cultic songs or psalms?

Meshel (1978) has suggested that the site itself was an Israelite/Judean cultic center on the northern boundary of the Sinai desert where local beliefs found their way into both written and iconographic sources. If he is correct, what we have is one of the innumerable deviant, often nonconformist variants of a provincial cult within the Israelite monarchy. In precisely such a context, a musician deity might have played a role of the sort evoked by Anat[[h?]]-Astarte-Asherah, which in turn derives from the musician deity Hathor (Albright, 1956). On the other hand, Hadley (1987) has proposed that what we have before us here is actually a caravansary situated at the north-south and east-west crossroads where an untold number of itinerants and travelers left traces of themselves in the form of wall or clay drawings or inscriptions. In that case, the figure with the lyre is merely an independent and probably secular musician. The latest interpretation, proposed by Ya'akov Meshorer (Meshorer/Qedar, 1999, 33), is of special interest for our discussion since it is to a great degree based on the presence of the lyre player in the discussed iconography. It appears that all iconographical motifs of the 'Ajrud jars — the Bes figure, cow suckling calf, tree of life, lion, figure smelling flowers, and the lyre player — appear on fourth-century-B.C. Samaritan coins (see chap. V/6). Although several centuries di-

IV.23. Storage jars with drawings, Kuntillet ʿAjrud:
(a) female lyre player, male figures and animals (above);
(b) male procession, TAUIA S78.4 and S78.46 (below)
(copies from Beck 1982)

vide the two iconographical corpora, we know that religious symbolism and semantics are persistent and that both textual and iconographical continuity — the 'Ajrud inscription "Yahweh of Samaria" (*yahweh šomron*, Heb.) and Samaritan images — exist. It is more than tempting to suggest that in Tell 'Ajrud we find the incipient symbolism of later Samaritan monotheism, which, like Judaism, venerates the *kinnôr* music and *kinnôr* instrument itself. In either case, then, the drawing represents a syncretistic cultural piece reflecting a primarily Phoenician-Israelite style. The environment that produced it was a pluralistic society positioned within the waning years of a great Canaanite-Israelite musical tradition involving the lyre, a tradition drawing to a close a period that actually began during the first half of the second millennium B.C.

B. Seals

Beginning in the fifth millennium B.C. in the ancient Orient, seals served as signs of possession and/or personal identification, though in many cases they also served as amulets and as personal adornment or jewelry. Not surprisingly, the thousands of seals found in Palestine/Israel are of enormous significance for cultural historians, and among them we find a relatively large number (about ten) associated with musical topoi, all of which date to a rather brief period, namely, the first half of the first millennium B.C. By contrast, Egyptian finds have yielded virtually no seals associated with musical topoi except for three portraying a worship scene with a trumpet player before a seated ruler (Wiese, 1990). About fifty seals with musical scenes have been found covering a span of about three millennia in the Babylonian sphere (Rashid, 1984). The stylistic and organological variety attaching to the seals found in connection with ancient Israel/Palestine represents the broad spectrum of cultures associated with ancient Israel.

Indeed, these seals are a rich iconographic source of information about the history of music during the Iron Age in this region as well as about the organological developments affecting the instruments themselves. The chronological unity just mentioned underscores the special sociohistorical status these musical artifacts enjoyed. The time period in question here is Iron Age II, the age of the most significant changes in this country and a time during which the city culture was revived and during which national ethnic groups were consolidated. Although the mixed style exhibited by most of the seals appears in its most pronounced form on the Philistine-Phoenician coast, it nonetheless can be viewed as characteristic for the entire country. The spirit of new beginnings was coupled with a spirit of both national and individual initiative, and the result was an atmosphere extremely congenial to increased artistic initiative and musical activity. This situation in turn produced these musically related seals, all of which are executed in the form of pictographs, even those dating to the period (eighth-seventh century B.C.) during which inscriptional glyptics came into use. Even though none of these seals has an inscription, they are probably still to be classified among the seals associated with private individuals and with certain officials. Four of the seals were found during documented excavations, and six are of unknown provenance.

Two seals reflect Philistine cultural influence. The Tel-Batash seal (illust. IV.24) is probably the oldest in the group, dating to the twelfth-tenth century B.C., while only half of the Ashdod seal (illust. IV.25) has been recovered. In this context, it is of some significance that the richest, geographically and chronologically most unified collection of archaeological evidence associated with music within this region comes from the Philistine cultural sphere, including at least fifteen musical instruments and ten artifacts otherwise associated with music. The conclusion one can

IV.24. Seal with lyre player, Tel Batash, HU-3593

IV.25. Seal with lyre player, Ashdod (original lost)

draw from this observation is that indigenous artisans must have been involved in the actual production of these items, or at least that the objects portrayed in them must have included an extremely pronounced indigenous element. In any event, the composition of both seals is extremely schematic, being executed largely in straight lines, and both seals portray a seated lyre player.

In every respect, the Ashdod seal (illust. IV.25) is related to the eighth-century seals from Cyprus, Rhodes, and southern Anatolia depicting what is known as the "lyre player group" (Porada, 1956). The instrument portrayed here is a U-shaped, symmetrical lyre. Several features, however, clearly deviate from those associated with the "lyre player group." These seals are rectangular rather than oval. The musician is nude rather than clothed. The lyre itself has two rather than three strings. The Ashdod seal lacks any drilled holes, and so on. The execution of the Ashdod seal also seems clearly inferior to the seals of the "lyre player group"; the chair is out of kilter, the hand position is incorrect, and the lyre itself is imprecisely rendered. This inferior execution together with the previously mentioned deviations suggests the seal was produced locally. Nonetheless, much suggests that the missing half of the seal probably depicted a dancer playing a frame drum as in the "lyre player group" (see Porada, 1956, illust. 5). The overall scene, which Buchner and Boardman (1966) have described as a "banquet with sacred meal," is rather depicting a cultic stand in front of a musician.

To my knowledge, the lyre on the Tel Batash seal (illust. IV.24) is the oldest known representation of a strictly angular symmetrical lyre with parallel strings. One significant and surprising observation connected with this portrayal is that it corrects our earlier view concerning the origin of this type of lyre; rather than originating in Assyria, it must have emerged much farther to the south. It was probably not until after Tiglath Pileser III conquered both Israel and Philistia that this lyre form reached the northwestern areas of Phoenicia and northern Assyria.

The third seal (illust. IV.26) depicts an angular symmetrical lyre of the Tel Batash type and is actually a bronze scaraboid (typical of northern Palestine) acquired by the Reuben Hecht Museum of the Haifa University. The peculiar portrayal of a similar instrument on a silver plate now in the Berlin Museum confirms the typology of this angular type of lyre, though scholars have recently concluded it probably originated in northern Palestine-northern Syria rather than in Egypt (Meyer, 1987). The Haifa seal portrays a seated lyre player together with what is probably a female

IV.26. Seal with lyre player and drummer, PU, H-1870

dancer playing a drum. This theme is certainly commensurate with the "lyre player group" and doubtless derives from the male-female duo of chordophone and membranophone familiar from the orgiastic cults in early Babylon (Rashid, 1984, illust. 58, 59).

The chordophone-membranophone duo already appeared earlier in this region (Anati, 1963) and is related to other duos of local provenance. This connection as well as the lyre type itself enable us to assign the Haifa seal almost certainly to the sphere of tenth/eighth-century Philistine artifacts. These Philistine duos date to a slightly earlier period than the well-known Phoenician chordophone-aerophone-membranophone trio, and it is worth recalling that the chordophone-membranophone duo, in which the instruments are always designated as *kinnôr* and *tōp*, appears in one of the earliest Old Testament passages associated with music, namely, Gen. 31:27. This duo symbolizes secular and cultic joy (Gen. 31:27; also Isa. 24:8; Ps. 149:3), and in at least one instance seems to be associated with an Assyrian theophany and sacrifice. We are probably safe in asserting that the duo represents a very early stage of ensemble playing.

The following two artifacts now represent a new group. The Nebo roll seal (illust. IV.27) and the stamp seal from the Tel Aviv University collection (illust. IV.28a-b) are strikingly similar in a number of features: the two musicians themselves — a male lyre player and a female double-pipe player — but also their clothing, their head covering, the emblem of the lunar god Sin

IV.27. Seal with lyre and double pipe player, Nebo, SBF-293
(roll seal with impression)

of Haran, the altar shaped like the Egyptian symbol of life Ankh, the holy tree, and the discrete groupings of ornaments. The female figure is playing a double oboe or double clarinet and certainly not a double flute, as has often been claimed (Giveon, 1978; Beck, 1986). Given the extent of the similarity between the two scenes, we can date the Tel Aviv seal to approximately the same period as that of the Nebo seal, and possibly even to the same workshop. Because the two seals clearly attest elements of the lunar cult, Giveon was probably correct in suspecting that this cult made significant headway into Israel during the Iron Age. The seals also show that this chordophone-aerophone duo played some role within that cult.

The limitations of the illustration itself prevent us from saying anything more spe-

(a)   (b)

IV.28. Seal with lyre and double pipe player, PU, TA-KhD3:
(a) side with lyre; (b) side with double pipe

cific about the double pipe's ergological features, for example, whether it had a mouthpiece or reeds and of what kind. The lyres, however, are interesting insofar as they have more strings than any of the previous examples, the Nebo seal having three, and the Tel Aviv seal having six. Both represent the asymmetrical lyre with rectangular resonator and parallel strings, a type apparently preferred in their local sphere of provenance. The Israelite prisoners on the famous relief in Sennacherib's palace in Nineveh (704-681 b.c.) are carrying the same type of lyre as those on these seals, the only difference being the slightly diverging side arms.

The symmetrical lyre with a rectangular resonator and a relatively small number of parallel strings was apparently quite popular in ancient Israel at the end of the second and the beginning of the first millennium b.c.; the same lyre type eventually became established in Assyria as well. Toward the end of the eighth century, however, it seems that the asymmetrical type with a rectangular resonator and six or more parallel strings superseded the earlier symmetrical instrument.

Given the instruments portrayed together on these seals, it is worth noting that the double pipe and lyre are also quite often portrayed separately in the ancient Orient. In fact, ancient Middle Eastern iconography only rarely attests the chordophone-aerophone duo in any event, and not at all before the fourth-third century B.C. The same observation applies generally to biblical texts as well. If we assume for argument's sake that the *ʿûgāb* was possibly an aerophone, it is noteworthy that the Bible mentions this duo in but a single passage, namely Job 30:31 (discounting for the moment the philosophical passage Gen. 4:21); it is perhaps not at all accidental that an equally rare reference to the lunar cult appears in immediate proximity (Job 31:26-28).

A standing lyre player flanked by symbols appears on two different seals, the first from Tell Keisan (illust. IV.29), the second from a private collection in Ramat Gan, Israel. This striking iconographical similarity extends from the portrayal of the musician himself, his instrument, and his clothing, to the symbolic ornamentation, and may even betray a common

IV.29. Seal with lyre player, [[Tell Keisan]], EB-3332

origin of the two seals in the same workshop; in any event, it does suggest that this seal (Braun 1999, illust. IV/3-10) dates to the ninth-seventh century B.C. This same pair is also clearly related to one from the BIF-collection (see Keel/Leu, 1991, Nr. 135) with the striding lyre player, which also is similar to the Tell Keisan seal. Scholars have offered various interpretations for the symbolic ornamentation in front of the lyre player, ornamentation similar to the Ankh symbol. Some think the symbol is actually the Phoenician letters gimel-daleth ("GD"; Briend/Humbert, 1980); others consider the context in interpreting it either as a symbol of the astral cult or as the Egyptian symbol of life (Keel/Shuval/Uehlinger, 1990, 328-30). Nor are these semantic distinctions inconsequential for the present study. The music of the ancient world simply accepted these ambiguities and passed them on accordingly. A seal from Jerusalem (PU, PC) is especially interesting in this regard, since it contains a peculiar symbolic mix including not only the symbols already familiar from the Tell Keisan group, but also the lunar symbol mentioned earlier as well as an astral/solar symbol. This admixture of symbolic elements on music seals seems to have been a local tradition in ancient Israel, and in any event certainly confirms that the lyre was an established part of the various cults that proliferated throughout the country. All these seals probably represent private professional seals belonging to priests who were also professional lyre players and guild musicians. The stylized instrument itself is an asymmetrical rectangular lyre with between two and six strings. Although the composition on several seals has been quite well executed, the BIF seal exhibits a considerably lower level of craftsmanship.

The last seal belonging to this group is the scaraboid of unknown provenance acquired by the Israel Museum (illust. IV.30). A personal-name seal that has been published in many different sources, its oval surface portrays an asymmetrical lyre with gently diverging, S-shaped side arms and a resonator with a rounded base with a rosetta in the center functioning either as a resonating hole or as simple decoration. The inscription reads: "Belonging to Maʿadanah, Daughter of the King." Avigad (1978) believes this portrayal is "the first true Hebrew rendering of this musical instrument, and perhaps closer to the *kinnôr* of King David or the *kinnôr* of the Temple 'orchestra' than any other known representation." Although epigraphical analysis does indeed date the seal to the seventh century B.C., closer analysis raises doubts about both its interpretation and even its authenticity:

IV.30. Seal with lyre, PU, IMJ-80.16.57

(a) No musical instruments are attested as isolated renderings, that is, as symbols, on artifacts prior to the Hellenistic period.

(b) Asymmetrical lyres with rounded resonators are attested neither prior to nor after this example.

(c) In no written sources is an Iron Age lyre from the Middle East described as having more than ten strings; Josephus's allusion to the twelve strings of the *nábla* dates from a period at least six centuries later (*Ant.* vii.12.3).

(d) Prior to the Middle Ages, no musical instrument is attested with a centered rosetta of this sort, either as a resonating hole or as an ornament;

when such does later appear, it does so only on zithers or zither-like instruments.

(e) Although the strings are rendered with considerable care and detail, they still exhibit troubling inconsistencies. Several extend above the yoke itself, the shortest is attached to the lyre arm, and as a whole the strings are distributed over the entire surface area between the two side arms.

(f) Probably most importantly, no lyres are known on which the ends of the side-arms supporting the crossbar are curved outside, which would be incorrect construction.

This brief survey of Iron Age seals allows us to draw several interesting conclusions:

(1) Iron Age seals attest a relatively large number of themes associated with music.

(2) These artifacts were found among the possessions of private individuals and as such reflect social tastes of the time, offering us a glimpse into the private lives of these individuals themselves as well as into the life setting of the musical topoi the seals depict, including that of both the musicians and their instruments. These assertions are fairly secure insofar as these seals were found largely during controlled excavations of private houses and grave sites. In all likelihood, their owners were themselves active in musical life. Moreover, although we cannot really determine unequivocally whether the seals were produced locally, they still offer a wealth of information about local lifestyles, tastes, preferences, and even about faith and tradition.

(3) With the exception of the questionable piece in the Israel Museum, all these seals portray performance situations; that is, they do not merely present symbols or isolated attributes, though such can certainly also play a role in the overall portrayal.

(4) We see once again that the lyre was clearly the dominant chordophone in ancient Israel. Given the present and problematical status of information and sources, the omnipresence of the lyre attested by archaeological evidence suggests yet again that whenever the Bible mentions chordophones, we are dealing with the lyre. Moreover, the lyre was the dominant instrument not only in the cult, but in private secular life as well.

(5) Even though these seals are quite small and offer only schematic

portrayals, we can nonetheless still distinguish three different lyre types: (a) the U-shaped symmetrical type with parallel strings; (b) the symmetrical type with a rectangular resonator and parallel strings; (c) the asymmetrical type with a rectangular resonator and parallel strings. The first two types, those with the smaller number of strings, date to an earlier period, approximately the twelfth-eighth centuries. The last type, with the greater number of strings, dates to a slightly later period, probably the tenth-seventh centuries. Much suggests that type (b) was made locally and that it eventually influenced the style in other areas, most notably the north. A rare find is a bone object (18th-17th cent. B.C.), which seems to be a plectrum, frequently used to strike the strings of the lyre (illust. IV.31).

(6) These seals portray the lyre not only as a dominant solo instrument, but also as the dominant ensemble instrument together with membranophones and aerophones; the duos depicted on three or four of the ten seals are probably continuations of the earlier chordophone-membranophone tradition. The notion of the duo was then altered and expanded in local workshops, for example, into the chordophone-aerophone duo, or into such topoi as that shown by the eleventh-century "musician-stand" from Ashdod. The duo ensemble ultimately developed into the Phoenician chordophone-aerophone-membranophone trio, which in turn profoundly affected the further development of this group. It appears that the Phoenician trio or quartet actually began two centuries earlier and further to the south, within the earlier sphere of ancient Israel/Palestine. These considerations, together with the geographical and chronological corrective involving the lyre with symmetrical rectangular resonator, show that the local musical culture clearly had a hand in the general development of the Middle Eastern musical culture.

IV.31. Plectrum, En-Gedi, IAA 67-484

4. Musicians and Dancers of the Philistine and Phoenician Coast

"Iamani from Ashdod, afraid of my armed force, left his wife and children and fled to the frontier of Musru [Ethiopia] . . . and hid there like a thief. I installed an officer of mine as governor over his entire large country and its prosperous inhabitants thus aggrandizing again the territory belonging to Ashur" (ANET, 284). Thus did Sargon II's (722-705 B.C.) campaign bring to an inglorious end the brief but glorious reign of the sea peoples. The culture we call Philistine went down with them, a culture reaching back into the first half of the twelfth century B.C.

No one seems to know exactly the geographic origins of the various ethnic groups whom Egyptian sources call the "foreigners from the sea." Suggestions include Cyprus, Crete, the Aegean sphere in general, and even Anatolia. In any event, after being defeated by Ramses III (1198-1166 B.C.), these Sherden, Tjekker, Danaoi, and Peleset (Philistines) were driven into the southern coastal regions of ancient Israel/Palestine. There, after a brief incursion into the north, they founded the Philistine Pentapolis, a confederation of the five cities of Gaza, Ashkelon, Ashdod, Gath, and Ekron. These Philistines were known even to biblical writers (1 S. 13:19) as mobile warriors, workers of iron, and successful merchants. Alongside these activities, though, they also developed an extremely rich cultic and artistic life that included music. Within that context, their indigenous artisans drew from a variety of sources in crafting a composite and independent cultural life. Combining both Canaanite and Egyptian elements, Dagon ruled in the Philistine pantheon, while Mycenaean influences found expression not only in the Great Mother Goddess, but also in the architecture of two adjacent temples. Assyrian features are also clearly discernible. In Gaza, Philistine rulers conducted festivals in the temple of Dagon that doubtless also included music, and biblical writers remind us that the great Dagon idol could be seen in Ashdod, the likely capital of the Pentapolis (1 S. 5:1-5). These Philistines apparently ruled as an elite, and despite the ongoing wars still managed to exert considerable influence on Judah's culture (Gitin, 1997; Amos 1:6-8). Musical life is more richly documented by archaeological evidence in Ashdod than in any other Philistine city. In this regard, one need only mention the famous musician stand (illust. IV.32a), the figurine of the lyre player (illust. IV.33), and the seal portraying a lyre player (illust. IV.25). These artifacts, together with the approximately twenty additional finds related to Philistine music, constitute one of the largest and richest collections of archaeological evidence documenting the indigenous music of a given Iron Age nationality. One of the two frames or stands belonging to this group depicts musicians, the other a dance; both are of particular interest in this context.

The stand from Ashdod is the only known monument from pre-Hellenistic Palestine portraying a musical ensemble. Two considerations can be noted here. First, at least to my knowledge, no one has yet been able to adduce similar groups from either Egypt or Assyria. Second, such ensemble renderings are on the other hand quite common within the Philistine area (Aign, 1963). Yet another consideration is that until now, this particular topos has been regarded as a clearly Phoenician-Cypriot product of the ninth-sixth centuries B.C.; the topos variously includes a trio or quartet with chordophone, aerophone, and membranophone (or idiophone) players. This particular artifact, however, has now been reliably dated to the end of the eleventh or beginning of the tenth century B.C. (DothanM, 1970), which means its origin must go back to a Philistine-Canaanite prototype.

In this piece, four different musicians (busts) are mounted into separated "windows." One of the figures seems to be playing the frame drum familiar from the columnal figures (illust. IV.32b). The second musician (illust. IV.32c) is playing a short double-pipe instrument held in a more vertical position than is usual according to local custom; this may indicate a different mode of playing, one recalling that of the Cycladic cultural sphere and anticipating modern Greek playing techniques. The third figure (illust. IV.32d) is playing a small symmetrical lyre with side arms extending up past the cross arm (Yaakov Meshorer, IM, restored the left arm). This particular lyre type is already familiar from the Cassite period (Rashid, 1984), and has been given a strikingly realistic rendering here in which the musician is playing the instrument in a new way, namely, while holding it at shoulder height. This playing position represents a prototype that as a matter of fact does appear in Cyprus shortly after the Ashdod lyre in the ninth century B.C. (Aign, 1963). The same small symmetrical lyre appears two to three centuries later in Kuntillet ʿAjrud (illust. IV.23) and in the eighth-century B.C. Ashdod terra cotta (illust. IV.33).

The fourth bust (illust. IV.32e) has a crownlike head covering and is holding what are probably small cymbals with handgrips similar to those from the Phoenician-Cypriot sphere, the kind which appears later in the Greek sphere in connection with the cult of Cybele and which are viewed

IV.32a. Clay stand with five musicians, Ashdod, IAA 68.1182

IV.32b. Idem, fragment with drum player

IV.32c. Idem, fragment with double pipe player

IV.32d. Idem, fragment with lyre player

170

IV.32e. Idem, fragment with cymbal player

IV.32f. Idem, fragment with full-size double pipe player

IV.33. Terra-cotta figurine, lyre player, Ashdod, IAA 63.924

as archaic. The central, dominant (fifth) figure on this stand is a full rendering of a male figure (illust. IV.32f) presumably representing the leader. He is holding the remnants of a double pipe to his mouth with both hands and is portrayed in *jour*-technique on the stand frame. His facial features are vague and grotesque, his eyes exaggerated, and on either side of his head one sees forms resembling huge ears, the so-called "patera" associated with the cult of Cybele. Finally, three schematically rendered, rectangular animals occupy the space above the figures.

The Ashdod stand is but one of many cultic stands "in a bewildering variety of shapes and sizes" attested throughout the Near East from the Chalcolithic to the Iron Age and culminating in ancient Israel/Palestine during the Late Bronze and Iron Age. "We may assume . . . that the small portable offering stands served a dual purpose in Israelite worship. First . . . [they] served as altars on which a wide variety of offerings were made, second . . . [they] bore symbolism or motifs that reminded the worshiper of Yahweh's continued presence" (Devries, 1987). What is striking about this particular stand, however, is that it contains none of the motifs generally associated with cultic iconography in ancient Israel/Palestine, nor were any found in the immediate vicinity of the stand. Some scholars associate this "musicians stand" with the scene from 1 S. 10:5, suggesting that "the figures probably represent musicians who were part of a Philistine cult, having a role similar to the Levites which were the singers in the Temple in Jerusalem" (Dothan, 1970). Although this group does indeed contain instruments similar to those played by the prophets who come down from the shrine in a prophetic frenzy in 1 S. 10:5, it is equally significant that similar groups of instruments are mentioned in Isa. 5:12 to describe the life of drunkards and in Job 21:12 as an accompaniment to the carefree life of the wicked (whereas the normal group includes the *kinnôr, nēḇel, ḥālîl*, and *tōp*, the passage from Job replaces the *ḥālîl* with a secular instrument, the *ʿûgāḇ*). Every other time the Old Testament mentions more than two instruments in an ensemble setting and yet still includes all three basic groups, the aerophone is a trumpet, and the context liturgical. Moreover, both the Ashdod terra cottas and the figurines on the stand exhibit facial features and hairstyles that, together with the previous considerations, do indeed make it plausible that "the figurines were intended to be representations of individuals" (Hestrin, 1971). This stand may well have belonged to a private household, and may be portraying a Philistine family at play or the prince's own court musicians (MazarA, 1980; Devries, 1987).

Yet another interpretive possibility, and one I find more compelling, draws on the George E. Mendenhall theory, which adduces various analyses of personal names and toponomy in associating the Philistines with the cult of Cybele. Doing so enables us to associate this particular stand with a relatively early stage in this cult's development. Given the present chronological and iconographical context, these musicians may be precursors of the later priests of Cybele, effeminate male figures who put themselves into an ecstatic frenzy through music and dance, accompanied by instruments characteristic of orgiastic situations in general (double pipes, drums, cymbals) and under the guidance of the standing figure with the obviously grotesque features. This leader is one of the two double-pipe players (these instruments apparently having double reeds) dominating the orchestra. The idiophone/membranophone group supports the instruments playing the melody, and the lyre, as was often the case, accommodates itself to the orgiastic atmosphere quite contrary to our conventional way of thinking (one need only recall the role of the lyre in the cult of Dionysus). Early iconography associated with the cult of Cybele offers an especially dramatic illustration of the orgiastic function of the lyre in such situations: One of the earliest representations of Cybele (Boghazköy, seventh century B.C.) portrays the goddess together with two young priests, one of whom is playing a double pipe and the other the *kithára* (Bittel 1968, 81). Indeed, the topoi associated with Cybele are also often accompanied by symbols similar to those on this stand, including both animal and patera motifs.

The small terra-cotta lyre player of Ashdod mentioned earlier (illust. IV.33; DothanM, 1971), a handmade figurine, was found in a temple precinct; the artist used black coloring to draw clothes, a head covering, and other details onto the body. Given the location in which it was found as well as the small cap and instrument, the person depicted probably functioned in some connection with cultic music. The actual lyre itself was about 40-50 cm. tall and had four strings; the musician held it at breast height with his left hand while his right hand, which unfortunately has been broken off here, plucked the strings, probably with a plectrum. This small, symmetrical instrument has a gently rounded resonator which the musician holds in a vertical position in front of himself, a lyre type icongraphic sources generally portray with the cross arm supported on top of the side arms. In any event, this particular portrayal is one of the first, if not the very first, to attest this form (cp. illust. IV.32d).

The Tel Qasile stand (illust. IV.34) portrays a series of dancing male figures with interlocking outstretched hands. Mazar has suggested, quite plausibly, that this scene is yet another example of the ritualistic or war-related dance otherwise so frequently attested in ancient oriental iconography and so similar to the *debbka* dance still performed today in the region (Bahat, 1970). This same or a similar dance form recurs in the Negev rock drawings (see illust. III.1), in second-millennium-B.C. Babylonian glypytics (Porada, 1947), and in Hellenistic iconography (Negev, 1986). Mazar (1980) is probably correct in assuming the presence of an artistic trend specific to the Philistine area around the eleventh-tenth centuries B.C. that produced these stands. As already mentioned, in their turn they probably represent prototypes of the later music and dance scenes attested within the Cypriot-Aegean cultural sphere.

Before closing this chapter we should approach the unresolved question of the incised *scapulae* (animal shoulder bones), which could or could not have served as sound tools — scrapers (see also chap. III/3). They appeared in Philistine and Phoenician areas at the close of the Bronze and the onset of the Iron Age. The earliest examples (twelfth-eleventh centuries B.C.) were discovered, as mentioned, by the Albright Institute and Harvard University expedition (S. Gitin and T. Dothan) in Tel Miqne/Ekron (see illust. III.13) and by E. Stern at Dor (Stern, 1993). In the last decade an additional remarkable corpus (eight items) of these *scapulae* was excavated at Tel Miqne and three more in Ashkelon by the Lawrence Stager (Harvard University) and Leon Levy expedition, all from the early Iron Age. The latest finds seem to present some additional information for the clarification of the central question of the function of these artifacts.

It is obvious that some of these finds could not be sound tools for two reasons — their surface was too short (less than 10 cm.) to perform a rubbing movement and the incision was executed in a way that did not allow the production of an acoustical effect (see illust. IV.35). These bones were probably used for account keeping or as a calender. Others with a longer polished surface and regular step-kind incisions can produce a fairly clear acoustical effect (illust. IV.36, 37). Taking into consideration that all the *scapulae* were found in cultic areas, it is quite possible that certain cults used them as sound tools. This could be the case with the Philistines and other sea people bordering the Philistines, for example, the Sikils, who for some time occupied such Phoenician-dominated territories as Dor. At present,

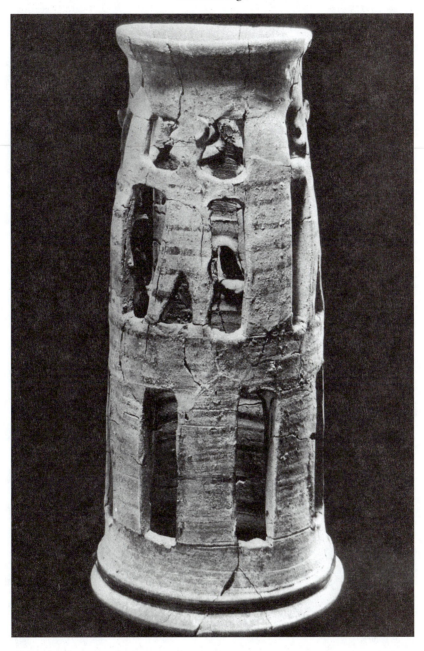

IV.34. Clay stand with dancers, Tell Qasile, IAA 76.449

IV.35. *Scapulae,* Tel Miqne/Ekron, Albright Institute of
Archaeology, Jerusalem, Object No. 11346

IV.36. Idem, Object No. 5557

IV.37. Idem, Object No. 108

however, while analyses do not attest exact traces of scraping, it is not possible to give a final answer regarding the acoustical use of these *scapulae*.

Phoenician materials from ancient Israel/Palestine have been voluminously discussed, and have quite undeservedly overshadowed witnesses to the Philistine culture. In reality, the purest form of Phoenician influence in ancient Israel/Palestine is found only north of the Carmel mountain range, an area constituting only a very small part of the Phoenician cultural sphere and of ancient Israel/Palestine as well. It does, however, constitute a kind of border area in which a pronounced musical culture developed from an admixture of both Phoenician and ancient Israelite elements, a culture whose influence ultimately extended even as far as Cyprus. While it is certainly also true that Phoenician influence extended into the south as well, the topoi we find there actually draw much more strongly from Canaanite, Egyptian, and Judean elements.

In the following paragraphs, I will enumerate topoi and individual works associated with Phoenician provenance and at the same time point out both the qualitative and quantitative distinctions in comparison with Philistine examples. The following four groups of artifacts and musical instruments can be addressed.

(a) Cymbals from the Late Bronze Age. Examples from the Phoenician and Philistine sphere (Acco, Shiqmona, Tel Batash, etc.) exhibit no distinguishing features when compared to other cymbals.

(b) Bell-shaped terra-cotta figurines of female drummers dating to the Iron Age. Workmanship influenced by northern Phoenician ceramics (Achzib, Shiqmona) is artistically more mature and sophisticated compared to examples from the central and southern areas of Philistia. On the other hand, organological considerations and features relating to actual performance prompt one to classify these works among the sister group of ancient Israelite/Palestinian figurines from Samaria and Nebo rather than among northern-Phoenician and Cypriot groupings. In this context, our attention is drawn especially to the slanted position in which the instrument is held as well as to the playing technique whereby one hand holds the instrument from the bottom and the other strikes the middle of the membrane. These observations suggest that an acculturation process involving both Phoenician and ancient Israelite-Edomite-Nabataean-Philistine elements took place in some if not in all areas of the country.

(c) The terra cottas with double-pipe players prompt similar conclusions. Here one can observe with even greater clarity how an autochthonous developmental line in ancient Israel/Palestine moved from the cylindrical, diverging double pipes played by female entertainers to the conical, parallel pipes played by men from the clergy or the military.

(d) The orchestra. As mentioned earlier, the topos as a whole has customarily been referred to as the "Phoenician orchestra." We can now see, however, that this designation is too narrow and too one-sided to do justice to the materials we have before us, and that we are probably better advised to speak of an "eastern Mediterranean orchestra" instead, since the actual groupings exhibit both Canaanite-Israelite as well as Philistine-Phoenician elements.

These observations, however, do not quite tell the whole story. The social character of the Phoenician artifacts is clearly of a different sort than that of the Philistine examples. The former represent primarily objects betraying the (more or less severe) leveling effects of mass-production techniques, objects that were found in every social class and every ethnic group throughout the country. The latter definitely represent individual artistic phenomena associated with the elite classes; their historical significance was often unique, and they functioned as prototypes for later artistic developments. As a result of these social inclinations the artistic and especially the ethnic character of the art works is also more pronounced. While the Phoenician finds are of a leveled down mass character, the Philistine art conveys a more profound individual ethnic message.

5. Conch Trumpets

Trumpets and similar instruments offer yet another example of the paradoxical relationship between written and archaeological sources. Not only are the ram's horn *(šôpār)* and the silver trumpet *(ḥᵃṣōṣᵉrâ)* both referred to as "instruments of the priests"; they are also the most frequently mentioned instruments in the Old Testament and the instruments about whose construction and playing techniques we are given the most complete information. At the same time, only one example of archaeological evidence for these instruments has come to light for the entire pre-Hellenistic period (see chap. III/ 3), and scholars must draw instead from several finds associated with neighboring cultures, including the Tutankhamen trumpet (Manniche, 1976), the Carchemish relief (NGD), the bronze figures from Anatolia (Rimmer, 1969), and the alabaster relief from Nineveh (Rashid, 1984).

The only trumpet-instrument frequently attested archaeologically in ancient Israel/Palestine is the one made from the shell of the *Charonia tritonis nodifera*. The conch trumpet was used at a very early stage in antiquity (from approximately the third millennium B.C. on), and Yemenite fishermen still use it today as a signal horn. In Spain and Micronesia, it still accompanies folk dancing and cultic dances (NGD). After its first appearance, it spread over large portions of all continents from Spain through southern Europe, northern Africa, southern Asia, Oceania, and into Central and South America. This sweep includes Palestine, and it was apparently one of the areas in which this conch-trumpet tradition flourished. The Minoans, and especially Crete proper, were famous for their conch-trumpet cult from about the second millennium B.C. on, and during the classical period this instrument was associated with Triton, the god of the sea. One extremely rare iconographic witness, from the grotto of Zeus on Idalon, is a gem depicting a priestess blowing a triton shell before an altar (Aign, 1963).

One can see that the approximately twelve conch trumpets from Palestine were intended to be used as sound devices because on most of them, the apex has been severed in a professional way. Only one, a tenth/ninth-century-B.C. piece from Hazor, has a small hole in one side about 3 mm. in diameter and rather close to the end through which the instrument was blown (illust. IV.38a-b). Experiments have demonstrated that this opening served as a fingerhole for changing the instrument's pitch, whereby a clear distinction can be discerned between the tones e' flat and e'. Although such openings or holes are attested elsewhere as well, they are extremely rare (Hedley, 1922). Only one of the conch trumpets from Palestine was able to produce an octave, and then only with great difficulty. Otherwise, these conch trumpets consistently produce tones only in the first octave.

The oldest conch trumpets from ancient Israel/Palestine are the one from Tel Nami (late Bronze Age) and those from Tel Qasile (twelfth-eleventh centuries B.C.) and Hazor (ninth century B.C.), whereas the most recent are those from Hellenistic Shiqmona. Perhaps not unexpectedly, all the conch trumpets found in ancient Israel/Palestine come from areas within the Philistine and Phoenician cultural spheres. Several, such as the conch trumpets from Tel Qasile and Tel Nami, were found within cultic contexts and thus probably functioned within the local cults. Others confirm that the horns were also used for purely communicative purposes. For example, the Hazor conch was found next to a destroyed wall, recalling

(a)

(b)

IV.38a, b.
(a) Conch trumpet;
(b) conch trumpet,
blowing end,
Hazor, IAA 78.5029

similar conditions during construction on the Jerusalem city wall (Neh. 4:12-14) where the shofar was used as a signal horn in times of danger (Yadin, 1960).

It should be pointed out that during the earlier period, the term *šôpār,* like many other designations for noise or sound devices, could refer to several different instruments, including but certainly not limited to the triton horn. This ambiguity may attach to Ps. 81:4-5, which tells us that the shofar was used to announce the new moon. Because the triton horn was also associated with the lunar cult (Sachs, 1940), this psalm may possibly be referring to the triton shell rather than to a ram's horn.

All these finds confirm that the conch trumpet was used for over a millennium in ancient Israel/Palestine, serving both as a cultic instrument and as a means of communication or signaling. Kurt Sachs is thus probably correct in asserting that the triton shell cannot really be associated with any specific function or specific ethnic group since "in reality the meaning of this device was subject to unprecedented change" (Sachs, 1965, 34).

If we are to believe the archaeological record, a great many changes occurred within the musical culture of ancient Israel/Palestine when the Israelite monarchy and other national states first became established. Certain musical instruments simply vanished. Others were now played in a different way and even changed their form. Still others simply continued on as before. Finally, completely new instruments appeared. One of the most important changes within instrumental music proper was the emergence of the chordo-aero-membranophone ensemble, familiar as the "Phoenician orchestra"; in this form, the ensemble dates to the eighth-sixth centuries B.C. and can be seen on a cult stand from Ashdod with its five musicians (see chap. IV/4). More recent analysis, however, suggests that this ensemble should probably be reinterpreted as an early form associated with the Cybele cult. That is, what we have hitherto called a "Phoenician orchestra" derives in fact from a Canaanite-Philistine-Israelite tradition.

Just which changes occurred and to what extent depend on which part of the country and even which national centers one examines. The orgiastic music of the Philistine-Phoenician coastal regions remained largely true to the Canaanite tradition, maintaining a preponderance of idiophone/membranophones as well as the chordophone-membranophone version of the ensemble, and using mobile, symmetrical lyres with only a small number of strings. In Edom, Moab, and Ammon, on the other hand, we find a more balanced style based on chordophones and aerophones and a more pronounced inclination to embrace innovations, including new lyre types with more strings, use of the latter in both solo and ensemble playing, and new kinds of wind instruments.

In the United Monarchy, it seems that most inhabitants were accustomed to a genuinely polystylistic music. Later, however, in the divided kingdoms of Israel and Judah, the relatively vigorous Canaanite tradition still present in certain groups was curtailed both in the larger sense and in instrumental music in particular, from the cult of the drum and horn to lyre playing and a capella singing; in this instance, it was the ethnoreligious isolation and the antipagan disposition of the Israelite-Judean theocracy that succeeded in imposing these restrictions (see Isa. 5:11-12; 23:16; Am. 6:5-6). Nonetheless, large portions of the population still practiced a more syncretistic musical style issuing from the "heterogeneity within homogeneity" characterizing music in ancient Israel/Palestine. This syncretism included the widespread use of lyre and reed instruments, a widespread diapason of the overall musical ethos, and the principle of varied modulation between motifs and motif series.

Such generalizations, of necessity, are based only in part on historically supported source material; in most cases, one must draw indirect conclusions and employ a more inductive method given the sometimes extremely sparse evidence at our disposal.

6. The Mystery of Absence, or an *argumentum ex silentio?* The Babylonian-Persian Period (587-333 B.C.): An Interlude

One encounters the greatest discrepancy between written and archaeological sources in this regard when one examines material from the Babylonian-Persian period. So great is this discrepancy that one cannot really write a chapter on this period at all, a situation all the more frustrating because it covers part of the period of the Second Temple. For this reason, I have opted for the following interlude instead.

In the year 587 B.C., one hundred thirty-five years after the collapse of the kingdom of Israel, Nebuchadnezzar also took Jerusalem, thereby bringing the kingdom of Judah to an end. He not only destroyed the temple, he also murdered the royal heirs and deported part of the population, primarily the political and cultural elite, to Babylon. This crippling catastrophe understandably left deep scars on the cultural life of the people. "By the rivers of Babylon — there we sat down and there we wept when we remembered Zion. On the willows there we hung up our *kinnōrôt*. For there our captors asked us for songs, and our tormentors asked for mirth, saying, 'Sing us one of the songs of Zion.' How could we sing the Lord's song in a foreign land? If I forget you, O Jerusalem, let my right hand wither! Let my tongue cling to the roof of my mouth" (Ps. 137:2-6).

Life in the conquered land, however, quickly blossomed anew. After the Babylonian Empire itself collapsed (539 B.C.), the deportees were pardoned by the Persian king Cyrus II, and many Judeans returned home. After receiving permission to rebuild the temple itself, they actually did so during the last two decades of the century. On balance, the liberal and tolerant politics practiced by the Persian kings in this region enabled the ethnic national entities in ancient Israel/Palestine to continue to develop both economically and culturally.

At precisely this juncture, however, we encounter serious problems with our sources, and an enormous discrepancy now emerges between tangible archaeological evidence and historical documents on the one hand, and biblical accounts on the other. According to the Old Testament, a glorious musical renaissance followed the construction of the Second Temple. It reports that an enormous and indeed a very precisely known number of musicians and singers returned from the Babylonian exile, including four thousand two hundred eighty-nine *kōhᵃnîm* (priests who played the *hᵃṣōṣᵉrâ*), seventy-four *lᵉviyim* (temple servants who played the *mᵉṣiltayim, nᵉbālîm,* and *kinnōrôt*), one hundred twenty-eight (or one hundred forty-eight) *mᵉšōrᵉrîm* (temple singers of the two great choruses associated with songs of praise), and more than two hundred *mᵉšōrᵉrîm* and *mᵉšōrᵉrôt* (male and female singers) of lesser rank (Ezra 2:36-41, 65; Neh. 7:39-44, 67). The account also mentions the grandiose orchestras, choruses, and processions of musicians associated with important occasions (Ezra 2:10; Neh. 12:27, 31, 36-39; Ps. 68:26). On other occasions, we are told that communal praise of God was enhanced by mass processions, "the *šārîm* (singers) in front, the *nōgᵉnîm* (minstrels) last, between them girls *bᵉtôp tôpēpôt* (drumming the drums)" (Ps. 68:26). Post-biblical Jewish literature then specifies more closely just how many of each instrument are allowed in the temple orchestra, asserting that "they played on never less than two *nᵉbālîm* or more than six, and on never less than two *hᵃlîlîm* or

185

more than twelve," that "there were never less than nine *kinnōrôṭ*, and their number could be increased without end . . . but of *ṣelṣᵉlîm*, there was but one," and that there were "countless instruments," to mention but a few stipulations. Ironically, the prototype for this temple orchestra was probably the Babylonian court orchestra.

These texts have led to the assumption that writers during this period were extremely well acquainted with the details of contemporary temple music, and that this information allows us to draw certain conclusions regarding both the instruments themselves and the style of music being produced. The result of this assumption is that studies based only on the Old Testament accounts themselves and on written sources from the Roman and Byzantine period often assert that "we are remarkably well informed" concerning music in the second temple (McKinnon, 1979/80), or that "the information is often very precise" (EJ). Furthermore, others conclude that chordophones became more prominent during this period while noisemakers receded (Werner, 1989). Ten-stringed harps were allegedly reintroduced (Seidel, 1989); given the archaeological evidence, one could, we are assured, reasonably assume also that cymbals could be heard in the temple forecourt, and that cymbals, lyres, and harps were used for this temple music *(idem)*.

The unfortunate truth is that archaeology has confronted us with a gap of approximately three hundred years with respect to precisely this period; virtually each of the ten or so artifacts that do date to this period come from neighboring cultures or other chronological stages. A similarly dismal gap emerges in extrabiblical written sources relating to the Babylonian-Persian period (cf. the Elephantine and Samaritan Papyri).

Given the present status of scholarship and resources, the question of Jewish liturgical music during this period must remain open. The lack of reliable information concerning, for example, temple music does not, however, mean that the Bible is utterly without value to the musical historian with respect to this period, since it does indeed offer bits of information concerning secular music. The book of Isaiah mentions music associated with paraliturgical occasions, thanksgiving, praise (12:5-6; 25:1; 26:1; 30:29; 38:9), communication (18:4; 27:13), and as a symbol for drunkards, sinners, and harlots (5:11; 14:11-12; 23:16-17). Indeed, Isa. 23:16-17 may well represent the first indirect libel the Old Testament issues concerning instrumental music: "Take the *kinnôr*, go about the city, you forgotten prostitute! Make sweet melody, sing many songs, that you may be remembered."

Neither musicological studies in the broader sense nor Judaic or biblical studies in the narrower sense have acknowledged this discrepancy between written and archaeological sources (Braun, 1994a). In fact, quite the opposite has been the case; the impression has arisen that available sources do indeed give us both a complete and a clear picture of the musical culture in ancient Israel/Palestine during this period. General historical studies actually describe the sources for the Babylonian and especially the Persian period as "extremely good" (Weippert, 1988).

The purely objective circumstances that developed following the catastrophe of 587 B.C. after Cyrus finally came to power were quite favorable, especially for Judea/Israel (Davies/Finkelstein, 1984). The liberal attitude and tolerance this ruler showed toward the region did much to encourage both ethnic-cultural and religious developments, the most obvious sign of such renewal being the reconstruction of the Second Temple during the waning years of the sixth century B.C. This reconstruction was of enormous significance, and in the larger sense constitutes nothing less than a genuine renaissance of Judean-Israelite cultic life (cf. the Decree of Cyrus, Ezra 6:3). Because the temple was rebuilt, one can legitimately conclude that both religious and cultural life, including music, blossomed anew. And indeed, the picture painted by written sources for this period, namely, the books of Ezra and Nehemiah, is glorious and radiant indeed (see above).

Nevertheless, the complete lack of archaeological information concerning music is still extremely difficult to explain, even when we consider various contributing factors and circumstances. It is true that archaeologists and historians have traditionally exhibited only modest interest in the Babylonian-Persian period in the first place, and that at least part of the absence of iconographic materials in Judean archaeological sites relating to this period may well have its roots in the influence exerted by iconoclastic powers within the Israelite-Judaic religious hierarchy (Stern, 1982). Over and above even these considerations, we must remember that the period itself encompasses only a short span of time. The lack of archaeological evidence remains troubling nonetheless.

Absence of such evidence relating to music seems to be more than merely an accidental situation that continued excavation and patience might remedy in the future. The situation surrounding the lute is exemplary in this sense insofar as after the three extremely interesting and revealing finds dating to the Late Bronze Age, not a single additional piece of evidence attesting the lute is found until the Hellenistic period. Nor does it seem to be merely coincidental that, given precisely this archaeological state of affairs, the Old Testament itself does not offer us an unequivocal name for this instrument. An equally revealing fact is the utter absence of finds relating to cymbals (see chap. III/6), possibly an indication that cymbals were in fact not at all common during this period, either within mass culture or within institutionalized worship.

What we seem to have before us is an archaeological situation utterly contradicting the notion that the musical culture in ancient Israel/Palestine during the Babylonian-Persian period, and especially within cultic contexts, was in fact rich, varied, and new.

Taking a step back for a moment, we should recall that the general availability of archaeological evidence relating to music in ancient Israel/Palestine is not exactly paltry. In fact, from a purely quantitative perspective it is actually quite good. We have almost four hundred individual pieces from normal excavations as well as approximately two hundred artifacts of unknown provenance. What this means is that in the larger sense, our understanding of the musical life in ancient Israel/Palestine, of the typology of instruments, and of their chronological classification is unlikely to change in the near future, if ever. Given this state of affairs, one simply cannot ignore the enormous archaeological gap that exists with respect to the Babylonian-Persian period. As long as we have no satisfactory explanation for this phenomenon, no one can expect any reliable interpretation of the texts relating to music in the books of Ezra, Nehemiah, and the Chronicles (see Table 1).

CHAPTER V

THE HELLENISTIC-ROMAN PERIOD

(Fourth Century B.C.–Fourth Century A.D.)

B y and large, the musical culture in ancient Israel/Palestine during the Hellenistic-Roman period does not escape the multilayered complexity and contradictory nature otherwise generally attaching to the term "Hellenization." The collapse of the traditional pagan religious canon is now less an issue than the confrontation between the Greek enlightenment on the one hand, and Judeo-Christian religious thinking on the other. This polymorphous cultural situation is also responsible for the multifaceted nature of music and musical life during the age. Pagan, Judaic, Samaritan, and early-Christian religious rituals all flourished in close proximity, and all made use of music and shaped attitudes toward music. The very notion of such cosmopolitanism, of "world citizenship," and of "biological equality" was fostered at every quarter by the overwhelming influence of Greek Stoicism. After the period when musical culture was largely specific to a certain city or nation, the setting created by the emergence of a genuine world power could hardly have been more propitious for the development of a rich, multifaceted, even comprehensive musical culture that would produce commensurately syncretistic, comprehensively cosmopolitan musical styles. The Syrian poet Meleager of Gadara proclaimed in an epigram that "Tyre reared me, though Gadara was my home, that new Athens in the land of the Assyrians. The world is the home of mortals, and chaos begot all human beings" (cited in Hengel, 1974). These sentiments are reflected in the inclination during this period to identify actors, artists, jock-

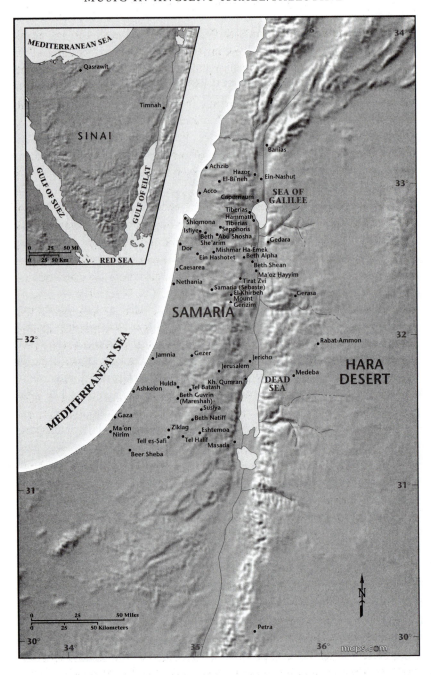

eys, and musicians in ancient Israel/Palestine not according to any ethnic or national group, but solely according to where they lived (see chap. V/5).

The availability of sources relating to musical culture changes dramatically during the Hellenistic period, and an entirely new musical world emerges before us. After the preceding disparity, archaeological and written materials complement one another and show that there was a break in the development of the musical culture. A rich, syncretistic style of music emerged especially within the sphere of purely artistic music, indicating that apparently musical life itself had now become stratified differently than during preceding periods.

Archaeological finds now include the entire spectrum of contemporary musical instruments. Bronze- and Iron-Age idiophones such as bells, cymbals, and rattles emerge anew as instruments of the masses, exhibiting both their old forms and new ones such as those exhibited by forked cymbals (often known as *crotala,* sg. *crotalum*) and castanets. We now encounter the first archaeological evidence for several Old Testament versions of otherwise widespread Near Eastern traditions, such as attaching small bells to a priest's garment (Ex. 28:33f.). The vigorous cultural exchange characterizing this period also included the introduction of foreign musical instruments; for example, the much larger, semi-spherical Greek *týmpanon* now replaced the traditional, smaller, round frame drum.

Chordophones and aerophones now undergo dramatic changes. After a long absence, lutes are reintroduced. Harps, primarily in the form of the small angular harp, are now also incorporated into musical life, possibly by way of Sidonian and other immigrants. On the other hand, the lyre loses its dominant role in musical life and is often used merely as a symbol, the first known example being found on Ptolemaic coins from Acco dating to the second century B.C. Oddly, even though zithers are often thought to have originated during the eighth century B.C. in the Phoenician sphere, and to have played a significant role in later Islamic culture [[*(qanun)*]], there is still no evidence attesting their presence during this period in ancient Israel/Palestine.

New wind instruments now appear with a technologically more advanced form likely reflecting a more highly developed level of artistic virtuosity. Such is the case with the double aulos; its new construction included bones overlaid with copper or some other metal and was innovative enough to prompt a critical comment in the Talmud (*b. Arak.* 10:2). In a typical confrontation between traditional aesthetics and innovative production technology, the Talmud declared that the innovation made it difficult to produce the instrument's traditional, ideal sound. Archaeological finds also clearly confirm that aulos players were now divided socially into professional virtuosos, semiprofessional musicians, and dilettantes. It is also during this period that we have the first witness to the cross flute in the Near East, depicted in this case on coins from Bâniyâs (Paneas or Caesarea Philippi, A.D. 169-222). Although the panpipe appears often in iconography, it seems to have been used more as a symbol than as an actual instrument. Shofars also appear in illustrations from the third-second centuries B.C. on; the first one, in fact, appears exclusively as part of a symbolic grouping consisting of Jewish cultic accoutrements (see chap. V/8). Although the trumpet is attested in Idumaic iconography for the first time in music history as a hunting instrument, it is still not unequivocally attested in any function associated with the temple, since the authenticity of the popular portrayal on the Arch of Titus is questionable. Finally, the Samaritan oil lamps with representations of portable pneumatic table organs represent some of the most important archaeological finds of this period. It is particularly interesting that the organs are always accompanied by two pairs of forked cymbals. In any event, these illustrations can certainly illuminate further the musical culture of the Samaritan community specifically and of Hellenistic Judaism in the larger sense.

For the first time now, we also encounter a Jewish musician by name, an actual Hellenistic klezmer. The aulos player Jacobius ben Jacobius is listed among cattle owners (155-144 B.C., Samaria/Fayum, Egypt, see Tcherikover, 1957, 171). Hygros ben Levi, a singer mentioned several times in the Talmud (*m. Šeqal.* 5:1; *m. Yoma* 3:11; *y. Šeqal.* 5:1; *b. Yoma* 38b), seems to have been an actual person as well judging by these accounts, which sound realistic and credible enough. He seems to have had an extraordinarily artistic vocal technique that involved varying his singing style by placing his thumbs in his mouth (*Šeqal.* 5:1), but was criticized for refusing to teach this special art to any other singers (*Yoma* 3:11). Finally, we now have the first iconographic evidence with an inscription portraying a female Nabataean *arghul* player (see chap. V/3).

The mutual interweaving and interpenetration of the various musical cultures in Hellenistic-Roman Palestine makes it virtually impossible to determine to which ethnic group or ritual association one should assign various instruments. On the one hand, the same instruments might be used in widely differing situations and for widely differing musical purposes in the same community. For example, Isa. 5:11-12 associates the *ḥālîl* with revelry, while Jer. 48:36 associates it with mourning. The book of Job associates the *kinnôr* and the *ʿûgāḇ* with both joy and sadness (21:12 and 30:31). On the other hand, the same or similar musical practices and instruments could be present in extremely diverse socioethnic groups where they nonetheless addressed similar psychological and emotional needs and accompanied similar sociofunctional events. When comparing the various ritual customs of the time, contemporary authors emphasize precisely this similarity between the accompanying musical practices. Plutarch, Tacitus, Philo of Alexandria, and other sources such as the books of the Maccabees all point out that the same music ceremony accompanied the rituals associated with the Nabataean and Jewish communities (see chap. V/3), and this ceremony was in turn quite similar to that associated with the cult of Dionysus (see chap. V/5).

Naturally enough, similar ceremonies of this sort also fostered similar musical styles. Psalms were sung not only in Jewish worship and in a modified form at the Dionysian cultic festivals, but also in secular situations such as drinking bouts accompanied by musical entertainment. Clement of Alexandria tells us that the Greek *skólion* with lyre accompaniment was actually quite similar to the singing of Jewish psalms (*Paed.* ii.4), while Erik Werner (1959) believes he has determined the mode of these songs, the *tropos spondeicus,* that is, the Dorian mode with avoided second or fourth degree.

The Hellenization of musical life in ancient Israel/Palestine also drew considerable impetus from specifically Greek musical institutions and cultural events such as the gymnasium, public sporting events, the hippodrome, and the theater wherever these were found, including in urban centers such as Jerusalem, Tiberias, and Caesarea. This development was especially strong during the reign of Herod the Great (37-4 B.C.), when "there were very great rewards for victory proposed . . . to those that were musicians also, and were called *thymelici;* and he spared no pains to induce all persons, the most famous for such exercises, to come to this contest for victory" (Josephus, *Ant.* xv.8.1). Such Hellenistic cultural influence was not limited to public life; it also found its way into private life. In Jerusalem, Gaza, Ashkelon, and Sepphoris, the private homes of pagans, Christians, and Jews alike could be decorated with mosaic floors and wall murals depicting a variety of musical themes.

Another source giving expression to the Jewish-Hellenistic syncretism characterizing this musical disposition is the apocryphal work of Sirach (second century A.D.): "Where there is singing, do not pour out talk; do not display your cleverness at the wrong time. A ruby seal in a setting of gold is a concert of music at a banquet of wine" (32:4-5); "the flute and the harp make sweet melody, but a pleasant voice is better than either" (40:21).

The relationship of the Romans (basically cosmopolitan) and the Jews (basically separatist) was not always harmonious. On the contrary, after the destruction of the Jerusalem Temple in A.D. 70, mutual enmity grew stronger. On one side, the Jews gladly attended and participated in public social events, although the Roman mimes and pantomimes frequently mocked Jewish habits and rules (Weiss, 1995). The Jewish religious establishment, on the other hand, increasingly prohibited Jews from attending the theater and other public events, and the Jewish communities became even more separated. This duality appears to have initiated the classical model of cultural isolation, which continued into the next two millennia.

The Talmud gives a colorful story about a Jewish musician and mime from Caesarea who appeared to Rabbi Abbahu in a dream, was asked by him to pray for rain, and, indeed, rain came. When asked by the Rabbi what his occupation was, the man, named Pentakaka, replied: "This man [referring to himself] commits five sins [Gk. — *pentekakos*] — he adorns the theater, engages the *hetaerae*, brings their cloth to the bath house, claps hands and dances before them, and beats the *babuia* (aulos)" (*y. Ta'an.* 1.4). This Talmudic passage not only tells us that the theater was syncretistic art and included drama, pantomime, dance, and instrumental music; it also confirms the existence of Jewish performing artists. Although this occupation was condemned by Jewish religious rules as a grave sin, it did not prevent Pentakaka's prayer from being accepted.

These syncretistic inclinations of local musical culture ran directly counter to both the Jewish and the Christian theocracy. One intimation of just how severe this conflict was is found in the book of Daniel, which obstinately repeats the same verse (3:5, 7, 10, 15) reminding the reader that foreign music and foreign instruments always announce the worship of the golden statue that King Nebuchadnezzar had set up. Although the content of the verses refers to the time of Nebuchadnezzar, the text itself was composed around 167-164 B.C., when the real reference was probably to Hellenistic-Roman temptations. Clement of Alexandria (*ca.* 150-215) composed a whole series of equally condemnatory passages against pagan music.

Amid all the animated cultural syncretism during the Hellenistic-Roman period, however, the most important development seems to be one of divergence rather than of fusion. Closer examination reveals traces of what will become two different worlds of contemporary music, one western, and one eastern, during the next fifteen hundred years. The most tangible reflection of this development may be found in two mosaics from the cult of Dionysus. The first, from the house of Sheikh Zouede, is a kaleidoscopic, pluralistic musical world bursting with color and orgiastic, pagan sentiment. The second, from Sepphoris, is an organized, controlled, monothematic musical world of Judeo-Christian disposition (see chap. V/5).

1. Apotropaic Bells

"On its [the priest's robe's] lower hem you shall make pomegranates of blue, purple and crimson yarns, all around the lower hem, with *pa'ªmônîm* of gold between them all around — a golden *pa'ªmôn* and a pomegranate alternating all around the lower hem of the robe. Aaron shall wear it when he ministers, and its sound shall be heard when he goes into the holy place before the Lord, and when he comes out, so that he may not die" (Ex. 28:33-35).

The *pa'ªmôn* (pl. *pa'ªmônîm*) is one of the few names of musical instruments in the Old Testament that enjoys interpretive consensus in being identified simply as a bell. This text from Exodus probably dates to the final century of the kingdom of Judah. Writing in the second half of the first century B.C., Josephus discusses the High Priest's vestments in his *Antiquities* and suggests that "the pomegranates represent lightning, the sound of the bells thunder" (*Ant.* iii.7.4, 7). Plutarch's account (40-120) of the Jewish High Priest's vestments dates to approximately the same period; he, too, mentions the numerous small bells around the hem, but associates them with the cult of Dionysus. The tradition itself is attested in ancient Oriental iconography from the fifteenth century B.C. For example, such bells are seen on the attire of a Syrian emissary on a grave mural from the time of Thutmose III (Grace, 1956, fig. 2) and even appear during the Roman period (Seyrig, 1939). In a Jerusalem grave, small bells were found with scraps of material still attached to them that could be the remnants of a hem (illust. V.8), so this custom was likely also followed in Roman Palestine. On the other hand, no iconographic witness to this tradition has come to light in Jewish sources prior to the Byzantine period. The first is a unique mosaic from a synagogue floor dating to the early fifth century found a few years ago in the Roman-Byzantine locale of Sepphoris, also famous for its Dionysus mosaics (see chap. V/5; Weiss/Netzer, 1996). Although the mosaic is badly damaged, one can still see the fragment of a garment with small bells attached to the hem; the accompanying inscription identifies the garment as belonging to the High Priest Aharon (cf. the copy in illust. V.11), evidence possibly attesting this cultic tradition for the period of the second Jerusalem temple.

Although scholars generally concur that these bells functioned in Palestine as apotropaic and prophylactic devices in connection with people and animals (Avenary, 1956; Schatkin, 1978), they had other meanings as well. Like the pomegranate, they also symbolized life and a bright future (Zech. 14:20). For Philo of Alexandria, they symbolized the cosmic harmony itself, for Rabbi Jonathan Beth-Govrin (y. Yoma 7:3), penitence. The two "horns" of the earliest example of such bells in ancient Israel/Palestine, namely, the ninth-century Megiddo-bell (illust. V.1), as well as the Bes countenance of the Tell Ḥalif and Tell eṣ-Ṣafi bells (illust. V.4; V.5a-b) seem to suggest they were also cultic accoutrements. The oldest finds include the eighth/seventh-century bells from Achzib and Ziklag (illust. V.2, 3). That Palestinian bells were also used cultically is suggested by the rather large number of bells found in graves, particularly from the Hellenistic period. In fact, both Plutarch and certain iconographic evidence confirm that bells were used in Palestine even in connection with the orgiastic cult of Dionysus (see illust. V.41d); the small bell attached to a chain as a pendant (illust. V.10) also shows that it was worn as an amulet. Secular uses were both decorative and communicative. The tiny bell from Caesarea (1 cm. diameter, illust. V.7) was used as jewelry, while the animal bell from Massada (illust. V.6) as a means of communication.

The bell remained a significant accoutrement of the Jewish faith up to the early Middle Ages, and was even associated with numerology in the reckoning of 12x6=72 bells on the hem of the High Priest. One might point out in this context that bells were probably not used very much in pre-Hellenistic Palestine, especially not in the Israelite-Judean liturgy itself. Both written and archaeological sources suggest as much. Apart from the two passages in Exodus, the Old Testament does not otherwise mention the pa'ᵃmôn; archaeologists have found only ten bells dating to pre-Hellenistic times in Palestine, and even some of these may well be imports rather than indigenous products, for example, the bell of Tell Ḥalif (illust. V.4).

Archaeologists have unearthed at least sixty-five bells dating to the Hellenistic-Roman period, and more than a hundred dating to the Byzantine period. Moreover, bells have been found throughout the country, with the largest concentrations coming from Jerusalem, Tarshish, Gezer, Achzib, and Beth-Shean. The largest bells measure over 6 cm. tall (illust. V.6), the smallest barely a centimeter (illust. V.7), though the size seems to have decreased in Hellenistic times. All are made of bronze and have an iron clapper. Although these bells occur in a wide variety of forms, and although each exhibits its own individual, even unique form, most can be classified according to three basic forms: (1) semi-spherical, cupola-shaped bells (e.g., illust. V.8); (2) conical bells with circular outlines or footprints (illust. V.10); (3) modern churchbell shapes with characteristically flared rims (illust. V.9). In general, these forms were as varied and imaginative as the bells' functions. Like other idiophones such as rattles and cymbals, bells bridged several different periods; over the course of several millennia and across multiple historical periods, various traditional elements and basic forms could be tenaciously maintained even though details regarding both use and form could vary or develop further.

V.1. Bell, Megiddo, OI M936

V.2. Bell, Achzib, IAA 601104

V.3. Bell, Ziklag, EE 1742

V.4. Bell, Tel-Ḥalif, IAA 80.697

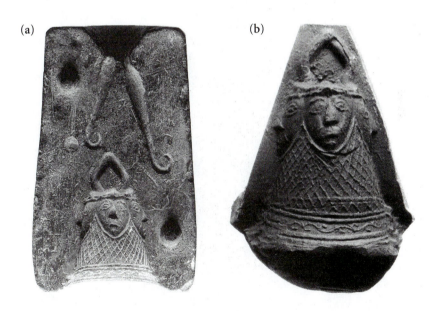

(a)   (b)

V.5. Bell, Tel-eṣ-Ṣafi, IAA S-215: (a) casting mould; (b) modern cast

199

V.6. Animal bell, Masada

V.7. Bell, Caesarea, IAA 51.686

V.8. Bell with cloth fragments, Jerusalem, IAA 34.3137

V.9. Bell, Abu Shosha, IAA 59.403

V.10. Chain with bell, Mishmar Ha-'Emeq, IAA 78.138

V.11. Mosaic floor, Sepphoris synagogue, Aharon in robe with bells,
copy from the IMJ Exposition

202

2. Idumean Hunting and Mourning Music and the Jewish Temple Trumpets

"It was early June, 1902, when we heard in Jerusalem that there was much illicit excavation for antiquities in the neighborhood of Bet Jibrin (Bet Govrin). . . . A certain Nubian could guide us intelligently over the site. . . . It proved to be . . . the most remarkable tomb ever discovered in Palestine. . . . We chanced to be the first traveling scholars to arrive on the scene after their excavations by the natives, . . . the paintings . . . were at the time of discovery in a perfect state of preservation. The heads which had been scratched out were effaced by the Shekh of Bet Jibrin, a pious Moslem, who entering the tombs, cried out haram, 'forbidden,' and drawing his knife from his girdle, scratched out the faces of the trumpeter, (and) the rider. . . ." Thus did the archaeologists John O. Peters and Hermann Thiersche (1905, 1-2) recount their discovery of the grave mural from Hellenistic Mareshah, capital of western Idumea, forty kilometers southwest of Jerusalem.

Although the actual illustrations on the murals themselves faded and became obscure soon after their discovery, the Fathers of the St. Stephen Convent in Jerusalem copied and photographed them, and Peters/Thiersch published them in 1905. Until about 1990, the originals were kept in the École Biblique, Jerusalem, but are now lost. In 1994, the IAA restored both the graves and the accompanying drawings under the leadership of Professor Amos Kloner.

The origins of the Idumeans have not been unequivocally determined. During the Hellenistic period, they developed an independent culture uniting extraordinarily diverse Near Eastern elements, including Philistine, Phoenician, Greek, Etruscan, Egyptian, and Jewish. Their capital, Mareshah, which Rome never recognized as a *pólis,* was built on the Greek model and served as an outpost for the advance of Hellenization into ancient Israel/Palestine, an advance that exerted its influence here in Sidonian-occupied Idumea by way of the Greek-Sidonian culture. Over the course of the Hellenistic period, Mareshah became a significant Near Eastern center of the arts, and as such has yielded a profusion of archaeological finds relating to architecture, the theater, the representative arts, and music.

A great many pieces of archaeological evidence relating to Idumean music have been unearthed, and much of this material is of considerable significance in showing the extremely advanced musical culture achieved by these people during the Hellenistic period. Nonetheless, scholars have largely ignored this musical culture, a fact all the more astonishing inasmuch as the drawings from the Idumean graves are some of the oldest finds relating to music in the entire sphere of ancient Israel/Palestine, and one of the most significant witnesses not only to the local musical culture, but to musical culture in the Near East at large.

The Idumean musical culture was by no means a merely fortuitous development or brief flash, but rather developed from a long tradition beginning back in the Iron Age. It seems that during the early first millennium B.C., during the time of Rehoboam (928-911, first king of Judah), a great many intellectuals and artists moved into the cities under his rule, including Jerusalem, Bethlehem, Gath, Mareshah, Lachish, and others. "The priests and the Levites who were in all Israel presented themselves to him from all their territories. The Levites had left their common lands and their holdings and had come to Judah and Jerusalem" (2 Ch. 11:8, 13-14). Local cultural centers developed in Edom, Philistia, and Judah in animated exchange with imported elements from Egypt, Greece, Sidon, Etrusca, and Cyprus, culminating then during the Hellenistic–early Roman period (third century B.C.–first century A.D.).

About thirty archaeological pieces contribute to our understanding of the Idumean musical culture, which grew out of the Edomite heritage. The tiny Edomite kingdom (eight-sixth centuries B.C.), hardly researched, seems to have possessed a unique style in both the visual arts and music. Apart from the murals of Mareshah, which I will discuss below, the following groups of artifacts were either part of this musical culture itself or contributed to its genesis.

(a) The seventh/sixth-century Edomite material from Qitmit and Tell Malḥata actually preceded the Idumean culture itself and constitutes a separate cultural entity. These unique terra cottas are without parallel in ancient Israel/Palestine; even within the larger Near Eastern context, they represent singular autochthonous works of art, full of imagination, expressiveness, and sophistication. Examples include the god's head with horns and rattle (illust. III.26), the plaque figure with the double-pipe player, and the man with the double pipe (illust. IV.19, 20).

(b) The Mareshah terra cottas portray lute and harp players (e.g., illust. V.35), which after an absence of more than a millennium now reappear within the sphere of ancient Israel/Palestine.

(c) The Beth Nattif plaques (illust. V.31, 32, 33) portray female figures with various idiophones such as cymbals, rattles, and castanets. These pieces probably represent a transformation of the earlier figurines portraying female drummers.

The Mareshah necropolis in which the murals were found is of the familiar underground Hellenistic chamber type. These opulent graves consist of an anteroom serving various purposes such as rituals, offerings, lounging, or even as a place where lovers might rendezvous, and of chambers with burial niches (Lat. *loculi,* Heb. [[*kochim*]]) into which the deceased were placed. Most scholars think the Mareshah graves are the oldest of this type in ancient Israel/Palestine. Given the singularity of the drawings found here (illust. V. 12, 13) and the innovations attested by the musical instruments they depict, Greek influence clearly had made extraordinary advances in this context, and a new autochthonous culture can now be seen emerging in ancient Israel/Palestine.

The third-century B.C. inscription in the first grave identifies the owner of the tomb complex as "Apollophanes, Son of Sesmaius, in the year 33, head of the Sidonians in Mareshah, known as a competent man and one who loved his family; he died in the seventy-fourth year of his life" (Peters/Thiersch, 1905). This man was thus a member of the Sidonian elite, which perhaps explains the hunting scene on the mural in the main chamber (illust. V.12).

Cypriot iconography already demonstrates to us that hunting was part of the lifestyle enjoyed by Phoenician and Hellenistic aristocracy (Perrot/Chipiez, 1885). The scenes in Cypriot examples, however, contain no musical elements. Music is a topos found in Assyrian iconography dealing with the hunt, where it played a cultic role during the libation after a successful hunt and where the entire associated action takes on more of a theatrical character (Rashid, 1984). The Mareshah scenes, however, manage to fuse the two topoi of music and hunting in a unique fashion.

Indeed, the proud trumpeter lends an aristocratic air to this hunting scene, accentuated not least by the belted tunic (the Macedonian *chlamýs*) and headband, both of which attest his high rank. His inclusion here evidently has some ceremonial significance. With his right hand, this *tubicen* (trumpeter) holds the trumpet in a strictly horizontal position while his left hand is held on his hip. This position underscores the ceremonial nature of his function insofar as in most portrayals, the player holds the *tuba* differently, pointed more upwards, and with both hands (Fleischhauer, 1964).

V.12. Mural, Beth Govrin, hunting scene with trumpeter, *in situ*

V.13. Mural, female harpist and
double-aulos player, *in situ*

Above the trumpeter's head we can discern the remnants of the word *sálpinx* (trumpet). To my knowledge, this scene represents the first portrayal of a trumpeter in connection with hunting, and as such attests an innovation in the function of trumpets, which in Greco-Roman culture are mentioned and portrayed as instruments associated with the cult, the military, and civilian life. The instrument in this scene is a Roman *tuba,* approximately 120-130 cm. long, slightly conical, about 2-3 cm. across at the mouth end and 10-15 cm. at the bell. The mouthpieces used with these instruments were made of bone or bronze, and enabled the instrument to produce up to six different tones. Several examples in the Magyari Nemzeti Museum in Budapest (e.g., no. 10.1951.3) show that they were made of hammered bronze. Nu. 10:2 already mentions this method of using hammered metal; in the case of Old Testament trumpets, the metal was *kese̱p miqšâ,* hammered silver. As with several other trumpet portrayals, this trumpet, too, has a stripe or line at the beginning of the bell, suggesting the presence of an attached part.

The Mareshah trumpet exhibits similarities not only with actual trumpets found at various excavations, but also with trumpets attested in iconography. This similarity is especially striking in the famous relief of the Arch of Titus in Rome from the year 72 (illust. V.14; this arch has been frequently reproduced). The famous arch depicts two trumpets next to the golden *mᵉnôrâ* (seven-branched lampstand) and the golden Table for the Bread of the Presence (Ex. 25:23-40). Unfortunately, it is impossible to determine whether these trumpets faithfully reproduce the two silver *hᵃṣōṣᵉrôt̲* of the Jerusalem temple (Nu. 10:1-8), or whether the Roman artists merely depicted the *tuba sacrum* already familiar to them. In either case, it is worth considering that the temple trumpets appear neither among the booty displayed in Rome after Titus's victory nor in his triumphal procession. Sources simply do not support the assertion that "also two sacred trumpets were carried around in the triumph" (Yarden, 1991). Indeed, the accuracy of the representations on this arch has in any event become subject to increasing doubt. For example, the menorah depicted here does not correspond to the Old Testament's own description of this cultic object in Ex. 25:31-40. What we probably have on the Arch of Titus are two typical Roman *tubae* which are virtually identical with the Mareshah trumpet.

A new source has recently been added to the iconography of trumpets associated with the Jerusalem temple (Weiss/Nezer, 1996, 20). In the early fifth-century synagogue mosaic from Sepphoris (copy in illust. V.15), "the trumpets are depicted as slightly curved tubes that widen gently at one

V.14. Arch of Titus, Rome, *in situ*

V.15. Mosaic floor,
Sepphoris synagogue,
two wind instruments with
superscription "trumpet,"
copy from IMJ Exposition

end. Each of the trumpets is decorated with two rings set at regular intervals" (Weiss/Netzer, 1996, 20). Although this description as well as the inscription on the mosaic (Heb. *hᵃṣōṣᵉrôṯ*, trumpets) are commensurate at least with the artists' intention, these instruments cannot be interpreted as trumpets. Trumpets were never "gently curved," but rather always completely straight or, as was the case with metal horns, severely curved. They never "widened gently at one end," but rather were clearly wider at the bell. They were never "decorated with two rings set at regular intervals," but rather always lacked such decoration; even if such "decoration" allegedly indicates the connection between individual parts of the instruments, the intervals are not at all regular. It simply is not possible to accept the trumpets in this mosaic as accurate representations of the trumpets described in the Old Testament. What apparently happened is that the artists in Sepphoris were already familiar with the common shofars (see chap. V/8) and simply accepted these horns as temple trumpets.

A second mural (illust. V.13) was found in the second grave, which in turn dates to a slightly later period (188-135 B.C.; Peters/Thiersch, 1905). Here the two musicians are standing directly next to the entry to the main burial chamber, and even appear to be entering the chamber itself as if they wanted to illustrate the scene from Isa. 14:10-11: "'You too have become as weak as we! You have become like us!' Your pomp is brought down to Sheol, and the sound of your *nᵉḇālîm*." In the larger sense, this scene may reflect the widespread notion throughout the Near East that the deceased are to be accompanied into the beyond and entertained there as well with feasting and music.

In any case, we see before us here a young double-aulos player and a female harpist dressed in provincial Near Eastern clothing, namely, the *chitón* and the belted *péplos*. Such clothing betrays the presence of Etruscan tradition, which is also reflected in the choice of instruments except that here, in Hellenistic Mareshah, the stringed instrument is the harp rather than the lyre common in older Etruscan sources (Fleischhauer, 1964). This tradition thus differs from that of Jewish funerals, where only wind instruments appear, as attested by the Talmud's assertion that "even the poorest in Israel should hire not less than two *hᵃlilîm* and one wailing woman" (*m. Ketub.* 4:4).

We have already mentioned the reappearance of the rare crescent harp and the role Idumea played in this connection. Not only is the entire harp depicted in the Mareshah scene, the drawing itself has also been carefully executed and clearly shows the instrument's various ergological features.

The resonator was located on the bottom of the instrument, and in this portrayal is largely concealed by the player. The resonator itself was probably not very large, and this fact might explain at least in part why this instrument, whose sound was less than pleasing, was not around very long. The instrument itself was about 60 cm. long, and both its form and the playing position reflect elements found in several different types of harps. Ergological features most closely resemble the smaller Ptolemaic version of the royal harp from the period of the Ramses, a harp played by aristocrats, kings, and gods (Manniche, 1975) but whose portrayal is always so transparently schematic that some scholars have even doubted it existed in the first place (Hickmann, 1982). The Mareshah harp, however, confirms both the existence and the *Sitz im Leben* of this type of harp. We can see that its playing position is the same as that associated with the shoulder harp of the new empire, and the small number of strings recalls the hetaera harp, which was viewed largely as an oriental curiosity and often associated with the *sambýkē* (Hickman, 1982; Behn, 1954; Marcuse, 1975, 38).

The realistic drawing from Mareshah quite possibly suggests that the version of this harp with four strings was a specifically Idumean feature. We encountered this harp earlier in the orchestra of Nebuchadnezzar (Dnl. 3:5, 7, 10, 13; fourth/third century B.C.). The *sambýkē* was often associated with the musical activities of harlots (*sambucistriae psaltriae;* Arnobius, third/fourth century), and the Greeks viewed it as a foreign instrument of Phoenician or some other, general Near Eastern provenance. Several sources, among them Euphorion and Athenaeus, also mention that the *sambýkē* had four strings. Landels (1966) has persuasively demonstrated that the *sambýkē* did indeed refer to a harp, in which case this word, which can refer to several different kinds of harp, can in the context of ancient Israel/Palestine refer only to the local type, namely, the small crescent harp.

This initial survey of Idumaic sources clearly illustrates the significance of this musical culture. Forms of instruments such as the harp, including the crescent type, and lutes, are already attested in Idumea during a time when the same types were a rarity in other parts of ancient Israel/Palestine and in part even in the rest of the Near East. The new uses for music attested in these finds is even more significant. For the first time in the history of music, the trumpet appears in connection with the hunt, and for the first time in ancient Israel/Palestine in the narrower sense, the aerophone-chordophone ensemble appears in connection with lament or mourning.

3. The Nabatean-Safaitic Culture

Musicologists have generally ignored the sibling Nabatean and Safaitic cultures even though the latter is of considerable significance both for Hellenistic-Roman Israel/Palestine and for the entire Hellenistic-Roman world. These musical cultures, located on the periphery of the Hellenistic-Roman world, are able to illuminate in a unique way the syncretistic nature of the Hellenistic-Roman musical culture as well as various local autochthonous features.

> The first people above Syria . . . are the Nabateans and the Sabaeans. . . . The metropolis of the Nabateans is Petra. . . . The Nabateans are a sensible people, and are so much inclined to acquire possessions that they publicly fine anyone who has diminished his possessions. . . . Since they have but few slaves, they are served by their kinsfolk for the most part, or by one another, or by themselves. . . . They prepare common meals together in groups of thirteen persons, and they have two girl-singers for each banquet (*mousourgoí dé dýo*). The king holds many drinking bouts in magnificent style, but no one drinks more than eleven cupfuls, each time using a different golden cup. (Strabo, *Geographikon*, xvi.4.21, 26)

Because ancient authors rarely say anything about music when discussing the peripheral regions of the Roman Empire, Strabo's portrayal here of the continual presence of music at symposia is quite noteworthy.

Several considerations make archaeological evidence from these cultures all the more intriguing. Most of these cultures lasted only a few centuries. They were restricted to small areas geographically, and on balance have left behind precious few archaeological traces. Remarkably, however, we have more than twenty archaeological pieces relating to music from these cultures. Music was clearly of enormous importance to them.

Toward the end of the fourth century B.C., the Nabatu, an Arabic group, settled near the city of Petra mentioned by Strabo and probably also occupied the neighboring regions of Edom and Moab. Their origins are not entirely clear, and they are first mentioned by Diodorus Siculus (first century B.C.), though he was describing events that occurred more than two hundred years earlier. By the time of Strabo, they had already been consolidated politically into a kingdom for at least a century. Although the Nabatean state itself did not last past the mid-second century (106), its vigorous trade relationships along the famous caravan routes associated with the incense trade as well as their highly developed know-how in various other areas of daily life enabled them to attain considerable wealth. They developed unique styles in architecture, art, and ceramics, as well as their own pantheon of deities (Zayadin, 1970). The Hellenistic elite that administered the well-oiled state bureaucracy may have represented a "minority in their own country" (Knauf, 1986). Recent archaeological finds have drawn enough attention to turn research in Nabatean culture into a specialized research area (Wennig, 1987).

A society of this cultural stature quite naturally had a well-developed musical life, with music playing a role in both secular and cultic situations. The Petra temple was of the ancient northern Arabic type and included the commensurate cult during which participants circumambulated or even danced around the square-shaped sanctuary in which cultic accoutrements were kept (Knauf, 1986). Herodotus describes this circumambulation (Arab. [[*tawaf*]]) in his report of the cult as practiced by a Syrian-Arabic emperor, who allegedly danced around the altar with several Phoenician women accompanied by various instruments *(órgana)* while playing cymbals *(kýmbala)* and drums *(týmpana)* (Herodotus, v.5.9). Here one might recall the constant use of bells throughout the Near East as well as the bells excavated in the Nabatean sphere; these devices were clearly indispensable in this cult.

Feasts and cultic banquets with fixed rituals and opulent meals were held regularly at the Nabatean court, with guests reclining in the comfortable *triclinia*, during the summer outdoors in the *porticus*, and during the winter indoors in the *odium* (Negev, 1986b). It was apparently at these meals that most of the musical entertainment described by Strabo took place, and we may safely assume that such music included not only singing but also purely instrumental performances. Two different, socially polar works of art relating to the Nabatean-Safaitic musical culture, representing probably the most significant archaeological finds to date, throw a great deal of light on the musical life of these two cultures (illust. V.16; V.18).

Scholars generally associate Strabo's description with the terra-cotta relief depicting a trio of musicians with two lyres and a double pipe (illust. V.16; Khairi, 1990). Although one can easily imagine that songs such as the *skólion* were sung at such banquets in Petra following Greek custom

212

V.16. Plaque terra cotta, trio (two lyre players and one double-aulos player), Petra, AM J.5768

(Clement of Alexandria, *Paed.* 2:4), such a scene does not seem to be intended here. This trio seems better suited for ceremonial musical accompaniment than for a banquet. They are given a rather strict rendering here, with virtually their entire bodies covered by cloaks or other tunics. They are also portrayed frontally next to one another in somewhat stiff, stylized positions. This trio, composed probably of two women and a man, just does not seem quite appropriate to a relaxed symposium that includes fine food, wine, and tempting songstresses. Everything about these figures seems to point to a ritual that, while certainly not an impossibility at the royal court, evokes more the context of a liturgy, possibly of a syncretistic nature, than a luxurious banquet. They are wearing long tunics with a heavy, woven or plaited hem, and possibly two different head-coverings (a wig and/or a turban). The middle figure is barefoot, a feature already familiar from Arabic cultic contexts. Finally, they have been given an almost genderless rendering. Syncretistic features are also recognizable in this scene. Although Greco-Roman features are clearly discernible and include the grouping of musicians themselves, the hairstyle of one of the female figures, and their tunics, other features are of an unmistakable regional, oriental provenance, including the almost total lack of physical body features, the frontal positioning, the foot positions, and the facial features (Avi-Yonah, 1981).

The well-preserved relief itself, measuring 9.2 × 8.7 × 2.5 cm. and dating to the period between the second and first centuries, exhibits excellent artistic execution and as such allows us to identify two different types of symmetrical Hellenistic lyres. The first is the Greek-Alexandrian type with a rounded resonator, lengthy and almost parallel side arms with a short crossbar, and five or six strings. The second is the Seleucid type, quite small (about 35 × 40 cm.), rectangular, with four to six strings attached to a gently curved yoke.

In this relief, the female musician playing the Seleucid lyre has a plectrum hanging down on a cord attached to her wrist, and yet the musicians are extending the fingers of their right hand as if they are about to pluck the strings. Does this mean that although this kind of instrument was indeed usually played with a plectrum, in this region it was actually plucked by hand instead? Judging from the size and string stops of the two instruments, one may have played treble, the other bass. If this interpretation is correct, the scene would offer a parallel to the two other lyre types in neighboring Judah, namely, the kinnôr and the nēbel, which many scholars also interpret as treble and bass instruments (see chap. V/7).

In any event, the two lyre types of the Petra relief are portrayed in a sociological-ethnically homogeneous constellation, and as such illustrate well the kind of musical syncretism that predominated during the Hellenistic age in Palestine.

The double pipe is apparently a double clarinet of the sort quite common throughout the Near East both then and today. The two tubes are of equal length, and each has what seems to be nine finger holes, an unusually large number, arranged in equal intervals along the length of the instrument, an equally unusual feature. This double-pipe instrument is still common today in Israel and Jordan, where it is known as the [[*mujwiz*]] (illust. V.17a).

The feature that makes this particular relief unique is its instrumental combination as a chordophone-aerophone ensemble. Even the trio grouping itself is a rarity, since up to this point iconographical evidence is available only for Seleucid duos consisting of a lute and double pipe or a harp and cymbals (Rashid, 1984), but not for trios. Although Egyptian ensembles did sometimes mix string and wind instruments, none included the lyre. To my knowledge, the oldest portrayals of a duo including the lyre and double pipe are found on two seals associated with the lunar cult and dating to the tenth-eighth centuries; one was found in Nebo, a Moabite city not far from Petra, and the other comes from an unknown site also within this region. I have elsewhere described this aerophone-chordophone combination as a "typical local ensemble born in the Assyrian-Phoenician-Philistine-Israelite acculturation process some centuries before the Phoenician trio" (Braun, 1990/91). The trio depicted on this relief may well document the continuation of precisely this regional tradition.

No mention of this combination of two chordophones plus one double pipe has yet been found in pre-Hellenistic literature. The Old Testament, for example, never mentions the double pipe in connection with liturgy, and an ensemble including both the double pipe and the lyre probably was never associated with the neighboring Jewish temple ritual. We do, however, have evidence of an ensemble including two chordophones plus an aerophone in texts coming from the general ambience of the Nabatean kingdom and, significantly, dating to precisely the same period as the Petra terra-cotta relief. The passage occurs in one of the Qumran thanksgiving hymns (1QH 11:22-24): "Then will I play (*'azammērâ*) on the *kinnôr* of deliverance and the *nēḇel* of joy . . . and the *ḥālîl* of praise without end." Here we encounter the three instruments recent musicologists have identified as two different types of lyre and a reed instrument, namely, the *kinnôr*, *nēḇel*, and *ḥālîl*. With regard to the Qumran scrolls, Eric Werner (1984) remarks that "the trouble with all these references to musical instruments is that they were usually meant as well as understood metaphorically." Talmudic Judaism and Christianity both occasionally referred to musical instruments metaphorically. During the period of the pre-Talmudic and pre-Christian Qumran sects, however, this process of metaphorical referencing was still in

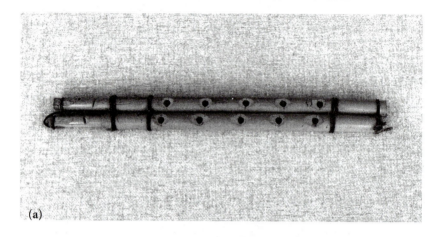

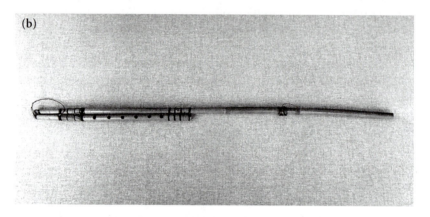

V.17. Modern traditional wind instruments: (a) [[*mujwiz*]];
(b) *arghul el-soghair* (Tel Aviv, AMLI Musical Instrument Museum)

its nascent stages, and the meaning or significance of the names of instruments was still grounded largely in actual practice. If that is still the case here, this passage represents a tangible example of the intertwining of real life and nascent metaphorical thinking.

The present status of research does not yet enable us to draw any reliable conclusions concerning how music was actually integrated into the cult. Does this ritual evoke an early Arabic folk cult with dancing, drumming, and horns? Or do the parallels between the Nabatean and Near Eastern temple style suggest more a ritual in the sense described by Avraham Negev (1977): "The ritual in this temple was probably performed in the following way: sacrifice was performed on an altar which stood in the middle of the *theatron;* incense was burnt at the roof of the inner shrine and a solemn procession was performed, using the two staircase-towers giving access to the roof; a festive meal then took place in the *theatron"?*

It is also helpful to recall here the procession of thanksgiving choruses and musicians associated with the dedication of Jerusalem's walls; "at the Fountain Gate, in front of them, they went straight up by the stairs of the city of David, at the ascent of the wall" (Neh. 12:31-43). One might also mention the Therapeutae, an ascetic Jewish sect not far from Alexandria who used music in connection not only with the liturgy, but also as accompaniment to the dancing at their symposia (Philo, *Vit. Cont.* 78-79).

In this case, music probably accompanied all three stages of the ritual. It was played during the offering at the altar, during the solemn procession up the stairs to the incense altar, and during the celebratory meal. It would come as no surprise, nor would it contradict any historical circumstances, to find that the Hellenistic Nabateans even conducted the two rituals in different temples, namely, the quasi-Arabic ritual of southern Syria on the one hand, and the quasi-Jewish ritual of Jerusalem on the other.

At the other end of these regional cultures in the Transjordan we have a stone etching (illust. V.18). This iconographic witness is part of the huge corpus, encompassing approximately fifteen thousand pieces, of inscriptions written in Safaitic, an ancient southern Arabic dialect, and occasionally illustrated by simple line drawings.

Bedouin nomads etched a great many of the drawings into basalt stones in the Harra Desert in northeastern Transjordan, apparently as tombstone inscriptions, marks of possession, or as a means of communication, though their exact meaning remains somewhat obscure. Even their dating is difficult, though most scholars date this "stone art" to the late-Hellenistic/early-Byzantine period (first century B.C.–fourth century; Knauf, 1988; Negev, 1981).

This drawing portrays a nude woman with clearly marked breasts and a profuse shock of hair. She is playing a double pipe while leaning back slightly, and this performance seems to require all her physical energy and mental concentration. Down and to the right, a somewhat smaller male figure dances in a worshipful, almost servile position with peculiarly

V.18. Basalt etching, Harra Desert, Amman, AM, J.1886

frayed feet. The Safaitic inscription reads: "By Aqraban ben Kasit ben Said the beautiful one *(dmyt)* plays the pipe *(zmrt)*."

The vitality and expressiveness of this simple stone art are so striking that it may well reflect the kind of ancient scene in which ecstasy or prophecy is induced musically. Indeed, it recalls the kind of scene described in the Acts of St. Thomas (Bounet, 1883):

> The aulos player *(aulétria)*, pipe in hand *(tous aulóus)*, went about playing to each person *(katálousa)*. But when she came to the place where the apostle was, she stopped before him and, circling his head, played for a long time. This aulos player, however, was of Hebrew lineage. . . . The apostle raised his eyes and began to speak the following song: The girl is the daughter of the light. . . . Through the movement of her feet, she creates joy. . . . The attendants who dance before her are seven in number. . . . And when he finished this song, everyone looked at him. . . . They saw that his face had changed, but

218

they didn't understand his words. . . . Only the aulos player understood everything, for she was by lineage a Hebrew.

At first glance, it may certainly seem odd to associate this female pipe
player from the Transjordanian desert with a legend that is not only possibly much younger, but also, according to an *ad verbum* reading of the text,
is set into a quite different geographical context. It might have been possible for St. Thomas to make the journey from Jerusalem to India by the Incense Highway, the same route the Nabateans used for centuries. However,
modern scholarship on the genesis of St. Thomas's *Acts* considers this
journey to be a legend of Near Eastern, probably Syrian, provenance; the
author of the *Acts* never really visited India. This is a typical case of mime-
sis, when the narrative and its Near Eastern locality are transposed into a
remote area — an accepted artistic device in early Christian literature; it
turns our written source into a quite convincing parallel to the discussed
iconographical source.

Music as a means to induce prophecy, rapture, and ecstasy is deeply
rooted in the cultural traditions of the ancient world. The classic examples
in the Near Eastern biblical context are the Israelite or Philistine minstrel
prophets of Gibea, who meet Saul (1 S. 10:5-11), and Elisha, who prophe-
sied to the kings of Israel, Judah, and Edom before the battle with Moab
(2 K. 3:14-20).

The cathartic power of ecstatic music was well-known in Roman Palestine. The legend of Thomas finds its parallel, or actually its roots, in the
Jerusalem Talmud, which was canonized during this period (fourth-fifth
century). The latter tells the story of a certain Jonah ben Abitai who comes
to Palestine as a pilgrim for the Water Festival. Because he lived in joy and
was a musician, God's Spirit prompted him to prophesy (*y. Sukk.* 5:1).

This particular drawing does not date later than the fourth century,
and is of enormous significance because it is the only known archaeological find relating to music from the Israelite-Jordanian region that associates a text with a specific drawing. As such, and unlike Egyptian and
Mesopotamian materials, it is unique in the entire Near East. It is also the
earliest iconographic piece attesting the idioglot Arabic clarinet with two
unequal pipes, the *arghul,* an instrument still common today.

The pipe in this drawing is apparently the *arghul el-soghair* (medium *arghul*). This
type has a melody pipe about 35 cm. long and a drone pipe about 60-70 cm. long

(illust. V.17b). Both laypersons and professional musicians especially among the Israeli Druze still play this popular instrument in folk music in connection with songs and dances. Unfortunately, we can no longer determine whether the Hellenistic *arghul,* like the contemporary instrument, was composed of nine parts (cf. illust. V.17b; Elsner, 1969).

This Safaitic inscription is the first unequivocal iconographic witness associating the playing of the double pipe with the word *zmrt,* and thus the earliest documentation of the term *zmr* in reference to the double-pipe instrument. To my knowledge, this scene is also the first time this word occurs in a secular context. Several centuries earlier, during the third/second century B.C., the term *z^emārâ* in Dnl. 3:5, 7, 10, 11 is used in a context suggesting the meaning "musical instrument" (Aram. *kōl z^enê z^emārā',* "all kinds of musical instruments"). This Safaitic inscription shows unequivocally that during the Hellenistic period, *zmrt* referred in the vernacular to the playing of wind instruments. This assertion contradicts a recent encyclopedia entry's insistence that in biblical texts this word never involves wind instruments, and that the Psalms use the word to refer exclusively to the playing of stringed instruments (*TDOT,* IV, 92, 96). In any event, this much is certain: here, much earlier than in the Medieval Arabic treatises (Collaer/Elsner, 1983, 4), a text mentions an instrument of the *arghul* type that at least at that time was designated by the term *zmrt.*

The root *zmr* occurs in yet another context of interest in this regard. The corpus of Nabatean-Safaitic names collected by Avraham Negev contains a series of personal names related to professional identity. In forty instances, the name *zmro* occurs, and has usually been translated as "without beard" or "beautiful person" (Negev 1991). One can assume, however, that the name *zmro* was that of a male or female pipe player. Because thirty-nine of these forty names appear in Safaitic rather than Nabatean script, one might conclude that these pipe players were members of the lower, Safaitic classes rather than of the priestly-economic Nabatean elite. Because all known texts involving juridical or religious matters are composed in the Nabatean language, and because Safaitic texts deal exclusively with daily secular life and private matters, it seems the Safaites had no access to the official ceremonial or to the liturgy (Negev, 1986).

One additional etched stone drawing might be adduced here, though the original is lost and is accessible today only as a copy (illust. V.19; Harding, 1969, 71, fig. 1). Its inscription is stylistically similar to that on the

V.19. Basalt etching, copy from Harding, 1969, Fig. 1

stone from the Harra Desert, and probably dates to the same period. Although it, too, includes the word *dmyt*, "picture" or "beautiful woman," no additional features are present that help us to understand this iconography. The drawing depicts a male rider and two female figures with lyres. The middle female figure is apparently at least partially nude and stylistically resembles representations of the local goddess Radu (Avi-Yonah, 1981). The manner in which she holds her lyre recalls the female harp player from Megiddo from the fourth millennium, demonstrating once again how deeply rooted regional traditions associated with the ritualistic use of stringed instruments could be.

The two women in this drawing resemble the Yemenite-Ethiopian

221

type, and both are playing the same instrument. This lyre is related to the East African type, the large Ethiopian *begganna* and its various derivatives ([[*litungu, arebab, gwe*]]; Kubik, 1982). The instruments in this drawing probably represent the earliest iconographic witness to this symmetrical type of lyre with a rectangular resonator and parallel strings, though here only one of the lyres has been sketched with strings at all, in this case with two. Although lyres of this type are attested from the seventh century on (Hickmann, 1960b), they are much smaller than the lyre in this drawing, which probably measured about 100 cm. Like the Safaitic instruments here, the larger lyres of the *begganna* and [[*gwe*]] type were held upright, while the smaller types were tucked under the player's elbow. Finally, the *begganna* had between five and ten strings.

The scene in this rock drawing is difficult to interpret. Is the lyre player on the ass a slave, and as such the spoils acquired by the rider on the horse, who in turn might then represent a returning warrior? Or is the male rider abducting his bride under the blessing of a goddess who plays the lyre?

4. Instruments of Avant-Garde Professionals and Conventional Folk-Musicians

We have already discussed above the striking reversal that took place in ancient Israel/Palestine at the beginning of the Hellenistic period. The exciting, fertile spirit of a new culture emerges at every juncture, not only in the grander, more significant historical events such as military campaigns, power shifts, the birth of new states, and population shifts, but also in localized phenomena such as the understanding of the cult or of law, in the cauldron of cultural and linguistic influences, and in the new directions in architecture and art. This new culture drew nourishment from occidental currents while still harboring the earlier oriental heritage, and indeed, this continuation of "non-simultaneity within simultaneity" and now even "foreign features within the local scene" is one of the most important characteristics of the Hellenistic cultural syncretism in ancient Israel/Palestine. This rich cultural give-and-take and cross nourishment was the substance driving the cultural development that ultimately turned this period into the golden age of music in ancient Israel/Palestine.

Given the free, lively, and profuse cultural exchange during this period, it comes as no surprise that it is in the sphere of musical instruments that archaeology has provided the most vivid evidence of this new cultural spirit. A graphic illustration of this situation can be conjured merely by considering the innovations prompted in part by the continued development of earlier musical accomplishments, and in part by the added participation of both related and more alien cultures. New musical cultures are born: the Idumaic, the Nabatean-Safaitic, the Samaritan. Various cultic ceremonies involving music now find their classic expression or are reborn: the Dionysian, the Judeo-Christian, the early Islamic. Even musical praxis in the larger sense often acquires new social functions and new forms of expression.

Apart from the bells that from the Iron Age onward had always carried forward the rich tradition of idiophones in ancient Israel/Palestine, it is now the simple or double-reed instruments with one or two pipes that appear most often throughout the country during the Hellenistic-Roman period. One of the most important finds in this context is an aulos fragment dating to the first half of the first century B.C.; it was found in 1972 during the excavation of a residential building on Mount Zion in Jerusalem (illust. V.20). The room in which it was found was decorated with profuse murals including birds, festoons, and trees, and may suggest the houseowner had a particular interest in art.

The fragment is actually a bone pipe 12.7 cm. long and 13 mm. in diameter; a bronze-overlaid horn- or endpiece 26 mm. in diameter is mounted on its 16 mm. coupling. This fragment represents the lower end of an aulos instrument that was originally about 60 cm. long. The rectangular opening was probably part of the revolving ring, the *kéras,* by means of which modal changes could be made. The entire piece, including the *kéras*-opening, strongly resembles the Meroë aulos fragments from the year 15 B.C. (Bodley, 1946), so much so that one can safely assume these instruments were made in the same place, possibly Alexandria. The position of the *kéras* opening, namely, 92 mm. from the opening of the hornpiece at the end, suggests this particular instrument was a drone aulos of the Meroë type. The bronze overlay of the Jerusalem fragment is particularly intriguing. Although it exhibits the same dimensions as that of the Meroë fragment, its execution is different. Round about the opening itself, it is folded over into or inside the extended ivory profile, testifying to an extremely sophisticated manufacturing technique. Written sources date the use of such metal overlaying in connection with musical pipes at least to the fourth century B.C. (Landels, 1968), and even a Talmudic legend mentions it. In yet another typical example of the conflict between technical progress and aesthetic ideals, the authors of the Talmud insisted that the gold-overlaid temple *'abbûb* did not recover its sweet, melodious sound until the gold was removed (*b. 'Arak.* 10:2).

223

V.20. Aulos (fragment), Jerusalem, Mount Zion, EE 442

A similar fragment can be found in the Museum of the University of Pennsylvania. This badly damaged specimen is small and much more simply executed, and was found during the 1926 Beth-shean excavations. Because it, too, has been dated to the Hellenistic age, these two fragments together suggest that bronze-covered aulos instruments were in fact quite common in ancient Israel/Palestine.

The Israel Museum in Jerusalem was recently fortunate enough to acquire two rare aulos fragments (illust. V.21). These, too, were probably made locally, and also exhibit strong similarities with the Meroë specimens. These fragments also have the bronze overlay, were about 50-60 cm. long in their original form, have a large number of finger holes, and exhibit quite sophisticated craftsmanship. The *hólmos,* a bulb or widened section where the *glṓttai* (reeds) were attached, was found intact, but its end is damaged, and it may be that a *hypóholmos* or second widened section was originally present as well. The smaller fragment has four finger openings and the larger one at least five plus a thumb opening, numbers dating the instrument to the Roman period.

A different kind of aulos was found in an unstratified layer during the 1929 excavations in Samaria (Sebaste). This type has no bronze overlay and dates to the third-first centuries B.C. (illust. V.22; first publication). Although Samaria was once the capital of Israel, its name later came to symbolize apostasy (Am. 6:1-6; 2 K. 17:29). During the Hellenistic-Roman period, it was the center of the Samaritan faith. Its population during this period was extremely heterogeneous; in fact, one might even call it international, the not unexpected result being that the Hellenistic-Roman in-

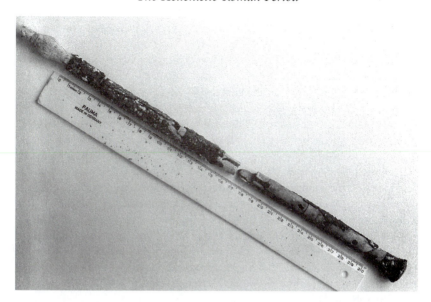

V.21. Aulos (two fragments), PU (Jerusalem?), IMJ 94.124-94

V.22. Aulos (fragment), Samaria, IAA 35.3548

fluence at work in other parts of the country became especially pronounced in Samaria as well. In the meantime, however, the status of the Hasmonean state to which Samaria belonged had fallen to that of a vassal *Civitas Stipendiaria.*

As luck would have it, the Samaritan aulos fragment has retained its fine polish even up to the present, and can be classified among the typical aulos fragments with four finger holes (Landels, 1981). The striking feature on this particular example, however, is that it actually has more finger holes; its five holes on the front side are 12 mm. apart, and the two on the back side 21 mm. apart. All the holes are 6 mm. in diameter, and were created with a very precise boring tool. A fragment from Delos is almost identical (Delos Museum, information from Dr. A. Belis) and this resemblance may even suggest that the Jewish musical community on Delos maintained close contact with Hellenistic Judea. Although in such cases, when only a fragment of an instrument is preserved, "only the most speculative and tentative suggestions can be made about the pitch" (Landels, 1981, 30), one might assume that this instrument was capable of producing intervals of the inharmonic or chromatic modes (with 1/4 and 1/3 tones). Such a capability would certainly have enabled a local musician to play the eastern modes on the instrument. Yet another bone fragment was found in Samaria that might have been part of the rare *plagíaulos,* a monoaulos or cross flute blown from the side (see Braun 1999, illust. V/4-5). Although this fragment does indeed resemble the plagioaulos fragments in the Museum of Musical Instruments at the University of Leipzig (no. 1218), some of its features indicate that this fragment may represent a local product. In any event, these Samaritan finds show that like Jerusalem, Samaria had local artisans producing the aulos.

Several aulos fragments were found in a Roman residential dwelling in Gezer among other items from daily life, including dishes and other ceramics (illust. V.23). One striking feature on these fragments is that the holes are irregularly carved, and the walls of the bone tubes themselves are quite thin. The best-preserved of these fragments is 133 mm. long and extremely thin, its diameter measuring only 8 mm. Unlike the fragments discussed to this point, this one was produced by hand, and the finger holes seem to have been first marked and then rather crudely carved. The holes are positioned at quite irregular intervals (20, 10, 29, 15 mm.), and the upper end may still have the remnants of an idioglot blowing device. The other two, smaller bone pipes were found near this first one, but have no finger holes at all and may represent parts of a drone pipe. These fragments evidently represent imitations that an amateur or nonprofessional made of the more sophisticated instruments. As such, they were probably originally used in a more popular setting. Moreover, the intonation schema such an instrument was capable of producing also suggests they produced tonal series different from those of professional "artistic music" and possibly employed a drone.

These pipe instruments from Jerusalem, Samaria, and Gezer clearly show that the art of playing wind instruments was highly developed dur-

V.23. Aulos (two fragments), Abu Shosha, IAA 81-1839

ing this period. Their workmanship and physical details, however, also show that a certain social stratification had taken place in musical praxis as well. Some of these instruments were produced with highly sophisticated professional techniques, others by rather primitive, even crude amateur methods. Similarly, the instruments were found in a variety of locations, including wealthy private homes, graves, and middens. And finally, because the instruments were made out of different materials and had their finger openings at sometimes widely differing intervals, they were capable of producing extremely different tonal qualitites and series. The musicians who played these instruments were as different as the instruments themselves. Some were high-ranking professional virtuosos. Others were semiprofessional folk musicians. As has always been the case in music history, the latter were the real guardians of traditional music.

The aulos was thus quite common in Palestine, and it comes as no surprise that the first documentation of a Jewish musician is associated with this instrument. A registry of Jewish livestock owners in the northern Egyptian settlement Samareia, which was probably settled by former inhabitants of Samaria-Sebaste, includes the "aulos player" Jacobius Son of Jacobius, who allegedly owned thirteen head of cattle, seven sheep, and one goat (Tcherikover, 1957 I, 17). We have already seen that during the Hellenistic period one could certainly encounter semiprofessional and amateur Jewish musicians of the sort who would later become known as klezmorim, Jewish folk-musicians who made a living at least in part by playing music.

Representations of the aulos in its classic form as a gently diverging double pipe with fixed hand position appear in Palestine's larger port cities

227

as early as the Persian period. One example is the black-on-red rendering on a vase fragment from Ashdod (illust. V.24). The quality of this drawing suggests it may have been done locally. Here a figure of Silenus, one recalling the type done by the Attic Cleophon painter, is playing a schematically rendered instrument.

Derivative types were probably also known in Palestine, such as the Phrygian aulos with two pipes, one of which had a mounted hornpiece as a resonating bell. One bone relief portrays a youth playing a Phrygian aulos (illust. V.25). This particular portrayal provides a clear rendering of both the instrument and its playing position. One of the pipes has finger holes and was used to produce the melody, while the other (with the horn) is held like a drone pipe. This relief may be portraying a figure from the Greek mimus, a theatrical form also popular in Palestine.

Such tablets apparently served as household decorative items for furniture, various kinds of boxes or containers, and other objects; Israel's museums have more than eighty such carved bone tablets on display similar to this one. Although not much is known about either the place of origin or the specifics of production for most of these tablets, much suggests they were made locally (Rosenthal, 1976). Such local production might provide one additional piece of evidence attesting the popularity of the aulos in Palestine during this period.

A new type of oboe appears almost simultaneously on several artifacts dating to the transitional stage of the Roman-Byzantine era. These *zurna* instruments were single conical pipes and may have appeared even earlier, though the witnesses are not reliable enough to permit unequivocal dating. Although these instruments are attested as early as the Iron Age as double pipes (see illust. IV.20), the single-pipe version is not reliably attested before the third-fourth centuries.

One additional witness to this instrument is found on a rare terra cotta (illust. V.26) which unverified sources identify as having come from a fourth-century Beth-shean workshop (*Fran Bibelns Land*, Exhibition Catalogue [Stockholm, 1955]). This seated figure exhibits Oriental-African facial features, has a beard, curly hair, and the feet of a goat, and obviously represents a local variation of the figure of Pan and the continuation of this Hellenistic-Roman tradition. The figurine is rather short (30-35 cm.) and holds the instrument downward in front of his body. During this period, the *zurna* instruments were presumably held in both positions, namely, horizontally and vertically. This dual playing position itself can be

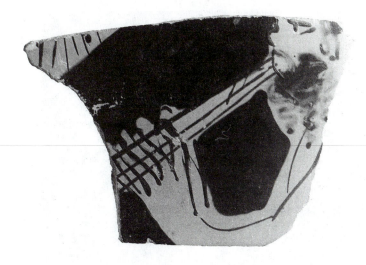

V.24. Vase fragment, black-on-red drawing, Ashdod, IAA 63.1873

seen as a continuation of the aulos tradition, which also attests the two positions. In these portrayals, the instrument has no pirouette, that is, no facilitating or auxiliary disk alongside the mouthpiece. This particular representation might indicate a transitional form to the later topos found on local mosaics during the post-Roman and early Byzantine period depicting a *zurna* player in a pastoral setting, a form attesting how common such *zurna* playing was in Palestine during the early Byzantine period (fourth-sixth century). One mosaic floor in a rather impressive residential dwelling from Medeba dating to the year 491 depicts various ornamental devices and animals, but also a barefoot shepherd (?) with clearly eastern facial features and wearing a short *chitón*. He is playing a conical *zurna* instrument about 50 cm. long held horizontally (illust. V.27b), a position characterizing the early period of such instruments but eventually altered. In this particular mosaic, the player holds the *zurna* with both hands and is actively moving his fingers while playing. This expressive example may have served as a model for later, similar mosaics such as the one from the Khirbet Schema Church (illust. V.27a), the Caesarea vault (illust. V.27d), and the mosaic portraying a *zurna* player together with a dog (?) from the Convent of St. Mary in Beth-shean (illust. V.27c). The latter mosaic offers a particularly clear rendering of the instrument itself, and for the first time

V.25. Bone relief, youth playing a Phrygian aulos, PU, HUHM (no number)

V.26. Plaque terra cotta, *zurna* player, IMJ 90.24.13

(a)

V.27a, b. Mosaic floor, *zurna* player: (a) Khirbet Shema (5th century), IAA;
(b) Medeba (491), copy in Kandeel, 1969, plate 27b

(b)

(c)

V.27c, d.
(c) Convent of St. Mary in Beth-shean,
in situ (560-570);
(d) Caesarea, Combined Caesarea
Expedition (5th-6th cent.)

(d)

it appears with the funnel-shaped end bell. The consistency with which these *zurna* players are portrayed with oriental features and in pastoral settings shows that the instrument was firmly established locally and quite popular among folk musicians (Braun 2003, in preparation).

The syrinx was at home in the same pastoral atmosphere, shown not least by its second name, the panpipe, which it acquired as an attribute of the pastoral Greco-Roman deity Pan. Recent etymological studies have revealed that the Greek word *sýrinx* is of Mediterranean or oriental origin, deriving possibly from Heb. *šrq,* "to pipe." Although the syrinx is attested in the Greco-Italian sphere from the sixth-fifth centuries B.C. on, no evidence for it in ancient Israel/Palestine appears before the year 12, the year in which an altar to Dionysus with a syrinx as the deity's symbol was erected in Scythopolis (Beth-shean), a center of Dionysus worship in the middle Palestinian region (illust. V.40). By the second century, the syrinx is fully established as the municipal symbol on coins from Paneas (see chap. V/7, Paneas coins).

The local organological tradition, however, does not appear graphically attested until the third century on a mural from a burial chamber in Ashkelon (illust. V.28). Two mythological figures — a chthonic goddess and a Gorgonian mask — appear among grapevines and combs along with local animals and birds as well as two youths who are picking the grapes. The scene as a whole seems quite realistic, especially the boys and the youth playing the syrinx. I would suggest, albeit with great caution, that the large number of pipes of almost equal length were capable of producing in their upper registers the microtonal mode for the melodic part of the syrinx music, while the pipes of the trapezoidal part produced supporting tones or drones associated with the basic tones.

The instrument in this scene has eleven pipes and represents what Gerlinde Haas has called the right-angle/trapezoidal bastard AB form of the syrinx (Haas, 1985). It appeared during the Hellenistic period but, unlike other forms, is not well attested. Portrayals of this type from Greece or Rome have anywhere from five to eight pipes, and isolated examples up to nine. The first AB-type with more than nine pipes appears in Ptolemaic Egypt (Hickmann, 1961a) and in our finds. Instruments with ten or more pipes apparently represent local versions, the large number of pipes possibly deriving from or reflecting local musical praxis in which the higher register had a tonal series with intervals smaller than half steps, and the lower register a tonal series with larger intervals.

V.28. Mural, burial chamber, Ashkelon, *in situ* (photo by J. Braun)

A second example of this Palestinian syrinx appears on a carved, decorative bone tablet of unknown provenance. It apparently portrays a Pan figure in the characteristic "plant costume" holding a palm frond in one hand and the instrument in the other (illust. V.29a). The local form of the syrinx appearing in this scene also suggests it is of local origin (cp. illust. V.28, pp. 234-35).

The symbolic character of the syrinx in Palestine seems quite clearly documented. Such is the case, for example, on the Eros terra cotta with Phrygian head decoration from the Royal Ontario Museum (illust. V.29c), or on the Mosaic of Sheikh Zouede (illust. V.41a). Nonetheless, it does not seem unreasonable to assume that these portrayals reflect a measure of realism. One small terra cotta of interest in this context is identified as being of Palestinian origin even though it was not found in the course of a regular excavation (illust. V.29b; catalogue of the Archaeological Institute of the University of London). This instrument, with its six characteristic notched pipes, offers unequivocal proof that the syrinx did indeed exist as a real instrument during this period.

The next developmental stage of instruments with multiple pipes would be the organ. Unfortunately, no evidence of such instruments in Palestine has come to light in either written or iconographic sources until

V.29a. Bone relief, Pan (?) plays a syrinx PU, HUHM A59

(b)

V.29b, c.
(b) PU, terra cotta,
London Univ., AI;
(c) PU, Eros with syrinx
terra cotta, Royal Ontario

(c)

now. The term [[*māgrēpâ*]], which until now scholars have generally interpreted as a kind of hydraulic instrument or something similar, appears only in the second-century Mishnah (*m. Tamid* 3:8; 5:6; *y. Sukk.* 5:3; 5:6; *b. 'Arak.* 10:2), though even this possible reference to the organ has been refuted (Sachs, 1940; Yasser, 1960).

Now, however, one can adduce a small corpus of approximately six terra-cotta oil lamps with reliefs portraying organs; these lamps have hitherto received no attention with regard to their musical topoi. One lamp was found during excavations in [['ein Hashofet]] (illust. V.30a), the others come from a private collection (illust. V.54). These finds are of particular importance for the Samaritan culture, and will be discussed in chapter V/6. Commensurate with tradition, these oil lamps portray not only the organs themselves, but also the slap cymbals *(krótalon)* whose small disks are frequently attested in Israel/Palestine in the Roman period (illust. V.30b).

These cymbals appear quite often during this period as instruments associated with the cult or with the more artistically inclined musical performances of the established religions, during Dionysian processions, and within the cult of Cybele. These idiophones represent a direct continuation not only of musical models from the Bronze and Iron Age, but also of various forms of artistic representation.

The terra-cotta reliefs from Beth Nattif are certainly of significance in this context. Large numbers of poured terra cottas and molds — clear evidence of mass production — were found in 1917, in Beth Nattif, a city in southern Judea with a mixed Jewish-Idumaic population and known during the Roman period as Bethletepha. These plaques, depicting female figures holding various idiophones, date to the second-third centuries and probably came from a local workshop (Baramki, 1936). The female figures, portrayed for the most part with clearly identifiable local stylistic features, are 13.8–14.5 cm. tall, and their iconographic type can be traced back as far as the Iron Age. One especially striking feature is their resemblance to the Iron Age female drummers from ancient Israel/Palestine. Both types are nude or wear transparent garments, both have jewelry or other adornment on their neck and hands, both are wearing headpieces or wigs. The same problems presented by the headpieces earlier also apply to the Beth Nattif figures; these figures might represent priestesses or temple servants on the one hand, lamenting women, dancers, or "funeral brides" on the other. In the present instance as well, however, one seems best advised to classify these terra cottas according to figure type and instrument type.

(a)

(b)

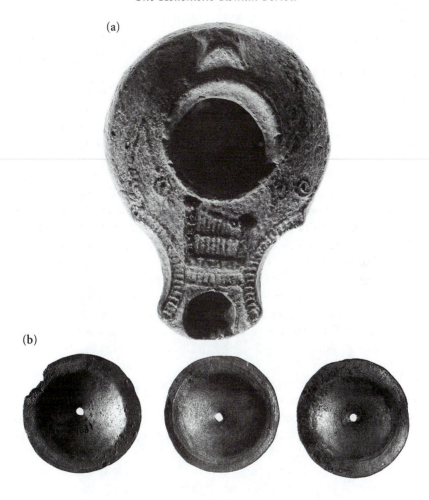

V.30. (a) Terra-cotta oil lamp, depicting organ and *krótalon*,
[['ein Hashofet]], IAA 71.5080; (b) cymbals, Ashkelon, IAA I1081

This particular topos has not yet been the subject of any scholarly discussion focusing on iconographical features, nor have the instruments themselves been identified. One priestess/temple servant (illust. V.31) is holding a metal rattle in her left hand whose form is already familiar from Ptolemaic Egypt (Hickmann, 1963). Roman priestesses used a kind of ba-

V.31. Plaque terra cotta, Beth Nattif, priestess (?) with metal rattle,
IMJ 69.27.567

ton with a poured-metal form similar to the head of a rattle (Sachs, 1965). The small saber in the woman's right hand seems to confirm her interpretation as a priestess. The female dancers or bacchantes portrayed on other relief figurines (illust. V.32) are beating small cymbals; they are barefoot, have neck jewelry, and are wearing transparent clothes revealing the body much like the Cybele dancer in the Villa Albani (Fleischhauer, 1964). These dancers, however, are much more static, and their arms seem raised in worship in the manner of the Iron Age figures. Yet another "dancer" (illust. V.33) is holding an idiophone, possibly castanets whose long, narrow form and rounded inner depression is carved in negative relief. Since this type of castanet is also found in the Ptolemaic kingdom, the topos itself represents a Hellenistic, Roman-Ptolemaic type whose local Levantine-Palestinian style is clearly discernible.

As discussed earlier, this period was one of profound cultural change. In such a context, the fate of chordophones would be of particular interest, especially since they played such a dominant role in all these musical cultures. To our great surprise, however, very few finds relating to the chordophone date to this period; in fact, we have only five artifacts and a few intaglios. Very few of these items have been documented with any precision, their local provenance is doubtful, and what organological innovations may be present are difficult to identify. Nonetheless, the radical changes attested elsewhere are still clearly discernible here as well. The lyre is clearly antiquated, and indeed eventually dies out. The lute experiences a renaissance, and its reappearance represents one of the most significant developments during the Hellenistic period in ancient Israel/Palestine. Here one can see how eagerly various parts of the region loaned and borrowed from each other's musical cultures, and how dynamic new influences were introduced into the musical culture at large.

The lute changed its form during the Hellenistic-Roman period. The neck was shortened, the resonator or sound-box became larger and broader, and more strings were added. By way of various interim forms, the instrument developed from the long-neck ancient Egyptian lute into the short-necked and pear-shaped lute, thence into the Arabic *úd* and ultimately into the later European forms.

One particular lute player is of great interest to us (illust. V.35). This terra-cotta figure was found in 1987 in Mareshah and dates to the fourth-third centuries B.C. (Kloner, 1991). As we saw earlier, during the Hellenistic period Mareshah (Tell Mareshah, Beth Govrin) was one of the capitals of

241

V.32. Plaque terra cotta, Beth Nattif, female dancer (?) with cymbals,
IMJ 69.27.568

**V.33. Plaque terra cotta, Beth Nattif, female dancer (?) with castanets,
IAA 38.205**

the Idumaic hipparchy, a Greco-Idumaic enclave on the southern border of Judea. The rich archaeological finds in this area profusely document the active and independent musical life that flourished in Idumea during the period. This particular lute player represents either Pan or, more likely, a satyr. In any event, he is holding a stringed instrument which is highly unusual in the Dionysian context; only rarely does one encounter the lute in association with Dionysus; and if stringed instruments do appear, then they are usually lyres rather than lutes. This case may represent a specific form indigenous to the local style of pagan Idumea, especially considering the long, autochthonous tradition the cults of both Cybele and Dionysus enjoyed in this area.

The Mareshah lute is an elongated, pear-shaped instrument whose resonator actually resolves into the neck. Portrayals of such lutes, often called *pandoúra* or *tríchordon,* are extremely rare. The two or three best known of these portrayals come from Ptolemaic Egypt (Hickmann, 1961a, illust. 105; Kinsky, 1930, plate 24:5). The Mareshah illustration is the earliest witness to this lute form, and may suggest that this particular variant from late antiquity with an elongated resonator actually originated in Ptolemaic Israel/Palestine or Idumea before moving out into other areas (Hickmann, 1961a).

During the course of its Hellenization, the Idumaic lute probably became shorter and smaller, and ultimately developed into the smaller form of the Tangara lute (third century B.C.; Fleischhauer, 1964, 98). The instrument played by a terra-cotta figure in the Eretz Israel Museum (illust. V.34) precisely resembles this smaller, pear-shaped lute with three strings. Unlike the female player of the Tangara lute, this player is using a rather large plectrum of the sort characteristic of Egyptian and, later, Arabic performances. The playing technique is also clearly discernible, the player executing rapid plectrum strokes with a quick movement of the wrist in the manner used by medieval *úd* players. The iconographic character is quite different as well. This lute player is nude and wears neck jewelry, whereas the Tangara player is sitting and is fully clothed; in this respect, our player recalls the terra-cotta tradition of female minstrels in ancient Israel/Palestine. Clearly this particular figurine does not evoke a scene of intimate house music or certainly a concert situation as in the case of the Tangara figure. These features evoke rather the loose, relaxed atmosphere of a banquet in a Near Eastern, Hellenistic port city at which the female minstrel might perform erotic love songs. It was precisely

V.34. Terra-cotta figurine, female lute player, PU, EIM 1870

V.35. Terra-cotta figurine, lute player, Beth Govrin, EE no. 1386

these pagan rites and the sensuality attaching to instrumental performances of this kind that made the orthodox rabbis and early church fathers so severely disinclined toward instrumental music.

Yet another sign of the profound changes that took place during the Hellenistic period is the first appearance of the harp since the fourth century B.C., contemporaneous with the renaissance of the lute. Significantly, every city in which terra-cotta figurines portraying harpists have been found was subject to strong Greek influences (illust. V.36, 37, 38); these cities include Idumaic Mareshah and the port cities of Dor and Jamnia.

The popular, small, portable angular harp was another type apparently quite well known in Israel/Palestine during the Roman period. Dor was a typical port city among the Greco-Roman provinces where Greek culture and deities were equally at home. It was previously a trade center of the sea peoples along the *Via Maris* and maintained active relations with virtually every part of the Mediterranean coast. The terra cotta found here (illust. V.36) depicts the figure of Cupid playing a harp. Although it is difficult to determine whether this piece was produced locally or im-

246

V.36. Terra-cotta figurine,
Cupid with harp, Dor,
IAA 85.34

ported, the topos itself, which portrays Cupid with the characteristic head covering together with a swan (or duck) and harp, attests an Egyptian cultural tradition. The figure of Cupid here, however, differs fundamentally from Ptolemaic-Seleucid examples insofar as it is holding the harp in a quite realistic playing position, striking the strings with his right hand by means of a plectrum; this particular performance technique is attested locally in other examples as well. The harp depicted in the Dor terra cotta is a small angular harp with a horizontal string holder and a vertical resonator. Found throughout the Near East, as a household instrument it was generally associated with women, and as a concert instrument with players of both genders. This instrument apparently represents the Greek *trígōnon,* an instrument preferred by young women and by professional and semiprofessional dancers and hetaerae as accompaniment for songs at celebrations and banquets. A second female harpist was found among imported Greek terra cottas in the port city of Jamnia, about 10 km. south of Jaffa (illust. V.38). Here the woman strikes the strings of a small, triangular harp, apparently a *trígōnon,* with her right hand (Fleischhauer, 1964). A terra cotta from Beth Govrin depicts a female harpist playing a similar instrument, though in this case the instrument is held upright (illust. V.37). The playing position in these final two examples is also of interest. In the first, the resonator is held vertically (illust. V.37), in the second, almost horizontally (illust. V.38). This distinction apparently also affected playing technique, since in the first example the player uses both hands, and in the second only one. Could these playing positions possibly reflect differences between concert performances on the one hand, and intimate chamber performances on the other?

V.37. Terra-cotta figurine, female harpist, Beth Govrin, EE Prof. A. Kloner

V.38. Terra-cotta figurine, female harpist, Jamnia, TAU, EE Prof. M. Fischer, YY97-92/7

248

The lyre appears on three terra cottas dating to this period. We have already discussed the Nabatean example with two lyres above (see illust. V.16). The second, described as a Samaritan lyre, is actually of unknown provenance and was acquired in Jerusalem by the Harvard Semitic Museum. I will discuss this piece in chapter V/6, and would say at this point only that this particular example (illust. V.53) depicts the lyre in a position in which it is impossible to play, much like several portrayals on the Gadara intaglios (illust. V.60a; V.61a), and clearly represents obsolete praxis. The third terra cotta is the fragment of an incense altar (illust. V.39) portraying Apollo nude and sitting on a *diphros*, or bench, with a lyre and his mother Leto. Here the rather large instrument is held upright, and seems to be portrayed during tuning or a pause rather than while actually being played. From now on, it will no longer be the lyres, but rather the portable, mobile lutes and harps suitable for virtuoso playing that will drive developments in musical life by providing professional virtuosos with more sophisticated performance possibilities.

V.39. Terra-cotta figurine, Apollo with lyre, Beth Govrin, EE Prof. A. Kloner

5. The Cult of Dionysus

Ancient Palestine, this tiny strip of land at the crossroads between Africa, Asia, and Europe, provided extraordinarily fertile ground into which the polytheistic ancient world could plant its bewildering variety of religious cults. One particularly interesting example is the cult of Dionysus, which experienced its golden age here in the breathtaking cultural fluidity of the last pre-Christian and first Christian centuries.

The most important center of the Dionysus cult in ancient Palestine was Scythopolis/Nysa (present-day Beth-shean), a city of the Roman Decapolis which according to mythological tradition Dionysus founded in honor of his nurse Nysa. This city, with the largest amphitheater in the Near East, was known far and wide during the second post-Christian century. During recent years, it has become one of the most significant excavation sites for materials associated with the Near Eastern tradition of Dionysus. A hexagonal altar 72 cm. high was unearthed in a basilica among various other items (Tsafrir/Förster, 1987/88, illust. 18). The *tabula ansata* recounts that a certain Seleucus erected the altar in honor of the founder of the city in the year 75 of the Scythopolis-Ra, that is, in the year A.D. 12. The symbolic ornamentation on the various sides of the altar includes a centrally positioned relief of Dionysus, two reliefs with horned figures of Pan, two with crossed thyrsi and one with a syrinx. At present, this altar represents the earliest evidence of music associated with the cult of Dionysus in ancient Palestine (illust. V.40).

The depicted instrument has seven pipes held together by a double ligature and represents a slightly modified fusion of the angular and winged form associated with what is known as the AB-group (Haas, 1985). The pipes in the upper register of this syrinx are more or less of equal length, while those in the lower register vary much more widely; this type is well attested in ancient Palestine, and its classic form with twelve pipes can be seen on the second/third-century grave drawing from Ashkelon (see chap. V/4). While exercising the requisite caution, I would suggest that the roots of this typical form of the syrinx in ancient Palestine may well be found in local musical praxis itself. In this view, the tonal series includes microintervals in the upper register and then much larger intervals — possibly even functioning as a drone — in the lower register. To my knowledge, the Scythopolis syrinx represents the earliest representation of this instrument in ancient Palestine; significantly even here, in its initial ap-

V.40. Dionysus, stone altar with panpipe, Beth-shean, *in situ*

pearance, it functions symbolically. Those who used this altar belonged to the well-to-do upper classes of a Hellenized, ethnically heterogeneous urban population (Nilsson, 1957).

It is probably on the Acco/Ptolemais coins from 125-110 B.C. that musical instruments first appear as symbols in ancient Israel/Palestine; they predate the altar of Dionysus by about a century (see chap. V/7). The front sides of these coins depict reliefs of Roman emperors resembling Apollo, while the reverse sides depict two different types of lyres. A certain series of portrayals employing musical instruments as symbols now begins. In the present case, the population of a commercial Near Eastern city adopted the musical instruments as a symbol from Greek coins. During the second Jewish revolt (132-35), the famous Bar Kokhba coins appear with their two different types of lyres and the pair of wind instruments (see chap. V/7); these coins were intended as an anti-Roman symbol enjoining both religious and political freedom. Several years later, in the second half of the second century, the Paneas/Caesarea Philippi coins were struck depicting the figure of Pan and various wind instruments, including the syrinx. These latter examples were in use among a broad segment of the urban pagan-Jewish-Christian population and were designed both to confirm loyalty to the central authority of the emperor and to function as a symbol of local municipal identity. At the same time, the organ now appears as a cultic symbol on an oil lamp from Samaria (see chap. V/6). One can thus legitimately say that it was during the period between the second pre-Christian and second post-Christian centuries that the symbolic portrayal of musical instruments became established among the various ethnic, religious, and social groups in ancient Palestine.

The most important materials associated with the cult of Dionysus, however, date to a later period than the altar in Scythopolis, in this case to the late Roman period between A.D. 70 and the mid-fourth century. The first example we will consider is the wonderful mosaic from the house of Sheikh Zouede from Gaza, now held by the Historical Museum of Ismailia. Although Jean Clédat discovered this mosaic eighty years ago near Gaza (Clédat, 1915), its significance for the musical culture of the time has prompted nothing more from scholars than a fleeting remark by Hans Hickmann (1949b, 85).

Sheikh Zouede's mosaic measures 4.75 × 3.0 m. and originally served as the floor of a triclinium (7.25 x 6.60 m.), or dining room, in a large building apparently belonging to a wealthy private individual and situated along the important caravan route between Egypt and Syria. The mosaic is divided into three parts; the largest portrays the triumphal procession of Dionysus with Bacchic and Heraclitic contamination. The mosaic as a whole contains a remarkable and rare plethora of musical instruments, more varied than even the most famous portrayals of this topos (illust. V.41a, b). The male centaur (illust. V.41c) is playing an instrument that can probably be associated with the Phrygian aulos, though in Hellenistic-Roman iconography it is usually the female centaur who plays this instrument. The coloring of the mosaic tesserae clearly shows that the drone horn, the *élymos,* is here a single-piece horn without finger holes rather than the pipe with a mounted horn typical of the Phrygian aulos. Hence what we have here is actually a drone horn, an instrument quite alien to the Roman tradition. What we cannot determine, however, is whether it has a trumpet- or oboe-type embouchure. In any event, the centaur also contradicts Roman performance technique insofar as he is holding the horn in his right hand.

Karl Gustav Fellerer (1956) has suggested that this particular playing technique, namely, with the horn in the right hand and the straight pipe in the left hand, was actually quite common from about the second century on. It seems to have flourished more on the periphery of the empire and may well have originated in such places where conventions associated with playing techniques were not as rigid. The second, linear pipe in this portrayal has either two or possibly three of the T-shaped *kéras* devices facilitating a change of tonal color. Yet here, too, the instrument clearly deviates from Roman praxis insofar as in the latter the *kérata* (plural of *kéras*) are always attached to the left pipe tube with the hornpiece or on both pipes. Here, the device appears only on the straight, left pipe.

The lyre held by the female centaur also contradicts Roman tradition. This lyre actually resembles the Egyptian lyres of the fourth and third pre-Christian centuries, the rare, geographically restricted lyres with extremely narrow, crescent-shaped resonators and curved side arms (Hickmann, 1960b).

The kind of lyre foot appearing on this instrument can also be seen on certain Roman sarcophagi (Matz, 1968, II, plate 174). As was the case with the horn on the Phrygian aulos mentioned earlier, the artist has emphasized the yoke arms by using a darker coloring, suggesting that here, too, we have a realistic portrayal of yoke arms made of horns of the sable antelope, the "oryxes, the horns of which are made into the sides of a lyre" (Herodotus, iv.192). The Jewish Bar Kokhba coins

(a)

(b)

V.41a, b. Sheikh Zouede mosaic floor, Gaza, Ismailia Historical Museum:
(a) photo; (b) relief drawing (from Hickmann 1949).
All photos of the mosaic by Prof. A. Ovadia

254

**V.41c. Sheikh Zouede mosaic floor, fragment, Dionysus
in chariot drawn by centaurs**

from the Roman period also depict such horns as side arms (see chap. V/7). In this particular instance, the lyre has six strings and six tuning pegs and is played with a plectrum. One question worth considering in this context is whether it is merely fortuitous that the male is playing the aulos, while the female is playing the lyre, or whether this distribution actually represents an interpretive change deriving from the period itself.

The presence of both the lyre and the Phrygian aulos in connection with the Dionysian chariot team clearly shows that Dionysian music was characterized by a profound and complex dualism. This chordophone-aerophone duality appears already in the cult of Cybele, where the lyre itself was firmly established (see chap. IV/4), and this cult now passes the dualism between stringed and wind instruments on to the cult of Dionysus. Although the complex instrumental symbolism attaching to the Dionysian musical *thíasos* (procession) has not yet been adequately researched, it cannot be understood as a simple wind instrument and percussion ensemble.

The central and constant iconographic feature of Dionysus's advent is precisely this team of centaurs guided by the small figure of Eros with Dionysus himself seated in the chariot. This *Dionysos teleté* is offering us a glimpse into an orgiastic ceremony or initiation into the Dionysian mysteries.

The next scenes in the Zouede mosaic are equally intriguing. In the first, Papposilenus (the silenus *par excellence* in the ancient Greek satyr plays) rides an ass accompanied by the dancing satyr Skirtus, who excitedly shakes a slap cymbal in each hand (illust. V.41d). In a scene positioned in the lower series, the same instrument appears between Pan and a satyr blowing a conch trumpet (illust. V.41e), where together with a syrinx it fills out the *horror vacui*. The portrayal is wonderfully detailed, and one easily discerns the ring holding the two slap cymbals together as is the case with the Egyptian-Coptic slap cymbals (Hickmann, 1949a). To the right, a disrobed maenad with opulent oriental adornment holds her tunic over her left arm and is ringing two bells. These figures, too, closely resemble Egyptian finds dating to the Roman period. One can hardly help but notice that this particular maenad is playing her bells with one hand over her head and the other behind her back precisely the way Spanish dancers do today when playing the castanets. This scene represents one of the rare portrayals of dancing accompanied by bells from such an early period. In the bottom row, a horned Pan also plays such slap cymbals (illust. V.41e); a second satyr has thrown an animal pelt *(nebrís)* over himself and is blowing a *kóchlos* (or conch trumpet, see chap. IV/5). Although Roman myths recount how this sea horn was played in the accompanying procession of Dionysus at the sea battle against the Indians (Nonnus, xxxiv.385), this instrument rarely occurs in connection with a triumphal procession.

This procession concludes with a dancing bacchante (illust. V.41f) holding a thyrsus in one hand while swinging a tympanum in the other. This instrument resembles those depicted on classical Greek vases and is simply a semispherical disk over which skin has been stretched. The bacchante parallels the nymph with tympanum and thyrsus spear on what is known as the Mildenhaller silver plate, which also dates to the Roman period (Merkelbach, 1988, illust. 85).

In summary, the Zouede mosaic offers us eleven portrayals of seven different musical instruments. They appear here both as genuine instruments that are actually being played and as symbolic representations. As such, this mosaic occupies an extraordinary position within the corpus of

V.41d. Sheikh Zouede mosaic floor, Satyr Skirtus with
slap cymbals and bacchante with bells

V.41e. Sheikh Zouede mosaic floor, Pan with
slap cymbals and satyr playing the horn

V.41f. Sheikh Zouede mosaic floor, bacchante with drum

iconography relating to Dionysus; one need only consider the two largest and most important groups portraying the Dionysian triumphant procession, namely, the Ptolemaic-Seleucid mosaics and the Italian-Roman sarcophagi, none of whose examples depict more than four different instruments at a time. One especially striking feature on the Zouede mosaic is the singular appearance of the slap cymbals, bells, and shell trumpets in connection with the Dionysian procession, three instruments otherwise profusely attested by archaeological finds within the Ptolemaic sphere. Finally, the syrinx is attested in connection with this procession in only one other instance, and significantly that example, too, is of Palestinian provenance (see illust. V.42).

The opulent scenery on the Zouede mosaic doubtless resembles Roman sarcophagi more than it does mosaics from northern Africa, and yet the topos itself, the anthropological type of the human figures, and the musical-organological features are ultimately rooted in quite realistic African-Ptolemaic models. Callixenus of Rhodes was an eyewitness of the spectacular theatrics accompanying such a triumphal Dionysian proces-

V.42. Lead sarcophagus fragment with Dionysus in chariot
drawn by centaurs (fragment), PU, EB

sion, and his account provides an extremely important written source
from Hellenistic Alexandria during the period of Ptolemy II Philadelphus
(285-247 B.C.). Callixenus describes a bewildering scene with a seemingly
endless procession of sileni, satyrs, nymphs, thousands of youths in purple
tunics, Dionysian statues, artists, and priests, wine containers, elephants,
two thousands bulls, eighty thousand cavalry riders and infantrymen, and
so on. Music and musical instruments were everywhere, as decoration,
symbols, fantasy objects, and then also as actual instruments both in solo
performance and as part of huge orchestras composed of sixty satyrs playing the aulos or of three hundred persons playing the *kithára* accompanying the presentation of images of kings and gods (cited in Athenaeus,
v.197-201).

Like many other parts of the cultural fabric, so also did beliefs, ceremonies, and artistic styles all start to loosen and change during the Hellenistic period. The active market economy and subsequent increased
wealth among certain portions of the population stimulated this process
even more. One consequence was a "revolution in communication." Alexandria maintained extremely active and far-reaching contacts with the
northern coastal cities along the *Via Maris,* including Gaza, Ashkelon,

Caesarea, Acco, and Tyre, and these contacts together with those with the Syrian Decapolis by way of the "Royal Highway" turned the Palestinian Roman provinces into one of the most significant crossroads in the ancient world. It was here that the Ptolemaic and Seleucid cultures met and mingled. From the Hellenistic period into late antiquity, the southeastern Mediterranean coast was a teeming center of musical activity and the place from which all sorts of cultural and artistic elements were exported elsewhere. This area produced the mystery cults with their own variety of music, as well as various new theatrical forms, and it was from here that countless cultic musicians traveled to all parts of the known world. Near Eastern mimes, dancers, and all sorts of musicians — functioning as entertainers themselves or as accompanists to dancers — were extremely popular as entertainers throughout the Roman Empire (Hitti, 1957; Mommsen, 1909). The first-century Roman satirist Juvenal speaks of these Near Eastern musical exports as a commonly accepted fact: "For a long time now, the Syrian Orontes has been flowing into the waters of the Tiber, bringing with it its languages and customs, its pipes and slanted strings, and let us not forget its native tympana and the girls who prostitute themselves!" (iii.58). The musical talents and proficiency, both vocal and instrumental, of the inhabitants of the Palestinian coast were famous throughout the Roman Empire and often drew the attention of authors. One anonymous fourth-century writer reports that "Laodicea exports its excellent jockeys to foreign countries; Tyre and Berytus send their actors; Caesarea its pantomimes, blessed with the gift of prophecy by the muses of Lebanon, and many aulos players. Gaza has excellent musicians . . Ashkelon excellent athletes" (Mueller, 1882, 519). This mention of Gaza is of particular interest to us in the present context. Gaza, home of the Zouede mosaic, was famous for centuries because of its excellent wines. During the fifth and sixth post-Christian centuries, it produced world-renowned philosophers and writers. During the fourth and fifth centuries, it may even have had its own production workshop for mosaics. Now we find that it was also famous for its musicians.

The extraordinary proliferation of music, dance, and theater in this region was not a mere fleeting phenomenon or singular development. It could have resulted only from centuries of development. Gaza must have had its own music school by the third or certainly the second pre-Christian century, and the overall musical praxis in Gaza doubtless also stimulated local visual artists as well; it was from this local music scene that these artists drew their examples, models, and even their own musical experiences.

The theme of the triumphal procession can be seen in a rather rare textual source providing us with an excellent example of cultural substitution in which the context and meaning are utterly changed, and yet the customary presentational forms remain essentially the same. 1 Maccabees 9:39 recounts a "triumphal procession" similar to the Dionysian, but now in a vastly different context and with a different meaning, namely, as a bridal procession. Dating to the second-third centuries, this passage describes the wedding of the daughter of one of the Nabatean nobles of Nebo as follows: "They looked out and saw a tumultuous procession with a great amount of baggage; and the bridegroom came out with his friends and his brothers to meet them with drums *(tympánōn)*, musical instruments *(mousikón)* and many weapons."

This same intercultural exchange of customs can also be found in descriptions of Jewish Palestinian wedding processions, which Shmuel Safrai describes as follows on the basis of Talmudic traditions dating to the time of Vespasian-Trajan (first/second century): "The bride's preparation consisted mainly of bathing, perfuming and anointing, and the arrangement of a complicated array of clothes and adornments. This completed, she was seated in a decorated carriage and, crowned with a wreath, driven through the main streets of the town to the accompaniment of song, dance, musical instruments and applause. When the bride was a virgin, it was customary for her to wear her hair loose" (Safrai/Stern, 1974).

The exact dating of the Zouede mosaic is still a matter of dispute, with suggestions ranging from the end of the second century (Clédat, 1915) to the beginning of the fifth century (Ovadia, 1991). I am inclined to date the piece to the pre-Byzantine period, that is, from the third to the first half of the fourth century, based on considerations of the musical-organological features discernible in this mosaic. These considerations include (1) the archaeological context, to which Jean Clédat already drew attention; (2) the actual sources of this theme, which goes back to the pre-Christian Ptolemaic culture; (3) the urban culture of Roman Gaza, which had been a center of excellent artistic and especially musical activity since at least the second century; (4) the fact that the Dionysian musical features of this mosaic apparently have no known precursor or model; and (5) the portrayal of the musical instruments themselves, which must be understood not as an archaic stylization, but as a largely correct and, to the extent the medium of the mosaic allows, also accurate rendering or illustration of musical praxis in Roman Palestine in the first-third centuries.

This processional theme also appears on a bronze sarcophagus fragment (64 × 40 cm.) of unknown provenance (illust. V.42), preserved at the École Biblique Jerusalem. Here Dionysus is seated in a chariot with a high back drawn by two minstrel centaurs and driven by a small figure of Eros. This team so closely resembles the Zouede mosaic that it probably represents a characteristic ancient Palestinian topos. This particular scene is framed by a wound rope or cord ornament of the sort found on other bronze sarcophagi as well. These sarcophagi represent typical products of local artisans and date to the period of the emperors, that is, to between the first and fourth century (Avi-Yonah, 1981). The overall typological similarity between this sarcophagus and the Zouede mosaic suggests that this sarcophagus was a product of regional artisans. The two instruments portrayed here add additional support to this assumption. On the one hand, the panpipe in this scene closely resembles the Palestinian bastard AB- or AA-type (Haas, 1985); on the other, the lyre played with a large plectrum certainly accords well with other examples of lyre iconography from the area.

The final witness in this context is the recently discovered and sensational mosaic floor from Sepphoris (Zippori), a piece exhibiting extraordinary artisanship and beauty (illust. V.43a).

Sepphoris, mentioned by Josephus and several other ancient authors, is located in Galilee a few kilometers from Nazareth. Like the Zouede mosaic, this one comes from a rather large, probably third-century house situated directly next to the local theater; as such, it probably belonged to a Roman or a Hellenized Jew (Chancey/Meyers 2000). Dionysian mysteries were often conducted or performed in the private residences of the wealthy in such cities, and this house was probably no exception. During this period, Sepphoris had a mixed Roman, Jewish, Christian population and was generally a city on the rise. Although Josephus does emphasize that pro-Roman sentiment ran high in Sepphoris (*B.J.* ii.18.11 and iii.2.4), it was nonetheless a center of Jewish cultural activity (Safrai/Stern II, 1976). Unlike the mosaics discussed above, this one draws more from Seleucid elements and more closely parallels the better examples of Antiochian works such as the Dionysus-Heracles drinking bout (Levi II, 1947, plate Ia).

Among the fifteen sections dealing with Dionysus and the U-shaped frame on the southern side, five scenes include musical instruments. Three of them portray familiar Dionysian musical topoi, including the drinking

V.43a. Mosaic floor, Sepphoris, *in situ*

bout between Heracles and Dionysus accompanied by a satyr playing a double aulos (illust. V.43b); the triumphal procession (the *Pompi*) in which yet another satyr plays the same type of aulos (illust. V.43c); and the presentation of gifts accompanied by a centaur playing a double aulos and a maenad beating a tympanum (the *Doresoroi*, illust. V.43d).

The two remaining scenes are rather unusual in the traditional Dionysian context. One is the *Komos* (illust. V.43e), the other a procession, perhaps an offering processional, though without any known mythological precedent (illust. V.43f). Both scenes depict female musicians playing the same double aulos found in the preceding scenes.

The term *kŏmos* is not fully understood. It is generally interpreted as a procession or tour following a symposium, a kind of "gay, raucous, drunken procession" (Pauly/Wissowa, 1957-90), often accompanied by fat dancing satyrs, music, song, and assorted other dancing (DeMarini, 1961). This ritual was still an active part of such banquets when the Sepphoris mosaic was produced, and the Syrian-Seleucid elements associated with it may be of some significance for the version we find on the mosaic. According to Isaak of Antiochia, the figure of Baalshamim, the "head of the gods," was "paraded around publicly with a tambourine and horn in Nisibis in

V.43b. Mosaic floor, Sepphoris, fragment, drinking bout
between Heracles and Dionysus

V.43c. Mosaic floor, Sepphoris, the
Dionysian *Pompi,* procession

V.43d. Mosaic floor, Sepphoris, *Doresori,* presentation of gifts

V.43e. Mosaic floor, Sepphoris, *Komos*

V.43f. Mosaic floor, Sepphoris, (sacrificial) procession?

the fourth/fifth century" (Bickermann, 1937, 114). Some archaeologists thus believe the scene depicted on the Sepphoris mosaic merely evokes "the 'joy' . . . of the Dionysiac rituals" (MeyersE et al., 1992). How else is one to explain this particular *kômos* scene, which contains neither drunkenness nor any procession nor any suggestion of a banquet situation? A similarly constructed scene appears on a mosaic in Sousse (Tunesia) depicting Virgil together with two muses (Dumbabin, 1978, illust. 130). Might one interpret the highly unusual *kômos* from Sepphoris perhaps as an allegory depicting the birth of a Dionysian *mysteria*, a drama, personified as a poetess inspired by a muse playing an aulos (perhaps Euterpe?) and a figure with a staff (Dionysus himself?)?

The scene of the procession with a female aulos player (illust. V.43f) is placed on the framing panel and, unlike the other scenes, has no title. The artist seems to have portrayed here the aulos player in a realistic setting including men, women, fruit baskets, poultry, a tripod, and other objects as part of what is probably an offering processional. This scene includes some elements which may indicate the presence of a Jewish tradition.

The wind instrument appearing in each of these five sections is consistently rendered, but no longer represents the Phrygian aulos found on the Zouede mosaic; instead, we now see a straight or linear double aulos, or more precisely a double tibia with pipes of unequal length (65 and 75 cm. long).

The instruments appearing in the triumphal procession, the drinking bout, and the *kômos* are of particular interest. The aulos itself as well as the position in which it is played have been rendered with extreme care, and we are able to discern on both pipes of these double tibia two different devices. The first are the T-shaped *kérata* already familiar from the Zouede mosaic by means of which the musician could close certain finger or tonal holes, thereby altering timbre and even mode. The second are the *cornicula* (sg. *corniculum*), long, pipe-shaped pegs jutting out in various directions by means of which the musician could change tonal color (Becker, 1966; Marcuse, 1975). The number of *kérata* and *cornicula* varies between one and seven, although the musician's hand may be concealing them in certain scenes. In other scenes they appear both on the bottom and on the top half of the instrument, between the musician's fingers and the mouthpiece. Both locations could be used during actual playing.

Unlike the instruments on the Zouede mosaic, those portrayed in the Sepphoris mosaic do not exhibit any discernible regional features. The kind of double aulos and frame drum chosen by the artist here resembles more the portrayals of the same instruments found in larger Greco-Roman cities and in the Seleucid sphere, suggesting perhaps that this mosaic artist was actually a foreigner living and working in Sepphoris.

Compared with the orgiastic atmosphere evoked by the Zouede mosaic, the scenes from Sepphoris are considerably calmer, even pastoral. Not nearly as many different musical instruments appear in the first place, and, significantly, there are no idiophones at all. An even more revealing observation is that the Dionysian iconography in both the triumphal procession (illust. V.43c) and the processional (illust. V.43f) has acquired discernible Christian and Jewish elements such as the halo around Dionysus himself, the ass and rider, and the cock offering. In reality, it was not uncommon for artists in Palestinian-Syrian border areas to mix pagan, Jewish, and Christian elements in their iconography: one need only recall the Dura-Europa synagogue with its David-Orpheus mural and Dionysian elements (Goodenough, 1964, IX). Erwin R. Goodenough has suggested that although the three main population groups in Roman Palestine, that is, the pagans, Jews, and Christians, all drew from a common inventory of symbols, they nonetheless interpreted those symbols differently. This explanation seems to apply quite well to the Sepphoris mosaic.

The Sepphoris mosaic and the Zouede mosaic differ in several fundamental respects. The overall style of the Sepphoris mosaic is more Antiochian-Greek, that of the Zouede mosaic more African-Roman. The instrumental accompaniments of the scenes in the two mosaics are also different: the Zoueda mosaic displays a rich variety of instruments, all of them of a more or less regional type, while on the Sepphoris mosaic only two instruments are depicted, and both belong to the Greek culture. So, for example, the orgiastic Phrygian aulos is played in the Zoueda scene, while in Sepphoris we have the classical double aulos. Finally, the semantic intentions of the two are in some ways almost diametrically opposed insofar as the Zouede scenes evoke an orgiastic-pagan atmosphere, those of the Sepphoris mosaic a considerably more pastoral, even Christianized-Judaized atmosphere. One of the medallions framing the Dionysian scene is perfectly intact and contains a remarkable portrait of a woman whom archaeologists have affectionately called the "Mona Lisa of the Galilee" (MeyersE et al., 1987; illust. V.43g). The woman seems to be surveying the entire scene and is portrayed so realistically that one cannot help but think she actually represents the house owner herself or perhaps one of the bacchantes or aulos players. In any event, if she does represent an actual person, she was doubtless one of those enlightened fourth-century women familiar with the Dionysian cult no less than with Christianity or Judaism. Certainly, though, she was a patron and admirer of art, music, and the sheer joy of life.

Our discussion of the instruments associated with the cult of Dionysus would be incomplete without our mentioning one extremely unusual phenomenon. All the musical instruments discussed in this chapter fit into the traditional Dionysian orchestra, with all its attendant local and chronological peculiarities already familiar from iconography throughout the region. One instrument, however, that rarely or never appears in the Dionysian ensemble, and indeed had disappeared altogether from the musical scene in ancient Israel/Palestine for almost a millennium, now suddenly reappears, and does so in this Dionysian context. I am referring to the lute. The lute terra cotta described in chap. V/4 above is of particular significance in this regard (see illust. V.35). This piece was found in Idumaic Mareshah, not far from Ashdod, an influential and important center of the early cult of Cybele and the Philistine Dagon cult. Although the lute never previously appears in any connection with Dionysus, the one on this terra

V.43g. Mosaic floor, Sepphoris, woman's portrait

cotta is played by Pan or by a satyr, clearly indicating some Dionysian connection. One can assume in this instance that the looser, even anticonser-
vative atmosphere surrounding the cult of Dionysus prompted and embraced such changes in the kinds of instruments associated with the
Dionysian ensemble in this region.

In the early Christian centuries Sepphoris started to change its ethnic-
religious image. A dominantly Jewish city in the pre-Christian centuries
and well into the third century, Sepphoris, renamed Docaesarea by
Antoninus Pius (138-61 C.E.), became more and more Hellenized toward
the fourth century (Chancey/Meyers, 2000). At this time, still with a remarkable Jewish population, it exhibited strong syncretist religious tendencies. Along with the above-discussed Dionysian mosaic, other artifacts
confirming the popularity of the Dionysian cult were discovered, among
them a small bronze figurine (second-third century) depicting a satyr
(Nagy et al., 1996, no. 17). The satyr is holding a panpipe of which three to
five pipes are visible. The quite mediocre craftsmanship of this artifact is in
great contrast to the superb mosaics.

Of special interest for the understanding of Sepphoris's cultural ambiance at this time is the zodiac on the mosaic floor excavated at the site of the Sepphoris synagogue (fifth century; Weiss/Netzer, 1996). This mosaic with a zodiac wheel in the center is part of a deeply rooted tradition in ancient synagogues, first attested at Hamat-Tiberias (fourth century; see chap. V/8; cf. Kuehnel, 2000). The Sepphoris synagogue mosaic, frequently compared in significance to the Dura-Europa wall paintings, is probably the best evidence of the pagan-Jewish-Christian cultural syncretism that blossomed from Hellenistic/Roman times to sixth-century-c.e. Palestine and produced numerous works of visual and, possibly, musical arts.

Part of the zodiac circle has been damaged, including the section representing the sign of Gemini. However, we can still see the figures of two youths symbolizing that sign; the youth on the right holds a large lyre (90-110 cm.) with three strings (illust. V.44). This is to my knowledge the only zodiac representation that contains a musical instrument. The lyre, considered the symbol of spiritual and physical consentaneity and harmony in both Jewish and Christian thought (Giesel, 1978), is placed in the twin section. Twins are the symbol of likeness. The Hebrew word for twins is *tᵉᵓômîm* (plural, from *tᵉᵓôm*), deriving from the word *teum*, which means "similarity, coordination, equalization, harmony." The zodiac was considered to be the "representative par excellence of the cosmos" and the symbol of God, the creator of the universe and order (see Kuehnel, 2000, 37). The concept of cosmic music, which was introduced by church father Anicius Manlius Severinus Boethius (ca. 480-524) and dominated the philosophy of music during the entire Middle Ages, came into use at the time when the Sepphoris synagogue was built. Should the Sepphoris zodiac lyre then be a symbol of this harmony and order? And do the Twins with their lyre symbolize the order of *musica mundana* and *musica humana*? According to Boethius, the first term refers to the "music of the spheres," the orderly mathematical relations observable in the behavior of the stars and planets, and the second to the ways in which such harmonious relations are printed on and exemplified in the soul and body of humans (Grout, 1973, 23).

The lyre depicted, while damaged at its upper part, may be classified as belonging to a type of symmetrical lyre with rounded base, an instrument popular at joyful folk feasts such as the Dionysos processions (cf. the lyre on illust. V.41). This lyre is very similar to the instrument depicted as that of the David-Orpheus on the Dura-Europos synagogue mural, and

V.44. Mosaic floor, Sepphoris synagogue, Gemini with lyre (drawing)

strongly differs from the stylized kitharas (large concert instruments) that appear on the Palestine Orpheus mosaics of the fourth to sixth centuries (Sepphoris, Jerusalem, Beth-shean; see Ovadia 1987) and in Gaza with the inscription "David" (illust. V.45).

At this time in ancient Palestine, the people participating in Dionysian processions and mysteries were anything but a homogeneous group, and they doubtless took great pleasure in the colorful, even spectacular portrayals of the various activities associated with the cult. Regional deities of the Nabateans, Philistines, and Phoenicians all embody certain Dionysian elements. When confronted with such deities, it is often simply impossible to determine whether a given example represents a Greek interpretation of a Levantine deity, or a local adaptation of a Greek deity (Safrai/Stern, 1976). Contemporary written sources confirm that Jewish sectors of the population were far from immune to such Hellenizing tendencies. Such was especially the case among the educated or intellectual class who wished for a reformation (1 Macc. 1:11). Such groups not only

V.45. Mosaic floor, Gaza, with inscription "David" and lyre player,
photo by IAA

accepted and frequented the Greek institutions of the gymnasium and sporting events (2 Macc. 4:11), but also embraced the Dionysian cult itself as the official state religion, welcoming it as a cultural device facilitating assimilation and an improvement of one's social status. Archaeological finds have confirmed that Roman, Jewish, and Christian inclinations were especially pronounced in Sepphoris (Sepphoris, 1988). At least to some extent, Jewish intellectual and spiritual leaders did permit participation in pagan cults. "Syncretism, or *shituf* [(Heb. 'participation'], as the rabbis called this recognition of plural divine control of the cosmos, was widespread" (Bickermann, 1988, 252-53). Many Jews in Egypt actually bore the name "Dionysus," and receipts have been found for fees paid by Jews in connection with the festivals of Dionysus (Tcherikover, 1957). This cult was also a source of conflict between Greeks and Jews. Second Maccabees 6:7 recounts "when a festival of Dionysus was celebrated, they [the Jews] were compelled to wear wreathes of ivy and to walk in the procession in honor of Dionysus." In 167 B.C., the Jewish temple itself in Jerusalem was desecrated through a Dionysian ceremony.

Whenever ancient authors compare the customs associated with Jewish and Dionysian rituals, they invariably focus on the music. In his *Quaestiones Conviviales* (iv.2), Plutarch remarks that "a few days later they [the Jews] celebrate yet another festival, this one now dedicated quite openly to Bacchus. One might call it a Kradephoria or Thyrsophoria because they enter the temple itself with palm fronds and thyrsus-staffs. We do not know what they actually do in the temple, but one might assume they conduct some sort of celebration to Bacchus since to invoke the god they use small trumpets of the sort the Argives use at their own Dionysian ceremonies. Others, whom they call Levites, play the cithara when they come out."

Plutarch mentions other parallels with the Dionysian ritual, including the garments of the Jewish high priest leading the procession, his long cloak with its many small bells (cf. Ex. 28:33-34), and the playing of drums in the temple (vi.1), a feature incidentally not attested by any Jewish sources. Certain features associated with the music played at such Jewish celebrations also reminded Tacitus of the Dionysian ritual; the priests, he recounts, sang psalms accompanied by tibia and tympanum, and he notes that "because these priests sang accompanied by pipes and cymbals and wore wreaths of ivy, and because golden wine was found in their temple, one thought they actually worshiped the *liber pater*, the conqueror of the Orient, despite the contradictory nature of their customs" (*Hist.* v.5).

At least one Jewish source recounts a ritual apparently including singing and dancing that did indeed evoke associations with Bacchic and ecstatic rapture. In his account of the Therapeutae, a small Jewish sect that established itself briefly near Alexandria, Philo mentions ritualistic vigils that included a meal and the singing of hymns by a double chorus (with and without dancing) as accompaniment to the processions and libations. Both men and women participated in this bacchic wine drinking and ecstatic singing and dancing, though the text does not make clear whether Philo intended these activities as allegories or whether they had some basis in reality (*Vit. Cont.* 80-89).

Of course, the musical customs of various socioethnic groups can be quite similar and yet still not indicate any genuine or substantive cultural kinship. Considering the geographical and chronological concentration of cultural factors obtaining in ancient Palestine, however, one should probably allow for at least a certain measure of cultural and musical syncretism. In any event, the variety of sources associated with the cult of Dionysus doubtless reflects the complexity of musical life throughout society in Roman Palestine. Although the two mosaics discussed above both emanate from the Dionysian cult, they present two different social, intellectual, spiritual, and musical worlds. In the multicultural polytheistic ambience of ancient Israel/Palestine, they symbolize the heterogeneous-in-the-homogeneous element of this culture.

6. Musical Instruments in Samaritan Areas

One of the most puzzling questions in musicological studies is one that in reality has never been genuinely discussed, with scholars tending simply to accept that the issue has been resolved and needs no further attention. The issue concerns which instruments the Samaritans used during the pre-Islamic period, and what kind of music they made with such instruments. Its resolution has been as primitive as it is unequivocal: the Old Testament forbids musical instruments (an indirect prohibition can be found in Hos. 9:1, a prophetic reference in Isa. 24:8), hence the Samaritans have no instrumental music. In its article on Samaritan music, the NGD mentions neither musical instruments nor instrumental music. As late as 1993, even the foremost Samaritan lexicon (Crown/Pummer/Tal, 1993) was still representing this restricted view, a view apparently based on nineteenth-century sources. One such source is the Palestinian travelogue of the Frenchman Claude Renier Conder, which was widely accepted by contemporary scholars: "He [Conder] stresses that the Samaritans sing their old hymns without any instrumental music, and appear not to have any such music" (Shur, 1992). Although it is true enough that contemporary Samaritan liturgical music does not have an instrumental component, and that the shofar is not used, we still do not know exactly when the prohibition against sounding the horn actually took effect. Studies of musical instruments in the ancient world and even modern studies of music in ancient Israel/Palestine or Rome completely ignore the Samaritan musical culture even though it certainly represents one of the most interesting cultural phenomena in the entire ancient Near East. Scholars generally agree that the Samaritan musical culture was closely associated with the original sources of liturgical singing, and much suggests that the history not only of Samaritan vocal music, but also of its instruments and instrumental music contains unique and certainly enigmatic information.

Because archaeological evidence has provided us with a considerable and significant corpus of diverse portrayals of musical instruments relating to the Samaritan culture, one simply cannot transfer the modern Samaritan prohibition against instrumental music onto the Samaritan past without entering into severe contradictions. Even if one does accept Samaria as the site where these artifacts were found, it is still extremely difficult to associate the various objects with any specific national or religious group given the extraordinarily heterogeneous population and advanced cultural syncretism that characterized Hellenistic-Roman Samaria.

The postexilic Judean-Samaritan schism (after the sixth century B.C.) worsened during the Persian and especially the Hellenistic period, when both theological and formal cultic differences became more pronounced. The Hellenistic period itself hastened this process, and the final separation came during the period of the Roman emperors. Despite this alienation, however, Jews, Samaritans, pagans, and Christians shared a common, albeit quite heterogeneous environment. Archaeological finds from the Samaritan sphere constitute a disinct, consistent, and identifiable corpus because of their iconographic-artistic stylistic unity and peculiarities, features setting them apart both artistically and within the narrower confines of musical history from all other known artifacts from ancient Israel/ Palestine. It is no accident that these very identifying features came to expression during the period when the sovereign Samaritan system of faith, cult, and symbols was finally consolidated. At that time, it was an expression of the Samaritans' autonomous ideological and artistic identity, an identity that faded away during the crisis years that were to follow in later centuries. Until further information becomes available, we have no reason to continue to ignore what the archaeological evidence unequivocally suggests, namely, that musicians within Samaritan circles in ancient Samaria did indeed produce instrumental music.

Two Samaritan coins, the only extant examples of this particular coinage, represent the earliest pieces of evidence in this regard (illust. V.46a, b). Dating to the fourth century B.C., they come from a rather large corpus of

V.46. Samaritan coins, PU, PC: (a) IAA 1442.1; (b) copy from
Meshorer/Qadar; 1999, No. 129

coins deriving in part from excavations in Samaria itself and in part from extant archaeological collections (Meshorer, 1999). One side of the coin depicts a seated, nude, bearded man plucking a large lyre (1.0–1.20 m. tall) with his right hand while his left hand damps the strings from the back side, a familiar playing technique associated with both Near Eastern and African lyres.

This instrument, which has been given a fairly detailed rendering, is an asymmetrical lyre with five or six strings strung in a fan shape. The last string before the longer side arm is attached directly to the arm itself, a highly unusual feature, and may be either a representation of a previously unknown method, by which the bass string was attached to the side arm of the instrument, or simply an inaccurate drawing. The drawing seems realistic insofar as the strings extend beyond the resonator. This asymmetrical lyre with its fan-shaped string arrangement, curved side arms, and rectangular resonator, has not been previously attested in ancient Israel/Palestine. Similar forms, albeit with straight rather than fanned strings, appear in this region in the second millennium B.C., which is why this instrument does indeed seem rather archaic (see Table 2). By contrast, the topos of a seated lyre player is certainly familiar enough in ancient Israel/Palestine and appears on seals, drawings, and gems (see illust. IV.23, 25, V.60d). The object at the feet of the player is difficult to identity, and may be either a fertility symbol or perhaps the letter "W" (Keel/Keel-Leu/Schoer, 1989).

The well-known Israeli numismatist Yaacov Meshorer believes "that this figure may represent some aspect of Samaritan religious practice. . ." similar to the Jerusalem Temple (Meshorer, 1999, 35). As attractive as this interpretation may well be, it is difficult to imagine a nude Samaritan temple musician portrayed without any indication or sign of his spiritual office. The player more likely represents a semidivine figure, perhaps Apollo-Orpheus-David, in the syncretistic spirit of the later Jewish-Christian iconography of this type. The image of the seated nude Apollo is a well-known topos of Greek vase painting, and the Greek religious cults were certainly embraced in Samaria alongside the Yahwistic faith. The musician's beard in any case deviates from what is normally associated with the figure of Apollo, and may be evoking the figure of David instead, who was extremely popular among the Samaritans. Features on several examples of Samaritan oil-lamp iconography are often even interpreted as the wagon, shaft, and other attributes associated with the transport of the ark, at which David played and danced (1 Ch. 15:29). And indeed, the unidentified object at the feet of the lyre player here does resemble a shaft of the sort appearing on the Samaritan oil lamps. The above-mentioned recent revelations by Meshorer (see p. 152) on the continuity of 'Ajrud and Samaritan iconographical topoi would explain a connection to the Iron Age lyre forms (see Table 2/8, 9, 10). The Samaritan lyre, however, cannot be so easily classified among the types already familiar in ancient Israel/Palestine. The only way to place this instrument into a musical context is to affiliate it with the Bronze Age instruments from the Negev and Megiddo (see Table 2/1, 2, 3, 4). This may give a possible foreign provenance to this mint, but it marks it as archaic even for the time of the 'Ajrud finds, which seem to indicate the origin of Samaritan iconography. Should Samaritan musical culture reach back as far as the Bronze Age? Or could this lyre player be an example of keeping an ancient mythological tradition, possibly Mesopotamian (cf. illust. III.2a), indicated by the stylized cuneiform signs on the lyre player coins (see V.46b)?

Another five centuries now pass before topoi related to music appear again in the Samaritan sphere that are attributable to the Samaritan culture itself.

Although until this time the shofar has appeared neither as part of Samaritan worship nor as a cultic symbol, it now appears in several artifacts in an idiomatic form deviating in many ways from Judean iconography and with features requiring that it be interpreted as a cultic symbol. As on many Judean oil lamps, it appears on Samaritan lamps as part of a symbolic grouping that includes the *m^enôrâ, šôpār, māḥtâ, lûlāv* and *'etrôg* (see chap. V/8), except that here the *šôpār* is placed symmetrically on either side of the menorah (illust. V.47). The same doubled position of the shofar appears on another artifact as well, actually one of the most significant finds associated with this Samaritan grouping, the mosaic floor of the Samaritan synagogue in El-Chirba (illust. V.48). After these two shofars were interpreted as trumpets (Magen, 1992), the conclusion reached in the ensuing discussion suggested that the El-Chirba artists doubtless intended to portray the two temple trumpets (Magen, 1993), since the Samaritans recognized only the Pentateuch, the part of the Bible that does indeed mention these two trumpets (Nu. 10:2-10). The iconography on the mosaic, however, refutes precisely this argument, since besides the two horns it also includes the *māḥtâ*, which is not mentioned in the first five books of the Old Testament. Moreover, the two quasi-trumpets in the El-Chirba mosaic also resemble the shofars in the Sepphoris synagogue (see illust. V.64). A

V.47. Terra-cotta oil lamp with two shofars, Samaria, IAA 32.2395

V.48. Mosaic floor, El Chirba, photo by Dr. Y. Magen

279

comparison with the horn or wind instrument in another mosaic panel from the Sepphoris synagogue (see illust. V.15) containing the superscription *ḥᵃṣōṣᵉrâ*, "trumpet," does not help here because of the structure of the horn depicted. Although the artist may well have intended to depict a trumpet, we cannot determine whether he was actually envisioning the trumpet or the shofar. What we can say in either case is that he portrayed a form of the shofar that was obviously quite familiar to him.

Other archaeological evidence, including Samaritan oil lamps, does not support this trumpet interpretation. They are rather robustly made and exhibit a different style. The shrine is portrayed on the lamp's nose end, and all the cultic accoutrements (shofar, *māḥtâ*, vessels, a table, and several unidentified objects) are distributed across the entire surface area. On one piece (illust. V.49), one can read the word *qûmâ*, "arise [O Yahweh]" (Nu. 10:35), confirming the cultic symbolism of this particular lamp. Here a single *šôpār* is depicted. On yet another lamp (illust. V.50), a trumpet is clearly visible next to the *māḥtâ*. Two crossed trumpets appear on the nose end of two additional lamps (illust. V.51), a position that may represent a realistic portrayal of how these trumpets were actually stored, since a similar position also appears on the Arch of Titus (see illust. V.14). In fact, this archaeological evidence seems to attest that both instruments, the shofar as well as the trumpet, had a place in Samaritan iconography.

Some historians think the remarkably well-preserved mosaic from the Beth-shean synagogue (see illust. V.63) is Samaritan (Shur, 1992). During a certain period, this synagogue did indeed fall within the ambience of the Samaritan culture, and a Samaritan inscription has even been found in a side room dating to a later period than the building itself. Still it is difficult to determine whether the synagogue was Jewish or Samaritan. Although the complete identification of this mosaic with that from Ḥammat Tiberias militates in favor of its Jewish origin, it is also possible that over the course of its history the synagogue itself changed hands.

One rare and singular find is an oil lamp (illust. V.52) depicting several different musical instruments. It includes a symmetrical lyre with a rectangular resonator and seven or eight parallel strings, two separate pipes of a double aulos with *kérata*, and cymbals. The image on the nose end of the lamp has been interpreted as the Table for the Bread of the Presence (see 1 K. 7:48; Sussmann, 1986/87). It is also possible that the image actually depicts shell-shaped percussion instruments filled with water (see

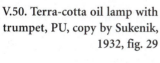

V.49. Terra-cotta oil lamp with shofar, Nathania, IAA 82-1051

V.50. Terra-cotta oil lamp with trumpet, PU, copy by Sukenik, 1932, fig. 29

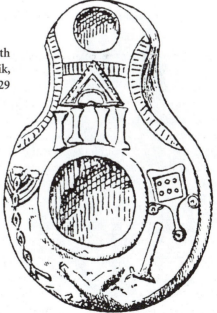

V.51. Terra-cotta oil lamp with two trumpets, private collection, Jerusalem

V.52. Terra-cotta oil lamp with double aulos, lyre, cymbals, water bowls, and unidentified symbols, PC, photo by Dr. M. Broshi

below); in that case, this lamp would be the only known Judean-Samaritan iconographical representation of these musical instruments, instruments one might interpret as having cultic connections based on parallels with other Judean-Samaritan lamps depicting exclusively cultic objects. This unique Samaritan witness is of enormous significance and seems to confirm the presence of an independent Samaritan musical instrument corpus. Yet another oil lamp (Sussmann, 1986/87, fig. 4) depicts a menorah in its upper part as well as symmetrically arranged cymbals on either side (representing perhaps Dionysian *paterae,* or offering dishes?); three small disks (cymbals?) are arranged in a circle. The instrumental groups on these two lamps portray several instruments quite realistically that in part have never been associated with cultic music; one must conclude that at some time the Samaritan population was familiar with precisely these instruments. The artists may have intended for these musical instruments from the Hellenistic-Roman period to represent the instruments of the first temple, and if such is the case, it is certainly understandable that they chose instruments from their contemporary musical environment.

Some of the instruments portrayed here also appear among the archaeological finds from the Samaritan sphere. Considering that two of the four known aulos examples in ancient Israel/Palestine come from Samaria (see illust. V.22; V.23), it is possible that Samaria even had its own aulos workshop.

Archaeological evidence relating to chordophones does not appear very often in the Samaritan context. One terra-cotta fragment from Harvard University's excavations in Samaria depicts a youth playing the harp (Reisner, 1924, plate 76:9), though the portrayal itself is extremely vague and unclear. By contrast, another terra cotta in the Harvard Semitic Museum (illust. V.53) thought to be of Samaritan provenance is quite expressive, depicting a bearded man in a tunic and wearing a priest's cap; he is playing a small symmetrical lyre (25-30 cm. high) held at shoulder height and with not more than five or six strings. The instrument has a cross arm and extending side arms, is both artistically and technically sophisticated, and was doubtless used by a professional musician. Given the head covering, the beard, and the professional quality of the musical instrument, this Samaritan lyre player can probably be viewed as a local temple servant, perhaps of the rank of a Levite. One point, however, should be made in this context; although the instrument itself is realistically rendered, the musician is holding it in an impossible playing position. The artist intended the instrument to be understood symbolically, that is, as identify-

V.53. Plaque terra cotta
(lyre player), Samaria (?),
HSM 907.64.474

ing the musician as a cultic servant or guild musician, and was not trying
to portray an actual playing situation.

Yet another group of unique artifacts is of particular significance in
this Samaritan context. Six third/fourth-century Samaritan oil lamps
(illust. V.54a-b; see also V.30a-b; Sussmann, 1978) provide iconographical
evidence of the Hellenistic-Roman organ, an instrument invented in Alexandria only a few centuries earlier. These lamps represent the first and at
this time only witness to the organ in ancient Israel/Palestine during this
period. In addition to the organ, each lamp also depicts two pairs of forked
cymbals (often called *crotalum*).

The placement of the iconography on these lamps is of particular significance.
With the opening located in the middle similar to other Jewish and Samaritan oil
lamps and the depiction situated on the sides and nose end of the lamp (in contrast to Roman lamps, which locate the iconography in the middle), the picture is
readable when the lamp is held with the nose end down (in contrast to Jewish and
Samaritan lamps). This stylistic peculiarity may indicate the presence of Greco-
Roman influence on the one hand, and an autochthonous Samaritan artisanship

284

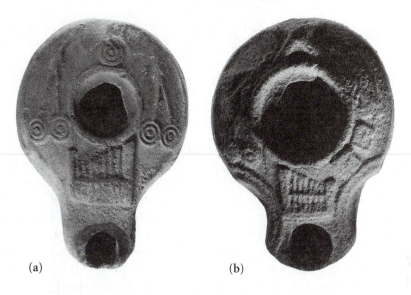

(a)   (b)

V.54a, b. Oil lamps with organ and slap cymbals, PU, PC

on the other. Even considering that the only archaeologically attested lamp among this group was a surface find, and that the others do indeed come from the antiquities trade rather than from regulated excavations, still the fact that all six appeared only in Israel and are attested nowhere else suggests they were produced locally. The instruments on the lamp's nose end are not harps, as suggested by archaeologists, but the upper, characteristic part of the organ, namely, the pipes, and the instruments on each side of the central opening are *crotala*. A cross strip of the sort found on early Roman organs holds the seven pipes together. Although the bellows, as is often the case, are not shown here, the openings at the upper ends of the pipes are clearly discernible. On the basis of other third/fourth-century iconography, this particular instrument probably represents the small pneumatic table organ played by women rather than the hydraulic organ. Each organ is portrayed with seven pipes probably because of the numerology associated with the number seven, the sacred number for both Jews and Samaritans. The number of pipes as well as the proportions between the shortest and longest ones (approximately 2:3) suggest that these organs represent the popular Hellenistic-Roman instruments capable of producing a tonal series of approximately equal half-steps encompassing an overall interval of a fifth (see Perrot 1971).

One characteristic of Samaritan organ iconography is that the organ is always accompanied by either one or two pairs of *crotala*. These small cymbals, whose form hardly changed after the Bronze Age, measured about 4-6 cm. across and are

285

richly attested in excavations even down into the Byzantine period, albeit without any remnants of their forked handle. The topos on these lamps attests the presence in antiquity of the kind of organ/*crotala* ensemble that became so popular later in the Middle Ages. This same grouping appears as early as the third century in a Syrian mosaic from Hama depicting it in a women's ensemble (Zaqzuq/Duchesne-Guillemine, 1970).

It is no accident that the organ appears on oil lamps in ancient Israel/Palestine. The symbolic pair of lamp and organ is attested as early as the second century on Carthaginian lamps (Perrot, 1971). The organ was the only musical instrument accepted by the church, and the early-Christian symbolism of the fourth-century eastern Alexandrian school (Gregory of Nyssa, Athanasius of Alexandria) understood it as reflecting the Holy Spirit, just as the Old Testament found the human spirit reflected in God's lamp, the menorah (Prov. 20:27).

Several questions remain in this context. Was the organ indeed an instrument associated with the Samaritan liturgy? Did the Samaritans identify it as an instrument of the first temple? Or did these oil lamps belong to an entirely different culture in the first place? Although we cannot answer these questions unequivocally at this time, the iconography on these lamps depicts a modern third/fourth-century organ together with *crotala* in a Near Eastern musical context. It is possible that this instrument was used in the Samaritan-Jewish liturgy during the Hellenistic-Roman period.

The Hama mosaic mentioned earlier depicts not only the organ, which alone is laden with information relating to the actual music scene, but also the entire corpus of Samaritan musical instruments attested archaeologically either individually or in groups on the artifacts already discussed. This document is of enormous significance for Near Eastern archaeology related to music from the pre-Roman period. It was found in 1960 in the Syrian village of Mariamin and is currently kept in the regional museum in Hama. This extremely realistic work of art portrays an entire women's ensemble in concert. One female musician is playing the pneumatic organ while two small angels operate the bellows. Alongside her a second female musician beats forked cymbals in either hand. We also see a double-aulos player holding a separate pipe in each hand, as well as a lyre player and a musician with bells. In the middle, a musician uses drumsticks to play what appear to be shells filled with water arranged on a table; this type of percussion instrument was common in the Near East, and the fifth/sixth-century Viennese Genesis identifies it as the instrument of a Pharaoh. It is no accident that the musical instruments attested on the Samaritan artifacts so closely resemble those on the Hama mosaic; we can see that Seleucid elements must have exerted considerable influence on Samaritan music.

These archaeological finds do not permit us to assert that during the Hellenistic-Roman period instrumental music could be found in Samaritan daily life as well as in its liturgy. At the same time, however, we are ill-advised to ignore the diversity and sheer quantity of archaeological evidence for instrumental music within the Samaritan sphere; moreover, within ancient Israel/Palestine as a whole, musical instruments are attested most voluminously and unequivocally precisely in cultic contexts. Similarly, we need to recall that it was here, in the Samaritan sphere, that the most advanced aerophones of the Hellenistic-Roman period were found, here that the most innovative developments took place with regard to musical instruments themselves, and here that evidence suggests an extremely sophisticated group of professional musicians was practicing their trade. Given this evidence, one simply cannot continue to assert that instrumental music was totally absent in the Samaritan culture.

7. Musical Instruments as Symbols of Cult, State, and Identity

One of the most pregnant expressions of cultural, national, ethnic, and cultic identity is the minted coin. In antiquity, iconography on such coins included the gods, mythological figures and subjects, cultic edifices and objects, rulers, divinized animals, and sacred plants. Musical instruments are portrayed both in the hands of mythological figures and cultic servants and as symbols either accompanying such figures or independently.

Lyres as integral parts of Greek culture, education, and ethics were portrayed on Greek coins beginning in the sixth century B.C. as symbols of the Greek folkway. At the beginning, lyres were portrayed with extraordinary care and quite realistically; over time, however, the portrayals became less realistic and increasingly symbolic, the result being that artists later often portrayed extremely dated or archaic, even abstract instruments. Indeed, the Bar Kokhba and [[Maʿadana]] lyres portrayed on modern Israeli coins are excellent examples of such idealized or archaic instruments (illust. V.55a, b, see illust. IV.30 and V.57a). What this idealization means

287

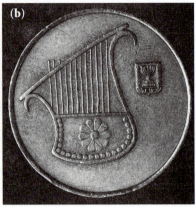

V.55. Modern Israeli coins with historical lyres: (a) from Bar Kohba coin;
(b) from [[Maʿadana]] seal

for the present study is that great care must be exercised when analyzing the iconography on such coins.

Musical instruments and musicians appear on three different groups of coins from ancient Israel/Palestine, the oldest group being that of the Acco-Ptolemais coins. Acco was a mature port city on the northern coast of ancient Israel/Palestine from at least the ninth-eighth centuries B.C.; for centuries, it was associated with the Phoenician culture and was one of the first city states to strike its own coins in Israel/Palestine around the mid-fourth century B.C. Coins struck during the period of the Antiochians (second century B.C.) with the legend *Antiocheon ton en Ptolemaidi* include a small group from the years 125/24, 112/11, and 111/110 B.C. depicting the head of Apollo on one side and a three-stringed lyre on the reverse side, a combination actually quite common during the Hellenistic period (illust. V.56a-b). Much suggests that these Acco lyres were produced locally rather than being mere copies of Greek lyres. This elegant, symmetrical instrument, which does not appear much earlier than the late Hellenistic period, had an elongated resonator, gently curved, S-shaped side arms, a small, characteristic inwardly curved hook on the yoke arms, and spherical ornaments on the cross and side arms. Even if the three strings depicted on the lyre in illust. V.56a (type A) do not represent the precise number, they do suggest a rather restricted number of strings, though a symmetrical lyre

288

(a) (b)

V.56. Acco coins depicting lyres: (a) type A, HAM 1156, (b) type B, HAM 1205

(type B) on yet another coin (illust. V.56b) has six strings. This unique model apparently had horn-shaped yoke arms and a resonator possibly made from a turtle shell. The six nodes where the strings were fastened to the cross arm are clearly discernible. Similar lyres, also with six strings, appear a mere two or three centuries later on coins from Syrian Antioch (Vorreiter, 1983, plate XV:1). Both the A and B types of lyres from Acco may have served as prototypes for the lyres associated with later portrayals, including the second group of coins from ancient Israel/Palestine, the Bar Kokhba coins. This double lyre imagery probably reflects the two forms this instrument had in ancient Israel/Palestine, and it ultimately came to characterize lyre iconography in this region during the Hellenistic-Roman period.

Coins associated with the second group represent some of the most significant documents of Jewish history; they bear the legend *šimon nassi yisrael* (Simon, Prince of Israel) and date to the period of the Second Jewish War (132-135). These coins were produced in great numbers as a result of a general recycling of Roman and other coins. The latter were restruck, this time with both national-religious as well as traditional Near Eastern symbols, including the temple facade, sacred greenery and fruits, the menorah, temple accoutrements, grape combs, palm fronds, garlands, and musical instruments. The Bar Kokhba coins appeared in private collections during the eighteenth century and were already being adduced in connection with musicological studies in 1817 (Jahn, 1817). They depict the two kinds of Acco lyre types mentioned above: type A (illust. V.57a, b), which is slender and has an elongated resonator made of two parts, probably of wood, and with thin side arms shaped in an elegant "S"; this type had three strings; and type B (illust. V.57c, d), a more cumbersome instrument, with side arms made from goat horns, between three and seven strings, a resonator apparently made from a wooden frame over which leather had been stretched, and with the strings attached to the resonator with an auxiliary piece.

Neither group portrays the strings extending beyond the resonator as is usually the case, suggesting that the portrayal itself has been stylized a bit. Only with extreme caution can one accept the usual assertion that the Bar Kokhba lyres accurately represent the instruments used during the period of the second temple. Apart from a few insignificant details, these lyres represent both the local prototype found in the Acco lyres and certain Hellenistic-Roman parallels. The A-type resembles a first-century statue group, the "Farnese Bull," from Tralles (modern Aydin) (Naples, Museo Nazionale), and iconography from Tyras (A.D. 35; Pick, 1910, plate XII:17), Caria (first century A.D., Anson, 1910, VI, no. 381), and Lycia (ca. A.D. 50, MMB, no. 643). The B-type resembles iconography from Rome (A.D. 85; Vorreiter, 1978/79, illust. 4:a) and Istrus (A.D. 15; Pick, 1910, I/2, no. 514). Numismatic studies offer no support in referring to the A-group as kithára/nēḇel and the B-group as chélys/kinnôr (Romanoff, 1944), terminology still used by some scholars even today (Mildenberg, 1984). Bathia Bayer (1968a) adduced voluminous written sources in determining that the A-type represented the kinnôr, the B-type the nēḇel. Contemporary sources assert that the kinnôr had ten thin strings and was played with a plectrum in an ensemble of no fewer than nine instruments (m. 'Arak. 2:3; Josephus, Ant. vii.12.3; m. Qinnim 3:6), whereas the nēḇel had twelve thicker strings and was struck or plucked by the hand alone. Its resonator was allegedly made of lotus wood ribbing, and an ensemble was to include at least two but no more than six instruments (m. 'Arak. 2:5; Josephus, Ant. vii.12.3; m. Qinnim 3:6). This information suggests that the kinnôr was a treble instrument, the nēḇel a tenor or bass instrument.

Illustrations V.57e and V.57f depict Bar Kokhba coins with wind instruments which have generally been interpreted as representing the two trumpets (hᵃṣōṣᵉrôt) of the Jewish temple. That written sources always mention these trumpets in pairs (Nu. 10:2) could be a serious argument in favor of this interpretation. Organological analysis of these particular representations, however, militates against it. The portrayals on all these coins

V.57. Bar Kokhba coins depicting lyres; type A (a) HUHM 049 and
(b) EIM K-4676; type B (c) EIM K-4663 and (d) K-4649; Bar-Kochba coins
depicting *zurna*/trumpets (?): (e) EIM K-4685 and (f) K-4689

clearly show that the slender part ends with a disk that can be interpreted only as the pirouette of an oboe-type double-reed *zumra* instrument. Similarly, the pipe, the bell, and the spherical expansion beneath the pirouette (a wind chamber or air reservoir?) are all characteristic of such reed instruments. This instrument shows more resemblance to the bladder pipe, which was always constructed with a wind chamber, a device already familiar during the Roman period in connection with Alexandrian flutes (Hickmann, 1961a) as well as with early bagpipes (Sachs, 1965), both of which probably originated in the Near East.

Josephus (*Ant.* iii.12.6) describes the contemporary temple instrument familiar to him as the *bukánē* invented by Moses, the Roman *bucina,* in the following way: it "was made of silver. Its description is this: In length it was little less than a cubit. It was composed of a narrow tube, somewhat thicker than an aulos, its mouthpiece *(stóma)* had so much breadth as was sufficient for admission of the breath of a man's mouth; it ended in the form of a bell, like the common *sálpinx* (trumpet)." It is clear from this rather vague description that Josephus was not really familiar with the construction of wind instruments. The wide mouthpiece is apparently the pirouette or disk at the blowing end of reed instruments, so this particular description cannot really be adduced in support of an interpretation of these instruments as trumpets. Scholars as early as Kurt Sachs, Sybille Marcuse, Erik Werner, and Laurence Picken already suggested that the instruments on the Bar Kokhba coins actually represent oboes with their unmistakable and characteristic pirouette. Still, this interpretation does not yet clarify the cultural-historical context suggested by the portrayals on these coins, since as far as we know oboes were never used in connection with the ancient Israelite cult, even if we accept the interpretation of the Hellenistic *ḥālîl* as an oboe-instrument.

In this context it should be mentioned that according to Horace, the most common double-reed instrument during the Roman period, the *tibia,* rivaled the trumpet itself. Two portrayals might be adduced in this connection, a fifth-century Etruscan grave and a Roman sarcophagus (Yarden, 1991, figs. 116, 117), which show a *tibia* functioning as a trumpet. Interestingly, the Bar Kokhba instruments do indeed resemble a much later wind instrument, namely, the Persian-Islamic *nafîr,* a small trumpet attested since about the eleventh century, about 60-70 cm. long, and capable of producing only two or three tones (see the fourteenth-century manuscript miniatures, Farmer, 1966, 84, illust. 72; also the Qazwini Manuscript, Staatsbibliothek Munich, Cod. Arab. 464). Known as the "war trumpet," this instrument was often played in pairs, as in Cameroun, but only during the holy Ramadan holiday. A remarkable feature of this instrument is that a spherical thickening a few centimeters from the embouchure conceals the connection between the mouthpiece and the straightened, middle portion of the instrument itself; this same thickened portion on the *nafir* and the wind instruments on the Bar Kokhba coin make the connection striking and unusual. Could the Bar Kokhba instrument represent a lost precursor of the *nafir*?

The third group of coins from ancient Israel/Palestine are those from Caesarea-Paneas dating to 169-220 (Meshorer, 1984/85). These coins are of extraordinary significance for music history in the region; not only do they afford some of the earliest representations of the cross flute, but they also show that a completely new development had taken place with regard to wind instruments.

Paneas (Caesarea Philippi, Paneion) is mentioned as early as the second pre-Christian century. In 3 B.C., Philipp, Herod's son, made it into the capital of his tetrarchy. It had a mixed pagan-Jewish population, and was a center of intellectual activity and of cultural exchange. Most of its coins depict Pan, its patron god (whence also the name Paneas), and sometimes also his cultic attributes, including the temple, *pedum* (shepherd's crook), syrinx, or some other wind instrument.

Several coins (illust. V.58a) portray the panpipe merely symbolically, as on the stone altar from Beth-shean (see illust. V.40), though the instrument portrayed here does not exhibit the form characteristic of ancient Israel/Palestine. This example has two double ligatures and pipes of equal length for the upper tones, suggesting Etruscan influence (Fleischhauer, 1964, illust. 1). Other cultic attributes, including the *pedum* (illust. V.58b) and temple, confirm that the artist intended this portrayal to function symbolically. Other coins within the Paneas group portray Pan himself playing the instrument (illust. V.58c). Although the instruments on these coins are extremely small, they are rendered with such clarity and so realistically that they are clearly identifiable as panpipe (illust. V.58b), cross flute (illust. V.58d), reed instrument (illust. V.58e), and possibly a long or notched flute (illust. V.58f).

Not much is known about the early history of the cross flute. The only witnesses are some second/first-century B.C.–second-century A.D. Etruscan, Roman, Alexandrian, and Indian reliefs and terra cottas, which make the discovery of a new corpus of evidence especially exciting. The cross flutes on the Paneas coins are played

V.58a-d. Paneas coins depicting (a) panpipe (from Meshorer, 1984/5), (b) pan-pipe with pedum (ANS), (c) Pan plays a panpipe (PC, photo by Z. Radovan), (d) cross flute (ANS)

by right-handed musicians and seem to be about 60-70 cm. long, that is, longer than Etruscan flutes. Unlike the Alexandrian and Roman instruments, they have no attached blowing devices. Hence one might surmise that they represent a new type of cross flute held either in a strictly horizontal position or lowered at a 20-25 degree angle similar to modern playing techniques.

Several other coins (e.g., illust. V.58e) depict oboes or *zurna* instruments identifiable from the bell, the conical shape of the pipe, and the playing position. Mistaking these instruments for flutes not only equates them with an instrument producing a completely different sound and associated with a completely different aesthetic milieu, but also affords a false understanding of the music and culture of this age.

Although double-reed instruments are only poorly attested by archaeological evidence, oboes during pre-Roman times were almost certainly used only as double-

(e)

(f)

(g)

V.58e-g.
(e) Pan playing a reed instrument
(IMJ 1134),
(f) Pan playing a long/notched
flute (Ashmolean Museum),
(g) Pan in a grotto with a panpipe
at his feet (ANS)

pipe instruments with almost cylindrical pipes. "From their distribution in antiquity, comprising the Mediterranean and the Near East, we conclude that oboes were created in the Semitic world, somewhere between Asia Minor and Arabia" (Sachs, 1940). Oboes with a conical pipe (the *zurna* type) are attested only by Edomite terra cottas, and even in these examples are not unequivocal. Apart from the Paneas coins, no other evidence has come to light. These coins thus enable us to establish a precise *terminus post quem non* for such oboe/*zurna* instruments, and it is thus also possible that these coins are depicting other aerophones as well, including perhaps long or notched flutes (illust. V.58f).

Several coins depict Pan with a wind instrument either in a temple or a grotto (illust. V.58g). Such grottos with third-century inscriptions can still be seen in modern Bâniyâs (Paneas) (illust. V.58h); statues of Pan himself apparently once stood in these grottos. Indeed, the Pan cult was an extremely fertile environment for wind instruments, and considering that forty-three of the sixty-one published coins from Paneas depict new instruments, one can see that musical praxis in Roman Paneas was both ex-

V.58h. Grottos of the Pan statues in modern Bâniyâs

tremely active and extremely innovative. The wide variety of flutes and oboes appearing in these representations of Pan shows that a new, modern musical culture had emerged and replaced the older culture centered on the syrinx and aulos.

A survey of the musical instruments depicted on coins from ancient Israel/Palestine suggests that they represent a singular group of idiomatic portrayals of musical instruments symbolizing various national, municipal,

296

or cultic identities. The symbolic affiliation of each mint described here is quite pronounced. The iconographical symbolism of the Bar-Kochba coins was frequently discussed: a sign of resistance to Roman occupation, Bar-Kockba coins used icons and legends that in a most direct way symbolize Jewish statehood, national independence, faith, and culture. Among other things, musical instruments — lyres and trumpets/*zurna*-instruments — are frequently depicted. Be the organological affinity of each as it may, these instruments were used both by the class of priests *(kohenim)*/Temple musicians *(levi)* and the wider segments of the population, which turned them into especially powerful symbols. Another example is the coinage of the city-states Acco and Panias. The lyre is placed on the Acco coin as a Hellenistic-Roman civic symbol. We have here the typical Roman mint: the Emperor's head on the obverse and a musical instrument on the reverse. On the Paneas coins the city's patron god Pan is often symbolized by the *syrinx* and other wind instruments played by him. The icons of the tessarae, intaglios, and gems, which include mythological images with lyres or musical instruments only, were probably produced for private ownership and may represent some kind of individual self-identification. This extraordinarily profuse, varied, and progressive collection attests a number of innovations affecting musical instruments during the period, and as such attests the presence of an active and independent musical culture.

Tesserae found near Caesarea Maritima, accessible today only as contour drawings, constitute a separate group of artifacts whose iconography is related to the coins just discussed (Hamburger, 1986). These small metal jetons measure 7-19 cm. across, are irregularly shaped, and were used for various purposes in ancient Rome, including tickets to public events or prostitutes, or in exchange for goods or money. Tesserae portraying dancers (illust. V.59a), flute players, or lyres (illust. V.59b-c) might have provided proof of membership in private groups or allowed one access to a private wedding. The lyres resemble the type-B lyres on the Bar Kokhba coins and show yet again how common this basic form was in ancient Israel/Palestine. The lyre with a dancing figure in place of its strings (illust. V.59c) was obviously intended to be taken symbolically (cf. again Isa. 23:16), and in general the lyre portrayals from this period do not always depict the instruments realistically. The iconography of the lyre confirms the change of its social standing from the instrument of cult musicians and higher classes in the Bronze and Iron Age to a symbol of the past or mass entertainment instrument of Hellenistic-Roman time.

   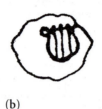   

(a)   (b)   (c)

V.59. Caesarea Maritima, tessarae depicting (a) female dancer with rattle,
(b) a lyre, and (c) female dancer in a lyre frame instead of strings
(from Hamburger, 1986)

The intaglios of the Sʿad collection (Henig/Whiting, 1987) also date to
this period and probably come from Gadara, one of the most important
cities of the Decapolis. Although they were found in unregulated excavations, these gems, like similar ones from Caesarea, are probably of local
provenance and were probably made locally. They represent typical artifacts of the Roman Near East and were worn as either jewelry or amulets.
The most splendid piece among the Gadara collection is a red jasper gem
depicting a young satyr playing a double aulos (illust. V.60a). One interesting feature of this portrayal is that the satyr is depicted precisely at the moment he presses his left index finger down onto the *kéras* or timbre peg;
this may correct the earlier view that the musician generally adjusted this
device *before* actually playing the instrument. Because of the extreme care
and detail with which this gem was made, there is little reason to doubt its
realism, and as a result, we must likely reassess our previous understanding
of these timbre pegs.

Yet another double pipe appears on a gem (illust. V.60b) depicting Eros riding a
sea centaur playing a double aulos. One can also mention the small, first-century
gem from Caesarea depicting a seated Pan or satyr playing an aulos with widely diverging pipes (Hamburger, 1968, no. 153).

A completely different, less realistic portrayal is found on another gem (illust.
V.60c) depicting the figure of Eros/Apollo gazing at a griffin with his hand on a
schematically rendered lyre positioned on a tripod. This portrayal seems to indicate a divinization of this abstracted instrument and may reflect the words of
Pseudo-Basil (ca. 330-379) who wrote in his commentary to Isaiah: "'Woe' it is

written 'unto them who drink wine to the accompaniment of cithara, aulos, tympanum and song' (Is. 5.11-12). You place a lyre ornamented with gold and ivory upon a high pedestal as if it were a statue or devilish idol, and some miserable woman, rather than being taught to place her hands upon the spindle, is taught by you, bound as she is in servitude, to stretch them out upon the lyre. . . . So she stands at the lyre and lays her hands upon the strings, her arms bare and her expression impudent. The entire symposium is then transformed, as the eyes of all are focused upon her and the ears upon her strumming; the crowd noise dies down, as the laughter and the din of ribald talk are quieted. All in the house are silenced, charmed by the lascivious song . . ." (McKinnon, 1987). Although Greek coins quite often depict lyres on pedestals (Richter, 1974, no. 149; Neverov, 1988, 76), the tripod as a Near Eastern cultic object suggests that this scene is of local provenance.

The fourth gem in this collection (illust. V.60d) depicts a seated Silenus playing a lyre before a priapic shrine. One noteworthy feature here is that the string holder on the resonator is clearly discernible.

Several finds dating to this period are of interest even though their origin is unknown. A second/third-century carnelian gem from the Haifa Museum (illust. V.61a) depicts a musician playing a five-string lyre from which "sacred bands" hang down. The middle string is portrayed quite realistically, and one can even see how it is stretched when played; similar portrayals rarely exhibit such realism. The lyre on the gem of IJM (illust. V.61b) has four strings; its side arms depict two dolphins and the resonator a crab form, suggesting that this portrayal is intended to be symbolic. The dolphin, a familiar Nabatean topos, may provide the key to this work's origin.

Musical instruments as well as music in the larger sense acquired a different cultural status during the Hellenistic-Roman period. This change can be seen in the sheer number and variety of objects used for adornment and personal identification depicting musical topoi. Musical symbols now indicate not only national or cultic identity, but also personal inclinations and traditional preferences.

V.60. Intaglios, Gadara, PU;
(a) young satyr (?) playing a double aulos,
(b) a centaur playing a double aulos,
(c) lyre with Eros (?),
(d) lyre player (S'ad Collection, Gadara)

(a)

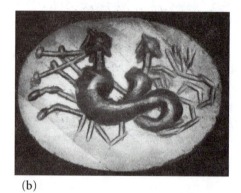

(b)

(c)

(d)

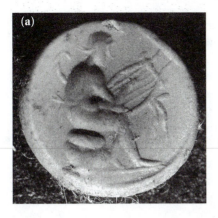

V.61. Gems, PU, (a) with lyre player, HUHM 1595, and (b) lyre, IMJ 90.24.14

8. The Shofar: Tool of Sound and Ritual, Symbol of Faith and National Identity

The shofar is the only instrument from the biblical period that has remained unchanged within the Jewish liturgy. The Old Testament mentions it 72 times, more often than any other musical instrument, and both musicological and general Jewish studies without exception identify it as a natural (animal) horn (see chap. I). The earliest portrayals of such horns in the Near East date to the second millennium B.C. (e.g., eighteenth century B.C. Parrot, 1961, illust. 389) and are thus considerably older than the first written mention in the Old Testament.

From the very outset, Jewish tradition has ascribed considerable symbolic meaning to the shofar. Edith Gerson-Kiwi has associated the shofar cult with the emergence of monotheism itself; *pars pro toto,* this horn became "the instrument . . . that brought human sacrifice to an end and sealed God's covenant with Abraham" (Gerson-Kiwi, 1980; cf. Gen. 22:13). The horn is capable of producing two or three tones evoking a tremulous, trumpeting sound of alarm. This sound is always described as *qôl* (literally: voice), *t⁽e⁾qî'â* (a trumpeting blast), *t⁽e⁾rû'â* (shout of jubilation), [[*r'a*]] (tumult, commotion), or *yabbāḇâ* ("sobbing, moaning; trembling"). All these terms underscore the magical, symbolical, and eschatological aura associated with its sound.

The Old Testament mentions the shofar in both cultic and secular

301

contexts. It appears as an omen of transcendental powers (Ex. 19:13; Ps. 47:6), on the Day of Atonement (Lev. 25:9), at the New Moon feast (Ps. 81:3), on the Day of Penitence (Joel 2:1), at the transfer of the ark (2 S. 6:15), during battle (Jgs. 3:27; 6:34; Josh. 6:4-20; 2 S. 2:28), at victory celebrations (1 S. 13:3), and during coups (2 S. 15:10). The shofar's function followed two lines of development in the Old Testament. The exile brought to an end its initial function as an instrument of war. Henceforth it functioned as a cultic instrument, and continues as such even today.

It is only since the Roman period that written sources (the Talmud and Qumran scrolls) have anything to say about the shofar's ergology and sound. The term *šôpār* actually refers to a goat's horn, later to a ram's horn, but never to that of a cow (*m. Roš Haš.* 3:2). The Mishnah (*m. Roš Haš.* 3:3-4) stipulates that it may be made in two different forms: "The shofar blown in the temple at the New Year was made from the horn of the wild goat, straight, with its mouthpiece (Heb. [[*piyâ*]]) overlaid with gold. . . . The shofars on days of fasting were rams' horns, rounded, with their mouthpiece overlaid with silver." The text does not clarify whether this [[*piyâ*]] is referring to a separate mouthpiece attached to the instrument or merely to the narrower end of the horn into which the player blew. In any event, some portrayals as early as the third-fourth centuries clearly show a mounted mouthpiece (see illust. V.62, 63). A rare iconographical witness dating either to the same period or possibly a decade earlier (to the beginning of the third century) attests yet another technical innovation involving the embouchure. Here the narrow part of the horn where the mouthpiece was attached is transformed into a cup-shaped piece (Heb. *kôs,* cup) serving as a mouthpiece made from the horn itself (see illust. V.67, V.69). This instrument represents what one might even call an idio-embouchure horn utilizing what has previously been thought to be an invention of modern technology.

The first depictions of the shofar do not appear before the third century, during the late period of the Roman emperors when Judaism was subject to the double influence of both Hellenization and early Christianity, but when the basic philosophical canon of the Jewish faith and its accompanying lifestyle was firmly enough established to allow various spheres of life to exist in an equilibrium; this situation applied especially to art in both its sacral and secular forms (Liebermann, 1942; Urbach, 1959; Goodenough, 1965, XII; Avigad, 1976; Neusner, 1981, to mention but a few of the most important studies of the cultural and artistic developments of Hellenistic-Roman Palestine).

Shofar portrayals do not depict merely the instrument *per se*, either in a liturgical or in a secular context. Rather, they depict it exclusively as a symbol together with other cultic accoutrements, including the menorah (seven-branched lampstand), the *māḥtâ* (incense pan), the *lûlāv* (palm frond), and *'eṭrôg* (citrus fruit), which "all together had a combined impact, which was important in itself" (Goodenough, 1954); as such, it could symbolize Judaism in the larger sense. Although these objects are variously positioned around the menorah as the dominant Jewish cultic symbol, only the shofar is present in every instance, whereas the other three may or may not be included. This omnipresence of the shofar clearly attests its eminent cultic status as well as the tenacity with which it maintained that status within the Jewish liturgy. Even though the menorah was already functioning as a symbol of Jewish identity prior to the emergence of Christianity, no iconography has surfaced prior to the end of the second and beginning of the third century for the symbolic grouping itself nor any evidence of the shofar before other parts of the group.

This symbolic grouping appears in numerous artifacts in both Roman and early Byzantine Palestine; they can be divided into two groups, in each of which the symbolic grouping has its own socioartistic significance.

1. Architectonic elements in public buildings, primarily synagogues (mosaic flooring, capitals, pedestals, and stone reliefs), and tombstones; the grouping symbolizes here social and ideological-national identification.

2. Smaller objects, among which the oil lamps discussed earlier are of particular importance, and where the symbolic grouping symbolizes personal self-determination in private contexts.

The earliest artifacts associated with the first group include a floor panel from Ḥammat Tiberias (fourth century) and two tombstones from Beth Sheʿarim from the early third century. The mosaic from the synagogue in Ḥammat Tiberias (illust. V.62a-c) contains marvelous portrayals of the complete symbolic group and probably represents a prototype of the ancient Israelite synagogue mosaic; actually, it has two identical groups positioned symmetrically at either side of a temple facade similar to those on the Khirbet Susiya and Beth-shean mosaics (Ovadia, 1987, no. 170; see the fragment in illust. V.63). The mosaic from Ḥammat Tiberias dates to the early period, a century or more earlier than the other mosaic masterpieces such as the Sepphoris mosaics (illust. V.64). This region was one of the richest in Roman Palestine and extended from the Golan Heights down along

(a)

V.62. Mosaic floor, synagogue, Ḥammat Tiberias:
(a) upper panel *in situ;*
(b) and (c) shofar, *māḥtâ,* and menorah fragment

(c)

(b)

V.63. Mosaic floor,
synagogue, Beth-shean,
IAA 63.932

V.64. Mosaic floor, synagogue, Sepphoris, copy from the IMJ Exposition

305

the Sea of Galilee to Beth-shean. During this period, the Sanhedrin convened in this area, and Jewish cultural, intellectual, and artistic life all flourished. These magnificent "imperial" mosaic floors appear here from the earliest emergence of the symbolic grouping in the larger sense down into the sixth century (Beith Alpha synagogue, sixth century), when the topos was interpreted more freely (cf. illust. V.65). Although all these artifacts exhibit a considerable degree of symmetry, each mosaic also exhibits individual features transcending the formal canon, and each offers a different composition and a correspondingly different portrayal.

All these artifacts, though especially those from Hammat Tiberias and Beth-shean, represent what at present must be considered the most complete depictions of the shofar from the Mishnaic period. The splendid, elegantly curved horns clearly reveal two different forms. The more opulently decorated horns on the left depict the New Year's shofar with its four golden rings; the horns on the right with the silver rings are the shofars used on fasting days. That is, this iconography actually reflects the Talmudic text itself to a certain extent (cf. b. Roš Haš. 27:1-2). The two mosaics also clearly show the different type of embouchure. On the New Year's shofar from Hammat Tiberias (illust. V.62b), one clearly discerns the mounted or, more precisely, inserted mouthpiece with the embouchure about three times wider than the end of the horn the player blows. The horn on the right has no mouthpiece (illust. V.62c). The New Year's shofar from Beth-shean seems to have the gold ornamentation (gold stone) as prescribed by m. Roš Haš. 3:3-5. The decorative rings on the horn associated with the day of fasting were apparently made of silver (white stone). A relatively small panel from the recently discovered Sepphoris synagogue (cf. the copy in illust. V.64) was part of a multithematic work measuring 280 × 450 cm. One can once again clearly discern in the symmetrical groupings the differences between the two types of shofar. In later examples from the sixth century, the canon is loosened somewhat, and the topos comprising a temple facade or shrine along with two symmetrically positioned symbolic groupings is treated a bit more freely. The mosaic from the Beith Alpha synagogue, for example, includes animals, birds, and trees and even distributes the attributes of the symbolic grouping more freely across the mosaic panel (illust. V.65).

Such iconography does not always accord with the Talmudic stipulations. Surprisingly, this noncompliance occurs even where one would initially think it would be followed most scrupulously, namely, in the synagogue itself. Not a single synagogue mosaic, for example, depicts the linear

V.65. Mosaic floor, synagogue, Beith Alpha, *in situ*

shofar which, as *m. Roš Haš.* 3:3-4 insists, must be sounded at the New Year. Similarly, the mosaic from Ḥammat Tiberias clearly depicts the gold and silver ornamentation on the two shofars, but not the mouthpieces. This particular portrayal apparently reflects a later regulation prohibiting any gold where the mouth is placed (*b. Roš Haš.* 27:1-2). The stipulation in *b. Roš Haš.* 27:2 clearly contradicts *m. Roš Haš.* 3:3-4 mentioned earlier, which explicitly prescribes that the mouthpiece of the New Year's shofar be overlaid with gold while that of the everyday instrument be overlaid with silver. The texts may be interpreting the term [[*piyâ*]] differently. In the case of the idio-embouchure shofar, overlaying with gold or silver is prohibited because it would involve part of the horn itself, thus raising the likelihood that the actual sound quality would be affected. In the case of a separate mouthpiece, however, such overlaying is permissible because the sound itself is then presumably less likely to be altered. The immediately following sentence confirms that the Talmud did indeed consider such a change in tonal quality to be of great significance and even dangerous: "Overlaid with gold from the inside: unacceptable; from the outside, should this alter the original sound: unacceptable; if it does not alter the sound: acceptable" (*b. Roš Haš.* 27:1-2). The Jewish ritual requires a natural tone; "whether thin, thick, or dry, the sound is acceptable, for all the tones of the shofar are acceptable" (*b. Roš Haš.* 27:2). The musical performance of the shofar could represent a unique aesthetic experience as well, and was acknowledged as such: "Whoever plays a song (Heb. *šîr*) on the shofar has fulfilled his religious duty" (28:1). The shofars depicted on the "imperial" mosaics represent the more sophisticated instruments on which such melodies could probably be played.

Additional mosaics depicting this symbolic grouping all date to a later period (fifth-sixth centuries). They come from all over the region and represent either fragments of larger works (illust. V.66) or smaller symbols on ornamental pieces (illust. V.67). Moreover, they were originally used outside the synagogue proper, for example, in ritual baths (illust. V.68). The northern tradition of the "imperial" mosaics is rarely attested, and even when it is, then only in part. For example, although the neighboring Isfiya synagogue contains two symmetrically positioned symbolic portrayals, they appear separated on the periphery of the mosaic. The only exception here seems to be the Jericho instrument (illust. V.67), whose idio-embouchure feature represents a clear deviation.

This symbolic grouping is often simply depicted alone or in an extremely abstract form on stone engravings and reliefs. Such is the case on two marble plates from Beth-shean that likely served as tombstones or sarcophagi. Although the grouping is portrayed in full here and with admirable artistry, it is decidedly stylized. The form of the shofar on the tombstone relief of "noble Karteria" represents the oldest instrument with an idio-embouchure (early third century; illust. V.69).

Unfortunately, scholars still cannot agree on the chronology of the oldest known representation of this symbolic grouping, the capital from Capernaum (illust. V.70), and offer suggestions ranging from the end of the second century B.C. to the sixth century. The location of the grouping itself is highly unusual; indeed, the grouping is actually almost concealed, suggesting perhaps that the artist intended a gesture of latent opposition.

An exception among these artifacts is a lead sarcophagus from Beth Sh'arim (illust. V.71), the only one among similar sarcophagi which bears the Jewish symbolic grouping. These sarcophagi were produced semifinished in Sidon and then decorated according to the wishes of the purchaser. On our sarcophagus, which dates to

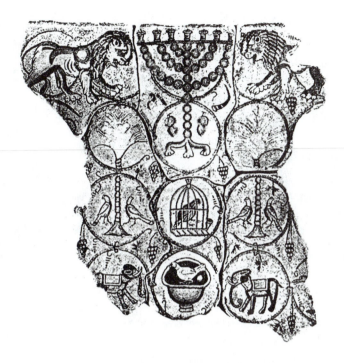

V.66. Mosaic floor, synagogue, Maʿon Nirim, IAA 57-869

V.67. Mosaic floor, synagogue, Jericho, *in situ*

V.68. Mosaic floor, ritual bath, Ḥuldah, IAA 53-583

V.69. Marble burial slab, Beth Sheʿarim, HUIA, no. 3412

V.70. Capital, synagogue, Capernaum, *in situ*

the first half of the fourth century, several Jewish symbolic groupings are embossed, all of which are artistically composed and carefully executed (Avigad, 1976).

The symbolic grouping also appears on pedestals (illust. V.72), capitals (illust. V.70), synagogue screens (illust. V.73), crudely cut tombstones (illust. V.74), and stone reliefs. Most of these examples date to the fifth-seventh centuries, and many are of unknown origin. One noteworthy feature is the appearance after the fourth century of many shofars bent almost into a right angle (illust. V.74). Several may depict attached mouthpieces as well (illust. V.73). On the whole, most of these portrayals are so schematic to begin with or so weathered and vague that one can no longer really discern the important details of the instruments.

V.71. Lead sarcophagus, Sidon/Beth Sh'arim, IAA 64.40

The second group of artifacts includes first of all the numerous terra-cotta oil lamps found throughout the entire country. Three subgroups emerge.

a. One extremely significant lamp fragment (illust. V.75) dates precisely to the third century. It was produced in the well-known Beth Nattif workshop and represents the Beth Nattif type of Jewish oil lamps (see also illust. V.76) with a small, smooth shofar, probably a goat's horn. The style of this type was probably influenced by the earlier Palmyrene and northern lamps from ancient Israel/Palestine (Gerasa, first-second centuries). This find shows that at the beginning of the third century, the grouping

V.72. Pedestal, Ashkelon, AA 58.285

V.73. Screen, synagogue, Ashkelon, Deutsches Evangelisches
Institut, Jerusalem, first fragment

V.74. Tombstone, Jericho,
Rockefeller Museum, R837

V.75. Terra-cotta oil lamp, fragment,
Beth Nattif, IAA 38.450

V.76. Terra-cotta oil lamp, PU, SBF 2277

with the shofar represented an established and semantically unequivocal symbol that could already be rendered in its full, established artistic form as on the mosaics discussed earlier.

b. One series of Jewish lamps does differ from this Beth Nattif type. As in Roman lamps, the image itself occupies the entire central part of the lamp, and the iconography can be read correctly only when the lamp is held with its nose end down. Both features characterize this group. Here the instrument is made from a ribbed sheep's horn. Two fourth-century Qasrawit lamps represent this group (illust. V.77). Although this type of lamp is frequently found in ancient Israel/Palestine, scholars generally agree that they were actually manufactured elsewhere.

c. The Samaritan oil lamps (see illust. V.30a; V.49, 50, 51, 52) constitute a separate group and exhibit a pronounced idiosyncratic character even though they actually represent a continuation of the Beth Nattif type with a centered opening and iconography positioned in a dispersed way not characteristic of Jewish oil lamps (see chap. V/6).

V.77. Terra-cotta
oil lamp, Qasrawit,
Ben Gurion University,
EE inv. no. 1460

One additional group of smaller artifacts includes rings, amulets, stamps, and pendants, but offers little information regarding the shofar, not least because of their uncertain provenance. All of these objects come from private collections and date approximately to the early Byzantine period. Most, however, like the pendant/amulet of unknown provenance (illust. V.78), are indeed of sociofunctional interest as symbols of religious or national identity. The bread seals, of which at least four have been found, are of particular interest in this regard (illust. V.79; see also Meyers/Meyers, 1975, pl. 15D). One individual find is a carved ivory tablet from Beth-shean with its severely curved, wound shofar and a menorah with a highly unusual, rounded base (illust. V.80).

Viewed as a whole, these artifacts show that the shofar was not merely a simple symbol of restricted meaning. It did not symbolize merely the idea of atonement or immortality as based on Abraham's sacrifice of Isaac (Goodenough, 1954). Nor did it symbolize merely a certain version of messianism (Roth, 1955). And it certainly was not merely a "decorative

V.78. Pendant, PU, Reifenberg private
collection, on loan to the IMJ

V.79. Bread seal, PU,
IMJ 87.56.526

V.80. Ivory carving,
Beth-shean,
Rockefeller Museum,
IAA 40.1523

317

convention" (Bayer, 1964/65). It was a holistic national-ethical symbol of identification appearing contemporaneously in various national and cultic artistic forms. Moreover, from the very outset, it was a fully developed, artistically mature symbol. The early witnesses to this symbolic grouping on the Beth Nattif lamps, the Ḥammat Tiberias mosaic, and the Beth Shean engravings, which possibly reflect foreign influence, appeared contemporaneously with the greatest masterpieces of Roman–Early Byzantine art. On the other hand, it seems clear enough that the artistic form of this symbolic grouping already began to degenerate soon after its initial appearance; the symbol itself was portrayed in an increasingly schematic and abstract fashion, and certainly with increasingly less realism (see illust. V.72).

Early sources do not say much about the shofar's sound. The Mishnah mentions only that the tone could be "long," "short," "calm" or "sustained," or could be a "blast" (*m. Roš Haš.* 3:3-4; *m. Sukk.* 4:5). The Qumran War Scroll mentions a mighty war alarm sounded in unison (1QM 8:10). The first graphic portrayals of these various sounds in the tenth-century Siddur (prayer book) of Saadiah Gaon (889-942) and the thirteenth-century Codex Adler give us a certain idea how the shofar signals sounded during the Roman period (illust. V.81a, 81b). Rabbinical writings do not agree concerning these signals. It was not until the fourth century that Rabbi Abiyehu of Caesarea fixed the terms *tᵉqîʿâ* as a long tone, *tᵉrûʿâ* as a quavering tremolo, and [[*šᵉbārîm*]] as broken tones (*b. Roš Haš.* 33:2; 34:1-2). All three forms are used today (see notation example illust. V.83). Special shofar blowers (*bāʿâl tᵉqîʿa*) may use the three possible natural tones of the instrument, namely, the octave, fifth, and fourth, that is, the second, third, and fourth partials (harmonics) of the tonic, which in turn depend on the length of the instrument. Concerning the length of the three signals, the Talmud says that "the manner of blowing the shofar is three blasts thrice repeated. A sustained blast *(tᵉqîʿâ)* is three times the length of a quavering blast *(tᵉrûʿâ)*, and a quavering blast *(tᵉrûʿâ)* is like three alarm blasts *(šᵉbārîm)*" (*m. Roš Haš.* 4:9; *b. Roš Haš.* 33:2; 34:1-2). Modern notation varies among congregations, and follows only the basic conclusion gleaned from these texts. One long tone, three short fifths or quartal leaps, several short, repeated, staccato tones, and then once again the initial long tone (cf. the notation example).

The inscription on a stone found near the temple wall suggests that during the Roman period, a specific place either at or near the wall was apparently set aside for the ritual sounding of the shofar: [[*l'beit hatʿqiʿâ*]], "at the house of blowing/sounding" (illust. V.82).

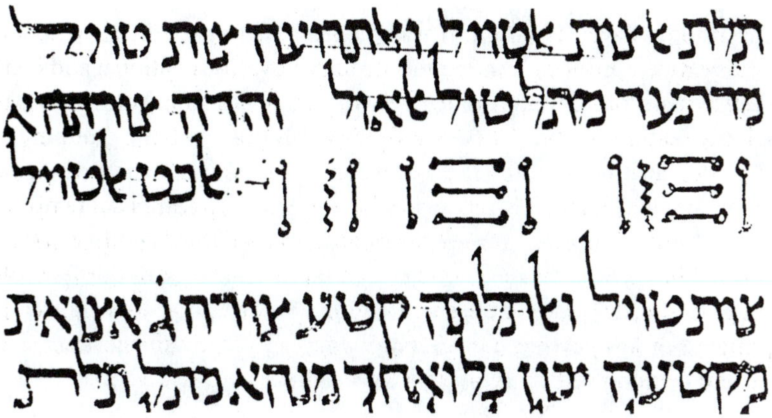

(a)

(b)

V.81. Graphic representation of the shofar signals: (a) Siddur (prayer book) of Saadiah Gaon, Oxford, Codex Hunt 448, fol. 149r, b; (b) Codex Adler, Jewish Theological Seminary, New York, Codex no. 932, fol. 21b

V.82. Stone inscription, Jerusalem, IAA 78.1415

Recorded at the Yeshurun Synagogue, Tel-Aviv (Egyptian Congregation),
by Ya'acov Snir, in preparation of a Ph.D. Thesis (1988) at the Bar Ilan University.

V.83. Musical example: (a) *t*ᵉ*qî*ᶜ*â,* (b) *š*ᵉ*b̠ārîm,* and (c) *t*ᵉ*rû*ᶜ*â*

Bibliography

Adaqi, Yehiel, and Uri Sharvit

1981   *A Treasury of Jewish Yemenite Chants.* Jerusalem.

Adler, Cyrus

1893   "The Shofar, Its Use and Origin," *Proceedings of the U.S. National Museum* 16: 287-301.

Aign, Bernhard

1963   *Die Geschichte der Musikinstrumente des Agaischen Raums bis vor 700 v. Chr.* Frankfurt/Main.

Aistleitner, Joseph

1959   *Die Mythologischen und Kultischen Texte aus Ras Schamra.* Budapest.

Albright, William Foxwell

1934   "The Kyle Memorial Excavations at Bethel," *BASOR* 56: 2-15.

1943   *The Excavation of Tel Beit Mirsim. AASOR* 21-22.

1944   "A Prince of Taanach in the Fifteenth Century B.C.," *BASOR* 94: 12-27.

1956   *Die Religion Israels im Lichte der archäologischen Ausgrabungen.* Munich/Basel.

1960   *The Archaeology of Palestine.* New York.

Alon, David

1976   "Two Cult Vessels from Gilat," *Atiqot* 11 (Eng. series): 116-18.

Amiran, Ruth
1967   "He'ara l'tipus hazalmit hamahzika, 'hefez agol' (A Comment to the Figurine Type with 'Round Object,'" *Eretz Israel* 8: 99-100 (Heb.).
1976   "Note on the Gilat Vessels," *Atiqot* 11 (Eng. series): 119-20.

Anati, Emmanuel
1955a   "Ancient Rock Drawings in the Central Negev," *PEQ* 82/1-2: 49-57.
1955b   "Una scena di danza nel Negev centrale," *Rivista de Scienze Preistoriche* 10: 70-75.
1963   *Palestine before the Hebrews.* New York.
1986   *Har Karkom: The Mountain of God.* Milan.

Anderson, R. D.
1976   *Catalogue of Egyptian Antiquities in the British Museum,* vol. 3: *Musical Instruments.* London.

ANEP. See Pritchard, 1954 and 1955.

ANET. See Pritchard, 1950.

Anson, L.
1910   *Numismata Graece,* 10 vols. London.

Assante, J.
1998   "The *kar/kid/harimtu:* Prostitute or Single Women," *UF* 30: 5-90.

Avenary, Hanoch
1956   "Magic, Symbolism and Allegory of Old Hebrew Sound Instruments," in *Collectanea Historiae Musicae,* vol. 2. Firenze, pp. 21-31.
1958   "Jüdische Musik," in *MGG1,* vol. 7, pp. 224-32.
1963   "Pseudo-Jerome Writings and Qumran Tradition," *Revue de Qumran* 13/4: 3-10.
1966   "M'ziltayim mashmiim (Sounding Cymbals)," in *Tatzlil* 6: 24-26 (Heb.).
1971   "Flutes for the Bride of a Dead Man: The Symbolism of the Flute according to Hebrew Sources," *Orbis Musicae* 1/1: 11-24.
1973-74   "The Discrepancy between Iconographic and Literary Presentations of Ancient Eastern Musical Instruments," *Orbis Musicae* 3-4: 121-27.
1979   *Encounters of East and West in Music.* Tel Aviv.

Avigad, Nachman
1976   *Beth She'arim: Report on the Excavations during 1953-1958,* vol. 3: *Catacombs 12-23.* Jerusalem.
1978   "The King's Daughter and the Lyre," *IEJ* 28: 146-51.

Avi-Yonah, Michael
1981   *Art in Ancient Palestine: Selected Studies.* Jerusalem.
1984   *The Jews under Roman and Byzantine Rule.* Jerusalem.

Bachmann, Werner
2000   "Frühbronzezeitliche Musikinstrumente Anatoliens," *OrA* 7: 150-158.

Bade, William Frederic, and Chester Charlton McCown
1947   *Tell en Nasbeh,* vols. 1-2. Berkeley/New Haven.

Bahat, Nomi
1970   "Musique et mouvement dans les ceremonies de mariage chez les druzes en Israel." Ph.D. thesis, Sorbonne, Paris.

Baramki, D. C.
1936   "Two Roman Cisterns at Beit Nattif," *QDAP* 5: 3-10.

Barnett, Richard David
1935   "The Nimrod Ivories and the Art of the Phoenicians," *Iraq* 2: 179-210.
1969   "New Facts about Musical Instruments from Ur," *Iraq* 31/2: 96-103.
1970   "Another Deity with Dolphins?" in James H. Sanders, *Essays in Honor of Nelson Glueck: Near Eastern Archaeology in the Twentieth Century.* New York, pp. 327-35.
1975   *A Catalogue of the Nimrud Ivories with Other Examples of Ancient Near Eastern Ivories in the British Museum.* London.
1982   *Ancient Ivories in the Middle East (Qedem 14).* Jerusalem.
1986   "Assurbanipal's Feast," *Eretz-Israel* 18: 1-6.

Bar-Yosef, Ofer
1974   "The Natufian Culture in Eretz-Israel," *Qadmaniot* 7/1-2: 3-23 (Heb.).
1979   "Excavations at Hayonim Cave 1975-79," *Mitkufah Ha'even* 16: 88-98 (Heb.).

Bar-Yosef, Ofer, and E. Tchernov
1970   "The Natufian Bone Industry at Hayonim Cave," *IEJ* 20/3-4: 141-50.

Baudot, Alain
1973   *Musiciens Romains de l'Antiquite.* Montreal.

Bayer, Bathja
1963a   *The Material Relics of Music in Ancient Palestine and Its Environs: An Archaeological Inventory.* Tel Aviv.

1963b	"Kunkhiyat haneshifa shel Hatzor (The Conch-Trumpet from Hazor)," *Tatzlil* 3: 140-42 (Heb.).
1964	"M'na'anim — schakschakot cheres? (M'na'anim — Clay-Rattles?)," *Tatzlil* 4: 19-22 (Heb.).
1964/5	"Hateud ha'archeologi schel haschofar b'eretz israel (Archeological Evidence on the Shofar in Eretz-Israel)," *Duchan* 6: 15-30 (Heb.).
1968a	"The Biblical Nebel," *Yuval* 1: 89-131.
1968b	"Negina v'zimra (Instrumental Performance and Singing)," in *Enzyklopedia Mikrait*, Bd. 5. Jerusalem, pp. 755-82 (Heb.)
1968c	"Eduyot Archeologiot (Archaeological News)," in *Fourth World Congress of Jewish Studies*, vol. 2. Jerusalem, pp. 421-22 (Heb.).
1982a	"The Titles of the Psalms," *Yuval* 4: 28-123.
1982b	"The Finds That Could Not Be," *BAR* 8/1: 19-37.

Beck, Pirhiya
1982   "The Drawings from Horvat Teiman (Kuntillet 'Ajrud)," 9/1: 3-68.

Becker, Heinz
1966   *Zur Entwicklungsgeschichte der antiken und mittelalterlichen Rohrblattinstrumente.* Hamburg, 1966.

Behn, Friedrich
1954   *Musikleben im altertum und frühen Mittelalter.* Stuttgart.

Beit Arieh, Itzhaq
1987   *Edomite Shrine: Discoveries from Qitmit in the Negev,* Israel Museum Catalogue No. 277. Jerusalem.
1988   "New Light on the Edomites," *BAR* 14/2: 28-41.
1995   *Horvat Qitmit: An Edomite Shrine in the Biblical Negev.* Tel Aviv.

Beit Arieh, Itzhaq, ed.
1999   *Tel 'Ira: A Stronghold in the Biblical Negev.* Tel Aviv.

Belis, Anne
1988   "Musique et transe dans le sortège sionysiaque," *Cahiers du gita* 4: 9-29.

Ben-Tor, Amnon, and M.-T. Rubiato
1996   "Hahafirot hamehudašot btel Hazor bešanim 1990-1995 (The Renewed Excavations at Tel Hazor in the Years 1990-1995)," *Qadmaniot* 29/1: 2-18.

Benzinger, Immanuel
1927   *Hebräische Archäologie.* Leipzig.

Bickermann, Elias J.
1937   *Der Gott der Makkabaer.* Berlin.

Bibliography

1988   *The Jews in the Greek Age.* London.

Bietak, Manfred
1985   "Eine 'Rhythmusgruppe' aus der Zeit des späten Mittleren Reiches: Ein Beitrag zur Instrumentenkunde des alten Agypten," *Jahrbuch des osterreichischen archäologischen Instituts in Wien* 56: 3-18.

Biran, Avraham
1986   "The Dancer from Dan, the Empty Tomb and the Altar Room," *IEJ* 36/3-4: 168-87.

Bittel, Kurt
1968   "Cymbeln für Kybele," in *Günther Wasmuth zum 80. Geburtstag gewidmet.* Tübingen, pp. 79-82.

Blades, James
1974   *Percussion Instruments and Their History,* London.

BMC
1899   *Catalogue of the Greek Coins in the British Museum: Syria.* London.

Bodley, Nicholas B.
1946   "The Auloi of Meroe," *AJA* 50/2: 217-40.

Bounet, Max
1883   *Acta Thomae supplementum codicis apocryphi.* Lipsiae.

Braun, Joachim
1990/91 "Iron Age Seals from Ancient Israel Pertinent to Music," *Orbis Musicae* 10: 11-26.
1994a   "Considerations on Archaeo-Musicology and the State of the Art in Israel," in C. Homo-Lechner, ed., *La pluridisciplinarit en archéologie musicale.* Paris, pp. 139-48.
1994b   "Biblische Musikinstrumente," in *MGG2,* vol. 1, cols. 1503-37.
1996b   "Musical Instruments," in *OEANE,* vol. 4, pp. 70-79.
1997   "The Lute and Organ in Ancient Israeli and Jewish Iconography," in *Festschrift Christoph-Hellmut Mahling,* ed. A. Beer et al.. Tutzing, vol. 1, pp. 163-88.
1999   *Die Musikkultur Alt-Israel/Palästinas: Studien zu archäologischen, schriftlichen und vergleichenden Quellen* (= *OBO* 164). Fribourg/ Göttingen.
2000a   "The Earliest Depiction of a Harp (Megiddo, Late Fourth Millennium BC)," in *OrA,* vol. 6, pp. 5-10.
2000b   "Some Remarks on the Music History of Palestine: Written or Archaeological Evidence," in *OrA,* vol. 7, pp. 135-40.
2000c   "Biblical Instruments," in *NGD* 2000, vol. 3, pp. 524-35.

2000d   "Jewish Music II: Ancient Israel/Palestine," in *NGD* 2000, vol. 13, pp. 29-37.

2000e   "Music, Musical Instruments," in *Eerdmans Dictionary of the Bible*. Grand Rapids/Cambridge, U.K., pp. 927-30.

2003 (in preparation)
     The David-Orpheic Lyra and the Pastoral Zurna-*Player in Third-Seventh Century Palestine*.

Braun, Joachim, and J. Cohen
1996   "Jüdische Musik," in *MGG2*, vol. 4, cols. 1511-69.

Brentjes, Burchard
1968   *Von Schanidar bis Akkad*. Leipzig-Berlin.

Briend, Jacques, and Jean-Baptiste Humbert
1980   *Tell Keisan: 1971-1976*. Paris.

Broshi, Magen
1976   "Excavations on Mount Zion, 1971-1972," *IEJ* 26/2-3: 81-88.

Buccelatti, Giorgio, and M. Kelly-Buccelatti
1997   "Urkesh: The First Hurrian Capital," *BAR* 60/2: 77-94.

Buchner, Alexander
1956   *Musikinstrumente im Wandel der Zeiten*. Prague.

Buchner, Giorgio, and John Boardman
1966   "Seals from Ischia and the Lyre-Player Group," *JDAI* 81: 1-62.

Casetti, Pierre
1977   "Funktionen der Musik in der Bibel," *Freiburger Zeitschrift für Philosophie und Theologie* 24: 366-89.

Catling, Hector William
1964   *Cypriot Bronzework in the Mycenaean World*. Oxford.

Caubet, Annie
1987   "La musique a Ougarit: Nouveaux apercus," in *Academie des Inscriptions et Belles Lettres: Comptes Rendus des Seances de l'année 1987*, novembre-decembre, vol. 4, pp. 731-53.

1994   "La musique du Levant au bronze rcent," in C. Homo-Lechner, ed., *La pluridisciplinarità en archéologie musicale*, pp. 129-35.

Chambon, Alain
1984   *Tell el-Far'ah*, vol. 1. Paris.

Chancey, Mark, and Eric M. Meyers
2000   "How Jewish Was Sepphoris in Jesus' Time?" *BAR* 28/4: 19-33.

Chehab, Maurice
1951-54   "Les terres cuites de Kharayeb," *Bulletin du Musée de beyrouth* 10
           (1951-52) and 11 (1953-54).

Clédat, M. Jean
1915   "Fouilles a Cheikh Zouede," *Annales du Service des Antiquites de
           l'Egypte* 15: 15-48.

Cohen, B.
1969   "The Responsum of Maimonides concerning Music," in idem, *Law
           and Tradition in Judaism.* New York, pp. 167-81.

Cohen, Rudolf, and Yigal Yisrael
1996   "Smashing the Idols: Piecing Together an Edomite Shrine in Judah,"
           BAR 20/4: 40-51.

Collaer, Paul, and Jürgen Elsner
1983   *Nordafrika* (= *MGB*, 1/8), Leipzig.

Collon, Domenic, and A. D. Kilmer
1980   "The Lute in Ancient Mesopotamia," in T*he British Museum Year-
           book,* vol. 4, pp. 13-28.

Cross, Frank Moore
1973   *Canaanite Myth and Hebrew Epic.* Cambridge.

Crowfoot, John Winter, et al.
1957   *The Objects from Samaria, Samaria-Sebaste,* vol. 3. London.

Crown, Alan D., ed.
1989   *The Samaritans.* Tübingen.

Crown, Alan D., Reinhard Pummer, and Abraham Tal, eds.
1993   *Companion to Samaritan Studies.* Tübingen.

Cuesta, Ismael Fernandez de la
1983   *Historie de la musica española: desde los origenes el "ars nova."* Ma-
           drid.

Dar, Shimon
1976   "An Egyptian Sistrum from Sinai," *Tel-Aviv* 3/2: 79-80.

Davies, W. D., and L. Finkelstein
1984   *The Cambridge History of Judaism: The Persian Period.* Cambridge.

Day, Peggy L.
1989   *Gender and Difference in Ancient Israel.* Minneapolis.

De Geuns, C. H. F.

1980   "Idumaea," *Jahrbericht van het voorasiatisch-egyptisch genootschap.* 26: 53-74.

De Marini

1961   "Komos," in *Encyclopedia dell'arte antica classica e orientale,* vol. 4. Rome, pp. 382-84.

Demsky, Aaron

1986   "When the Priests Trumpeted the Onset of the Sabbath," *BAR* 12/6: 50-52.

Deubner, Ludwig

1929   "Die vierseitige Leier," *Athenische Mitteilungen* 54: 194-200.

Dever, William G.

1983   "Material Remains and the Cult in Ancient Israel: An Essay in Archaeological Systematics," in *The Word of the Lord Shall Go Forth: Festschrift for D. N. Freedman,* ed. C. L. Meyers and M. O'Connor. Winona Lake, Ind., pp. 571-87.

1984   "Asherah, Consort of Yaweh? New Evidence from Kuntillet 'Ajrud," *BASOR* 255: 21-37.

1998   "Archaeology, Ideology, and the Quest for an 'Ancient' or 'Biblical' Israel," *NEA* 61/1: 39-52.

Devries, Lamoine F.

1987   "Cult Stands: A Bewildering Variety of Shapes and Sizes," *BAR* 13/4: 26-37.

Dixon, D. M., and K. P. Wachsmann

1964   "A Sandstone Statue of an *Auletes* from Meroe," *Kush* 12: 119-25.

Doelger, F. J.

1934a   "Gloeckchen im Ritual der Arvalbrueder?" *Antike und Christentum* 4: 243-44.

1934b   "Die Glöckchen am Gewand des jüdischen Hohenpriester," *Antike und Christentum* 4: 233-42.

Dornemann, Rudolph Henry

1983   *The Archaeology of the Transjordan in the Bronze and Iron Ages.* Milwaukee.

Dothan, Moshe

1970   "The Musicians of Ashdod," *Archaeology* 23/4: 310-11.

1971   "Ashdod II-III: The Second and Third Seasons of Excavations 1963, 1965," *Atiqot* 9-10. Jerusalem (Eng. ser.).

1983   *Ancient Synagogues: Hammat Tiberias, Early Synagogues and the*
          Hellenistic and Roman Remains. Jerusalem.

Dothan, Trude
1982   *The Philistines and Their Material Culture.* Jerusalem.
1989   "The Arrival of the Sea People: Cultual Diversity in Early Iron Age
          Canaan," in S. Gitin and W. G. Dever, *Recent Excavations in Israel:*
          Studies in Iron Age Archaeology. New York (= *AASOR* 49), pp. 1-14.

Dothan, Trude, and Moshe Dothan
1992   *People of the Sea.* New York-Toronto.

Duchesne-Guillemin, Marcelle
1984   *A Hurrian Musical Score from Ugarit: The Discovery of*
          Mesopotamian Music. Malibu.

Dumbabin, Katherine M. D.
1978   *The Mosaics of Roman North Africa.* Oxford.

Dyk, P. J. van
1990   "Current Trends in Pentateuch Criticism," in *Old Testament Essays,*
          vol. 3, pp. 191-202.

Edelman, Diana V., ed.
1991   *The Fabric of History: Text, Artifact, and Israel's Past.* Sheffield.

Eichmann, Ricardo
1988   "Zur Konstruktion und Spielhaltung der Altorientalischen
          Spiesslauten: von den Anfangen bis in die seleukidisch-parthische
          Zeit," in *Baghdader Mitteilungen* 19. Berlin, pp. 583-625.

Elgabish, Joseph
1975   "Shiqmona, 1975," in: *IEJ* 25/4: 257-58.

Ellermeier, F.
1970a   "Beiträge zur Frühgeschicht altorientalischer Saiteninstrumente," in
          Archäologie und Altes Testament: Festschrift für Kurt Galling, ed. A.
          Kuschke and E. Katsch. Tübingen, pp. 75-90.
1970b   "Die ersten literarische Belege für die Doppeloboe in Ugarit,"
          Theologische und orientalische Arbeiten 2: 10-21.

Elsner, Jürgen
1969   "Remarks on the Big Arġġûl," in *Yearbook of the International Folk*
          Music Council, vol. 1, pp. 232-39.

Engel, Carl
1864   *The Music of the Most Ancient Nations.* London.

Engel, Hans
1987   *Die Sellung des Musikers im arabisch-islamischen Raum.* Bonn.

Engle, I.
1979   "Pillar Figurines in Iron Age Israel." Ph.D. thesis, Pittsburgh.

Farmer, Henry George
1966   Islam (= *MGB*, 3/2). Leipzig.

Fellerer, Karl Gustav
1956   "Darstellungen von Musikinstrumenten auf dem koelner Mosaik,"
            in *Das römische Haus mit dem Dionysos-Mosaik von dem Südportel
            des Kölner Doms,* ed. F. Fremersdorf. Berlin, pp. 65-69.

Fine, Steven
1997   *The Holy Place: On the Sanctity of the Synagogue during the Greco-
            Roman Period.* Notre Dame.
2000   "Iconoclasm and the Art of the Late-Ancient Palestine Synagogues,"
            in Levine/Weiss, 2000, pp. 183-94.

Finensinger, Sol Baruch
1926   "Musical Instruments in the Old Testament," *HUCA* 3: 21-76.

Finkelstein, Israel
1988   *The Archaeology of the Israelite Settlement.* Jerusalem.
1999   "State Formation in Israel and Judah," *NEA* 62/1: 35-52.

Finkelstein, Israel/Na'aman Nadav
1994   *From Nomadism to Monarchy.* Jerusalem.

Finney, Paul Corby
1978   "Orpheus-David: A Connection in Iconography between Greco-
            Roman Judaism and Early Christiantity?" *Journal of Jewish Art* 5: 6-
            15.

Fitzgerald, Gerald M.
1931   *Beth-Shan Excavations 1921-23: The Arab and Byzantine Levels.*
            Philadelphia.
1925   "Report on Excavations in the Northern Cemetery of Beth Shan."
            MS (Archives of the University Museum, Philadelphia).

Fleischhauer, Günter
1966   *Rome und Etruskien.* Leipzig (= *MGB*, 2/5).

Foerster, Gidon
1985   "Representations of the Zodiac in Ancient Synagogues and Their
            Iconographical Sources," *Eretz-Israel* 18: 380-91 (Heb.).

1987 "The Zodiac in Ancient Synagogues and Its Place in Jewish Thought and Literature," *Eretz-Israel* 19: 525-34 (Heb.).

Forkel, Johann N.
1788 *Allgemeine Geschichte der Musik,* vol. 1. Leipzig, pp. 99-184.

Foxvog, D. A., and A. D. Kilmer
1980 "Music," in *ISBE,* vol. 3, pp. 436-49.

Freedman, David Noel
1985 "But Did King David Invent Musical Instruments?" *BR* 1/2: 48-51.
1987 "Yahweh of Samaria and His Asherah," *BA* 50/4: 241-49.

Fulco, William J.
1976 *The Canaanite God Resep.* New Haven.

Galling, Kurt, ed.
1977 *Biblisches Reallexikon.* Tübingen.

George, Beate
1978 "Hathor, Herin der Sistren," *Medelhavsmuseet* 13: 25-31.

Gerson-Kiwi, Edith
1957 "Musique dans la Bible," in *Dictionnaire de la Bible,* sup., vol. 5, pp. 1411-68.
1974 "Horn und Trompete im Alten Testament: Mythos und Wirklichkeit," in *Studia Instrumentorum Musicae Popularis,* pp. 57-60.
1980a *Migrations and Mutations of Music in East and West.* Tel-Aviv.
1980b "Cheironomy," in *NGD,* vol. 4, pp. 191-96.

Giesel, Helmut
1978 *Studien zur Symbolik der Musikinstrumente in Schrifttum der alten und mittelalterlichen Kirche.* Regensburg.

Gitin, Seymour, and Trude Dothan
1987 "The Rise and Fall of Ekron of the Philistines," *BA* 50: 197-222.
1998 "Philistia in Transition: The Tenth Century BCE and Beyond," in S. Gitin et al., ed., *Jerusalem,* pp. 162-83.

Giveon, Raphael
1971 *Les Bedouins Shosou des Documents Egyptiens.* Leiden.
1972 "Hator k'elat hanegina besinai (Hathor as Music Goddess)," *Tatzlil* 12: 5-9 (Heb.).
1978 *The Impact of Egypt in Canaan.* Freiburg-Göttingen.

Glueck, Nelson
1940 *The Other Side of the Jordan.* New Haven.

1965   *Deities and Dolphins: The Story of the Nabataeans.* New York.

Goodenough, Erwin Ramsdell
1953-68   *Jewish Symbols in the Greco-Roman Period,* vols. 1-13. New York.

Gordon, Cyrus H.
1961   "Canaanite Mythology," in S. N. Kramer, ed., *Mythologies of the Ancient World.* New York, pp. 181-218.
1965   *Ugaritic Textbook.* Rome.
1996   "Recovering Canaan and Ancient Israel," *CANE* 4: 2779-88.

Grace, Virginia R.
1956   "The Canaanite Jar," in Saul S. Weinberg, ed., *The Aegean and the Near East.* New York, pp. 80-109.

Greenfield, J. C.
1974   "The Marzeah as a Social Institution," *Acta Antiqua Academiae Scientiarum Hungaricae* 22: 457-65.

Greifenhagen, Adolf
1929   *Die Darstellung des Komos im VI. Jahrhundert.* Königsberg.

Gressmann, Hugo
1903   *Musik und Musikinstrumente im Alten Testament.* Giessen.
1927   *Altorientalische Bilder zum Alten Testament.* Berlin-Leipzig.

Grout, Donald Jay
1973   *A History of Western Music.* rev. ed., New York.

Gutmann, Joseph, ed.
1981   *Ancient Synagogues: The State of Research.* Ann Arbor.

Haas, Gerlinde
1985   *Die Syrinx in der Griechischen Bildkunst.* Wien, Koln, Graz.

Hachlili, Rachel
1971   "Figurines and Kerno," in Dothan, M., 1971, pp. 125-35.
1989   *Ancient Synagogues in Israel: Third-Seventh Century CE.* Haifa. 1989.

Hachmann, Rolf
1989   "Kamid-el-Loz 1963-1981: German Excavations in Libanon," *Berytus* 37: 7-187.

Hadley, Judith M.
1987   "Some Drawings and Inscriptions on Two Pithoi from Kuntillet 'Ajrud," *VT* 37/2: 180-213.

Bibliography

Haifa Exhibition
1990/91   *Musical Instruments in Biblical Israel,* Exhibition Catalogue, Haifa
1990/91 (reprinted as *Music in Ancient Israel,* Haifa, 1972, and Music in the Ancient World, Haifa, 1979, both HMMAL).

Haïk-Vantoura, Suzanne
1991   *The Music of the Bible Revealed.* Berkeley-San-Francisco.

Hamburger, Anit
1968   "Gems from Caesarea Maritima," *Atiqot* 8 (Eng. ser.): 1-25.
1986   "Surface-Finds from Caesarea Maritima-Tesserae," in I. Levin und E. Netzer, *Excavations at Caesarea Maritima Final Report* (= *Qedem* 21), pp. 187-204.

Hamilton, R. W., and S. A. S. Husseini
1935   "Excavations at Tell Abu Hawam," *QDAP* 4: 1-69.

Hammond, Philip C.
1973   *The Nabateans — Their History, Culture and Archaeology.* Gothenburg.
1982   "The Excavations at Petra 1974: Cultural Aspects of Nabatean Architecture, Religion, Art, and Influence," in A. Hadidi, ed., *Studies in the History and Archaeology of Jordan,* vol. 1. Amman, pp. 231- 38.

Hanbury-Tenison, Jack
1985   "A Late Chalcolithic Bowl Stand from Pella, Jordan," *PEQ* 117/2: 100-101.

Harding, G. Lankester
1950   "A Roman Family Vault on Jebel Jofeh, Amman," *QDAP* 14: 81-94.
1953   "The Cairn of Hani'," *ADAJ* 2: 8-56.
1969   "A Safaitic Drawing and Text," *Levant* 1: 68-72.

Harris, William
1982   "'Soundng Brass' and Hellenistic Technology," *BAR* 8/1: 38-41.

Hedley, C.
1922   "How Savages Use Sea Shells," *The Australian Museum Magazine,* 163-67.

Hengel, Martin
1974   *Judaism and Hellenism: Studies in Their Encounter in Palestine during the Early Hellenistic Period,* vols. 1-2. Tübingen-Philadelphia.

Henig, Martin, and Mary Whiting
1987   *Engraved Gems from Gadara in Jordan.* Oxford.

Hestrin, Ruth

1971   "Figurines and Kernoi," in Dothan M., 1971, pp. 125-37.

1987a   "The Cult Stand from Ta'anach and Its Religious Background," in *Studia Phoenicia*, vol. 5, pp. 61-77.

1987b   "The Lachish Ewer and the 'Asherah," *IEJ* 37/4: pp. 212-23.

Hickmann, Ellen

1982   "Eine ägyptische Harfendarstellung aus hellenistisch-römischer Zeit," in *Jahrbuch für musikalische Volks- und Völkerkunde*, ed. J. Kuckutz, vol. 10. Wiesbaden, pp. 9-19.

Hickmann, Hans

1946   *La Trompette dans l'Egypte Ancienne*, Cairo.

1949a   *Catalogue general des Antiquites égyptiennes du Musée du Caire: Instruments de Musique*. Cairo.

1949b   *Cymbals et Crotales dans l'Egypte Ancienne*. Cairo.

1960a   "Laute," in *MGG1*, vol. 8, pp. 345-56.

1960b   "Leier," in *MGG1*, vol. 8, pp. 517-28.

1961a   "Ägypten" (= *MGB*, 2/1). Leipzig.

1961b   "Vorderasien und Ägypten in musikalischem Austausch," *ZDMG* 3: 23-41.

1963   "Rassel," in *MGG1*, vol. 11, pp. 7-12.

Hillers, D. R.

1970   "The Goddess with the Tambourine: Reflections on an Object from Ta'anach," *Concordia Theological Monthly* 51/9: 606-19.

Hitti, Philip K.

1957   *History of Syria including Lebanon and Palestine*. London.

Holland, T. A.

1977   "A Study of Palestine Iron Age Baked Clay Figurines with Special Reference to Jerusalem: Cave 1," *Levant* 9: 121-55.

Hornbostel, Erich M., and Curt Sachs

1914   "Systematik der Musikinstrumente: Ein Versuch," *Zeitschrift der Ethnologie* 46: 553-90.

Jacobson, Thorkild

1970   *Towards the Image of Tammuz and Other Essays on Mesopotamian History and Culture*. Cambridge, Mass.

1987   *The Harps That Once . . . .* New Haven.

Kadman, Leo

1961   *The Coins of Akko Ptolemais*. Jerusalem.

Kandeel, H.
1969   "Excavations of the Mosaic in Masarisa Courtyard," *ADAJ* 14: 61-66.

Kantor, Helene
1956   "Syro-Palestine Ivories," *JNES* 15: 153-74.

Karageorghis, Vassos
1982   *Cyprus from the Stone Age to the Romans.* London.

Karamatov, Fajsulla
1983   "Uzbek Musical Instruments," *Asian Music* 15/1: 11-53.

Kartomi, Margaret J.
1990   *On Concepts and Classification of Musical Instruments.* Chicago-London.

Kaufmann, Walter
1981   *Altindien* (= *MGB*, 2/8). Leipzig.

Keel, Othmar
1972   *Die Welt der altorientalischen Bildsymbolik und das Alte Testament am Beispiel der Psalmen.* Zurich.
1974   *Die Weisheit spielt vor Gott: Ein monographischer Beitrag zur Deutung des* mesahaqat *in Spr. 8:30.* Freiburg/Göttingen.
1976   "Musikinstrumente, Figuren und Siegel im judaischen Haus der Eisenzeit II," *Heiliges Land* 4: 35-43.

Keel, Othmar, H. Keel-Lau, and S. Schroer
1989   *Studien zu den Stempelsiegeln aus Palästina/Israel,* vol. 2. Göttingen.

Keel, Othmar, M. Shuval, and C. Uehlinger
1990   *Studien zu den Stempelsiegel aus Palästina/Israel,* vol. 3. Göttingen.

Keel, Othmar, and C. Uehlinger
1992   *Göttinnen, Götter und Gottessymbole.* Freiburg, Basel, Wien.

Keel-Leu, Hildi
1991   *Orderasiatische Stempelsiegel: Die Sammlung des biblischen Instituts der Universität Freiburg* (= *OBO* 110). Freiburg, Göttingen.

Kelm, George, and Amihai Mazar
1982   "Three Seasons of Excavations at Tel Batash — Biblical Timnah," *BASOR* 248: 1-36.

Khairy, Nabil J.
1990   *The 1981 Petra Excavations,* vol. 1 (= *Abhandlungen des Deutschen Palästinavereins* 13). Wiesbaden.

Kilmer, Anne Draffkorn
1974   "The Cult Song with Music from Ancient Ugarit: Another Interpretation," in *RlA*, vol. 68, pp. 69-82.

Kilmer, Anne Draffkorn, and Domenice Collon
1980-83   "Laute" and "Leier," in *RlA*, vol. 6, pp. 512-17 and 576-82.

Kilmer, Anne Draffkorn, Domenice Collon, and Stefano de Martino,
1995-96   "Musik," in *RlA*, vol. 8, pp. 463-91.

Kilmer, Anne Draffkorn, Richard L. Crocker, and Robert R. Brown
1976   *Sounds from the Silence, Phonodisc: Recent Discoveries in Ancient Near Eastern Music.* Berkeley.

King, Philip J.
1988   "The Marzeah Amos Denounces," *BAR* 14/4: 34-44.

Kinnkeldey, Otto
1960   "Kinnor, Nebel-Cithera, Psalterium," in *Joshua Bloch Memorial Volume.* New York, pp. 40-53.

Kinsky, Georg
1930   *A History of Music in Pictures.* London-Toronto-New York.

Kircher, A.
1650   *Musurgia Universalis.* Rome.

Kletter, Raz
1996   *The Judean Pillar-Figurines and the Archaeology of Asherah* (= *BAR* International Series 636). Oxford.

Kloner, Amos
1991   "Maresha," *Qadmoniot* 24/3-4 (95-96): 70-85.

Kloner, Amos, and J. Braun
2000   "Hellenistic Painted Tombs at Marisa: Burial-Hunt Music," in *OrA*, vol. 6, pp. 47-52.

Knauf, Ernst A.
1986   "Die Herkunft der Nabataer," in Lindner, 1986, pp. 74-78.
1988   "Ein safaitisches Felsbild vom gebel Qurma und die 'Meder' in Bosra," *Damaszener Mitteilungen* 3: 77-82.

Koehler, L. W., W. Baumgartner, and J. J. Stamm
1967-90   *Hebräisches und aramäisches Lexikon zum Alten Testament,* vols. 1-4. Leiden, 1967-90.

Koitabischi, Matahisa
1999   "Music in the Texts from Ugarit," in *UF*, vol. 30 (1998). Munich.

Bibliography

Kolari, Eino
1947   *Musikinstrumente und ihre Verwendung im Alten Testament.* Helsinki.

Kraeling, C. H., and L. Mowry
1960   "Music in the Bible," in E. Werllesz, ed., *Ancient and Oriental Music.* London, pp. 282-312.

Kraus, Samuel
1910-12   *Talmudische Archaeologie,* vols. 1-3. Leipzig.

Kubik, Gerhard
1982   *Ostafrika* (= *MGB,* 1/10). Leipzig.

Kühnel, Bianca
2000   "The Synagogue Floor Mosaic in Sepphoris: Between Paganism and Christianity," in Levine/Weiss, 2000, pp. 31-43.

Kuhnen, Hans-Peter
1990   *Palästina in griechisch-römischer Zeit* (= *Handbuch der Archäologie Vorderasiens,* vol. 2/2). Munich.

Kutcher, Raphael
1990   "The Cult of Dumuzi/Tammuzi in Ur III," in J. Klein and A. Skaisted, eds., *Bar-Ilan Studies in Assyrologie, Dedicated to Pinhas Artzi.* Ramat-Gan, pp. 29-44.

Lamon, R., and Geoffrey M. Shipton
1939   *Megiddo I, Seasons of 1925 Strata I-V.* Chicago.

Landels, John G.
1963   "The Brauron Aulos," *ABSA* 58: 116-19.
1964   "Fragment of Auloi Found in the Athenian Agora," *Hesperia* 33/4: 392-400.
1966   "Ship-Shape and Sambuca-Fashion," *The Journal of Hellenic Studies* 86: 69-77.
1981   "The Reconstruction of Ancient Greek Auloi," *World Archaeology* 12/3: 298-302.
1999   *Music in Ancient Greece and Rome.* London/New York.

Langdon, Stephen
1921   "Babylonian and Hebrew Musical Terms," *JRAS,* pp. 169-91.

Lawergren, Bo
1998   "Distinctions among Canaanite, Philistine, and Israelite Lyres and Their Global Context," *BASOR* 309: 41-68.

Lemaire, Andre
1984   "Who or What Was Yahweh's Asherah," *BAR* 10/6: 42-51.

Levi, Doro
1947   *Antioch Mosaic Pavements,* vols. 1-2. Princeton.

Levine, Lee I., ed.
1981   *Ancient Synagogues Revealed.* Jerusalem.

Levine, Lee I., and Ze'ev Weiss
2000   *From Dura to Sepphoris: Studies in Jewish Art and Society in the Late Antiquity.* Portsmouth, Rhode Island.

Lieberman, Saul
1942   *Greek in Jewish Palestine.* New York.
1950   *Hellenism in Jewish Palestine.* New York.

Liebowitz, Harold
1967   "Horses in New Kingdom Art and the Date of an Ivory from Megiddo," *JARCE* 6: 129-34.
1980   "Military and Feast Scenes on Late Bronze Palestinian Ivories," *IEJ* 30/3-4: 162-69.

Lindner, M., ed.
1970   *Petra und das Konigreich der Nabataer.* Nürenberg.

Lipschitz, N., and G. Biger
1991   "Cedar of Lebanon (Cedrus Libani) in Israel during Antiquity," *IEJ* 41: 167-75.

Loud, Gordon
1936   "News from Armageddon," *ILN,* pp. 1108-10.
1938   "The Pavement Artists of 5000 Years," *ILN,* p. 975.
1939   *The Megiddo Ivories.* Chicago.
1948   *Megiddo II: Seasons of 1935-1939.* Chicago.

Luckenbill, Daniel David
1924   *The Annals of Sennacherib.* Chicago.

MacAlister, R. A. Stewart
1909   "Twentieth Quarterly Report on the Excavations at Gezer," *PEFQ* 41: 13-25.
1912   *The Excavations at Gezer 1902-1905 and 1907-1909,* vols. 1-3. London.

MacDonald, Ean
1932   *Beth-Pelet II.* London.

338

Magen, Itzhaq
1992 "Batei kneset shamroniyim (Samaritan Synagogues)," *Qadmoniot* 25/3-4 (99/100): 66-90 (Heb.).
1993 "Tshuva (Response)," *Qadmoniot* 26/3-4 (103/104): 68 (Heb.).

Malamat, Avraham
1999 "Zemarim/neganim mhazor nešlahim lemari (Singers/Players from Hazor Sent to Mari)," *Qadmaniot* 32/1: 43-44.

Manniche, Lise
1973 "Rare Fragments of a Round Tambourine in the Ashmolean Museum, Oxford," *Acta orientalia* 35: 29-36.
1975 *Ancient Egyptian Musical Instruments*. Munich.
1976 *Musical Instruments from the Tomb of Tut-'ankhamun*. Oxford.
1987 *The City of the Dead: Thebes in Egypt*. London.
1988 "The Erotic Oboe in Ancient Egypt," in Hickmann, Ellen, and D. H. Hughes, *The Archaeology of Early Musical Cultures*. Bonn, pp. 189-98.
1991 *Music and Musicians in Ancient Egypt*. London.

Marcuse, Sybil
1975 *Musical Instruments: A Comprehensive Dictionary*. New York-London.

Matz, Friedrich
1968-74 *Die Dionysische Sarkophage*, Teil I-IV. Berlin.

May, Herbert Gordon
1935 *Material Remains of the Megiddo Cult*. Chicago.

Mazar, Amihai
1973 "Mikdash plishti b'Tel Qasile (A Philistine Temple at Tel Qasil)," *Qadmoniot* 21/1: 20-23 (Heb.).
1980 *Excavations at Tell Qasile I* (= *Qedem* 12).
1985 *Excavations at Tell Qasile II* (= *Qedem* 20).
1990 *Archaeology of the Land of the Bible, 10,000-586 B.C.* New York.
1997 "Four Thousand Years of History at Tel Beth-Shean: An Account of the Renewed Excavations," in *BA* 60/2: 62-76.

Mazar, Benjamin
1976 "The 'Orpheus' Jug from Megiddo," in *Magnalia Dei: Essays on the Bible and Archaeology in Memory of Ernest Wright*, ed. F. M. Cross et al. New York, pp. 187-92.

Mazar, Benjamin, and Trude Dothan
1966 *En Gedi: The First and Second Season of Excavations 1961-62* (= *Atiqot* 5, Eng. ser.).

Mazar, Eilat
1993   "Akhziv," *Excavations and Surveys in Israel* 12/99: 6-7.

Mazar, Benjamin, and Trude Dothan
1966   *En Gedi: The First and Second Season of Excavations 1961-62*
            (= *Atiqot* 5, Eng. ser.).

McCown, Chester Charlton
1947   *Tell en Nasbeh*, vols. 1-2. Berkeley/New Haven.

McGovern, Patrick Edward
1986   *Late Bronze Palestine Pendants*. Sheffield.
1987   "Central Transjordan in the Late Bronze and Early Iron Ages: An
            Alternative Hypothesis of Socio-economic Transformation and Col-
            lapse," in Adnan Hadidi, ed., *Studies in the History and Archaeology
            of Jordan*, 3. Amman, London, and New York, pp. 267-74.

McKinnon, James
1965   "The Meaning of the Patristic Polemic against Musical Instru-
            ments," *CM* 1: 69-82.
1968   "Musical Instruments in Medieval Psalm Commentaries and Psal-
            ters," *JAMS* 21: 3-20.
1979-80   "The Exclusion of Musical Instruments from the Ancient Syna-
            gogues," *PRMA* 106: 77-87.
1986   "On the Question of Psalmody in the Ancient Synagogue," in *Early
            Music History*, 6: *Studies in Medieval and Early Modern Music*.
            Cambridge, pp. 159-91.
1987   *Music in Early Christian Literature*. Cambridge.
1998   *The Temple, the Church Fathers and Early Western Chant*. Ashgate.

Megaw, J. Vincent S.
1960   "Penny Whistles and Prehistory," *Antiquity* 34: 6-13.

Mendenhall, George H.
1986   "Cultural History and the Philistine Problem," in Lawrence T.
            Garaty and Larry G. Herr, eds., *The Archaeology of Jordan and
            Other Studies Presented to Sigfried H. Horn*. Berrien Springs, Mich.,
            pp. 525-46.

Merkelbach, Reinhold
1988   *Die Hirten des Dionysos*. Stuttgart.

Meshel, Zeev
1976   "Kuntilat 'Ajrud — An Israelite Site on the Sinai Border,"
            Qadmoniot 36/4: 119-24.
1978   "Kuntilat 'Ajrud: A Religious Centre from the Time of the Judean

Monarchy on the Border of Sinai," in *Israel Museum Catalogue 75* Jerusalem.

1979   "Did Yahweh Have a Consort?" *BAR* 5/2: 24-35.

Meshorer, Yaakov

197.   "Klei negina b'matbeot Eretz-Israel (Musical Instruments on Eretz-Israel Coins)," *Tatzlil* 11: 140-43 (Heb.)

1982   *Ancient Jewish Coinage*, vols. 1-2. New York.

1984-85   "The Coins of Caesarea Paneas," *IMJ* 8: 37-58.

Meshorer, Ya'acov, and Shraga Qedar

1999   *Sumerian Coinage.* Jerusalem.

Meyer, Jan-Waalke

1987   "Die Silberschale VA14117 — Ägyptisch oder Phönizisch?" in *Studia Phoenicia*, pp. 167-80.

Meyers, Carol L.

1987   "A Terra-cotta at the Harvard Semitic Museum and Disc-holding Female Figures Reconsidered," *IEJ* 37/2-3: 116-22.

1988   *Discovering Eve: Ancient Israelite Women in Context.* New York-Oxford.

1993   "The Drum-Dance-Song Ensemble: Women's Performance in Biblical Israel," in Kimberly Marshall, ed., *Rediscovering the Muses: Women's Musical Tradition.* Boston, pp. 49-67.

Meyers, Carol L., and E. M. Meyers

1975   "Another Jewish Bread Stamp?" *IEJ* 2/3: 154-55.

Meyers, Eric M., E. Netzer, and C. L. Meyers

1987   Artistry in Stone: The Mosaics of Ancient Sepphoris," *BA* 50/4: 223-31.

1992   *Sepphoris.* Winona Lake, Ind.

MGB

1964-89   *Musikgeschichte in Bildern: Begründet von Heinrich Besseler und Max Schneider*, ed. Werner Bachmann. Leipzig.

MGG1

1949-79   *Die Musik in Geschichte und Gegenwart*, vols. 1-14 and supplement, ed. F. Blume. Kassel/Basle.

MGG2

1994-   Ibid., second new rev. ed., ed. L. Finscher. Kassel-Weimar.

Mildenberg, Leo

1984   *The Coinage of the Bar-Kochba War.* Frankfurt/Main.

Miller, Patrick D., et al., ed.
1987   *Ancient Israelite Religion: Essays in Honor of Frank Moore Cross.*
          Philadelphia.

Mitchell, T. C.
1992   "The Music of the Old Testament Reconsidered," *PEQ,* July-
          December, 124-43.

Mitchell, T. C., and R. Joyce
1965   "The Musical Instruments in Nebuchadnezzar's Orchestra," in D. J.
          Wiseman et al., ed., *Notes on Some Problems in the Book of Daniel.*
          London, pp. 19-27.

MMB
1965/66   *Münzen und Medaillen AG Basel, Auktion Sammlung Niggeler,* Vier
          Teile. Basel, 1965/66.

Mommsen, Theodor
1909   *The Provinces of the Roman Empire from Caesar to Diocletian.* Lon-
          don.

Moscati, Sabatino, ed.
1988   *The Phoenicians.* Milan.

Mound and Sea
1986   *Mound and Sea: Akko and Caesarea Trading Centres,* ed. Reuven and
          Edith Hecht. Haifa University Museum, Haifa.

Mueller, Karl (Carolus Muellerus)
1882   *Geographi Graeci Minores,* vols. I-II. Paris.

Muhly, James D.
1985   "Phoenicia and the Phoenicians," in *Biblical Archaeology Today:*
          Proceedings of the International Congress on Biblical Archaeology, Je-
          rusalem 1984. Jerusalem, pp. 177-91.

Nagy, Rebecca Martin, et al., ed.
1996   *Sepphoris in Galilee: Crosscurrents of Culture.* Raleigh, North
          Carolina.

NEAEHL
1993   *The New Encyclopedia of Archaeological Excavations in the Holy*
          Land, ed. E. Stern, vols. 1-4. Jerusalem, 1993.

Needler, Winifred
1949   *Palestine, Ancient and Modern: A Handbook and Guide to the Pales-*
          tine Collection of the Royal Ontario Museum. Toronto.

Bibliography

Negev, Avraham
1977   "Nabateans and the Province of Arabia," in *ANRW*, vol. 2/8, pp. 520-686.
1981   "Nabatean, Greek, and Talmudic Inscriptions," *IEJ* 31: 66-71.
1986   *Nabatean Archaeology Today.* New York-London.
1991   *Personal Names in the Nabatean Realm* (= *Qedem* 32). Jerusalem.

Neusner, Jacob
1981   "The Symbolism of Ancient Judaism: The Evidence of the Synagogues," in Gutmann, ed., 1981, pp. 7-17.

Newberry, Percy Edward
1893   *Beni Hasan, Part 1: Archaeological Survey of Egypt,* ed. F. L. Griffith. London.

NGD
1980   *New Grove Dictionary of Music and Musicians,* ed. Stanley Sadie, vols. 1-20, London.

NGD 2000
2000   *New Grove Dictionary of Music and Musicians,* ed. Stanley Sadie, vols. 1-28. London.

NHdb
1989   *Neues Handbuch der Musikwissenschaft,* ed. C. Dahlhaus, vol. 1. Laaber.

Nilsson, Martin P.
1957   *The Dionysiac Mysteries of the Hellenistic and Roman Age.* Lund.

Nixdorff, Heide
1971   *Zur Typologie und Geschichte der Rahmentrommeln.* Berlin.

Nonnos
1963   *Dionysiaca.* The Loeb Classical Library, Greek with English translation, by W. H. D. Rouse, vols. 1-6. London–Cambridge, Mass.

Noy, Tamar, and B. Brimer
1980   "Adornment of Early Natufian Burials," *IMN:* 55-64.

Norborg, Åke
1996   *Ancient Middle Eastern Lyres.* Stockholm.

OEANE
1997   E. Meyers et al., ed., *The Oxford Encyclopedia of Near Eastern Archaeology,* vols. 1-5. New York-Oxford.

OrA 6
2000   Hickmann, E., and R. Eichmann, ed., *Studien zur Musikarchaeologie,* 1: *Orient Archaeologie* 7. Rahden/Westf.

OrA 7
2000   Hickmann, E., I. Laufs, and R. Eichmann, ed., *Studien zur Musikarchaeologie,* 1: *Orient Archaeologie* 6. Rahden/Westf.

Oren, Eliezer D.
1982   "Ziglag — A Biblical City on the Edge of the Negev," *BA* 45/3: 155-66

Ory, J.
1939   "A Painted Tomb near Ashcalon," *QDAP* 8: 38-44.

Ovadia, Asher
1991   "The Mosaic Pavements of Sheikh Zouda," in *Festschrift Joseph Engemann.* Bonn, pp. 181-91.

Ovadia, Asher and Ruth
1987   *Mosaic Pavements in Israel: Hellenistic, Roman and Early Byzantine.* Rome.

Palisca, Claude von
1978   "G. B. Doni — Musicological Activist, and His 'Lyra Barberina,'" in Edward Olleson, ed., *Modern Musical Scholarship.* London, pp. 180-205.

Pandermalis, Dimitrios
1997   *Dion: The Archaeological Site and the Museum.* Athens.

Panofsky, Erwin
1955   *Studies in Iconology.* New York.

Pardee, Dennis
1988   *Les textes para-mythologique, Ras Shamra-Ougarit IV.* Paris.

Parr, Peter
1978   "Pottery, People and Politics," in *Archaeology in the Levant,* ed. Roger Moorey and P. J. Parr. Warminster, pp. 203-10.

Parrot, Andre
1961   *Assur.* Munich.

Patrich, Joseph
1984   "'Al-'Uzza Earrings," *IEJ* 34/1: 39-46.

Pauly-Wissowa, eds.
1957-90   *Paulys Real-Encyclopädie der klassischen Altertumswissenschaft,* vols. 1-24. Munich.

Perrot, George, and Charles Chipiez
1885   *History of Art in Phoenicia and Its Dependencies.* London.

Perrot, G., and C. Chipiez
1890   *History of Art in Phoenicia and Its Dependencies,* vols. 1-2. London.

Perrot, Jean
1971   *The Organ from Its Invention in the Hellenistic Period to the End of the Thirteenth Century.* London.

Peters, John P., and Hermann Thiersch
1905   *Painted Tombs in the Necropolis of Marissa.* London.

Petrie, William Matthew Flinders
1928   *Gerar.* London.
1930   *Beth-Pelet (Tel Fara).* London.
1931/1932/1933/1934/1952
              Ancient Gaza I-V. London.

Pfanner, Michael
1983   *Der Titusbogen.* Mainz am Rhein.

Pfeiffer, August F.
1779   *Über die Musik der Alten Hebräer.* Erlangen.

Pick, B.
1899-1910   *Die antiken Münzen von Nordgriechenland,* Bd. 1. Berlin.

Pickard-Cambridge, Arthur
1962   *Dithyramb: Tragedy and Comedy.* Oxford.

Picken, Laurence
1975   *Folk Musical Instruments of Turkey.* London.

Pilz, Edwin
1924   "Die weiblichen Gottheiten Kanaans," *ZDPV* 47: 129-68.

Poethig, E.
1985   "The Victory Song Tradition of the Women of Israel." Ph.D. thesis, Union Seminary, New York.

Porada, Edith
1947   "Seal Impressions of Nuzi," *AASOR* 24.
1956   "A Lyre Player from Tarsus and His Relations," in *The Aegean and the Near East: Studies Presented to M. Goldmann.* New York, pp. 185-211.

Portaleone, Abraham ben David
1612   *Shilte ha-gibborim.* Mantua.

Praetorius, Michael
1914-19   *Synagma musicum,* Bd. I-III. Wittenberg.

Prausnitz, Moshe W.
1955   "Ay and the Chronology of Troy," in *University of London Institute of Archaeology 11th Annual Report.* London, pp. 1-10.

Pritchard, James Bennett
1943   *Palestinian Figurines in Relation to Certain Goddesses Known through Literature.* New Haven.
1950   *Ancient Near Eastern Texts Relating to the Old Testament.* Princeton;
1954   *The Ancient Near East in Pictures Relating to the Old Testament,* Princeton.
1955   Supplement to *ANET* and *ANEP.* Princeton.
1975   *Sarepta: A Preliminary Report on the Iron Age.* Philadelphia.

Proceedings
1997   *Proceedings of the International Archaeological Conference: Cyprus and the Aegean in Antiquity, Nicosia, December 1995.* Nicosia.

Pummer, Reihard
1987   *The Samaritans.* Leiden.

Qassim, Hassan
1980   *Les Instruments de Musique en Iraq.* Paris-New York.

Quasten, J.
1930   *Musik und Gesang in den Kulten der heidnischen Antike und christlichen Frühzeit.* Münster.

Rachmani, L. Y.
1966   "On Some Recently Discovered Lead Coffins from Israel," *IEJ* 36: 234-50.

Randhofer, Regina
1995   *Psalmen in einstimmigen vokalen Überlieferungen: Eine vergleichende Untersuchung jüdischer und christlicher Traditionen,* vols. 1-2. Frankfurt/Wien.

Rashid, Subhi Anwar
1970   "Das Auftreten der Laute und die Bevölkerung Vorderasiens," in *Hundert Jahre Berliner Gesellschaft für Anthropologie, Ethnologie und Urgeschichte, 2. Teil: Fachwissenschaftliche Beiträge.* Berlin, pp. 207-19.
1984   *Mesopotamien* (= *MGB,* 11/2). Leipzig.

Ravina, Menashe
1963   *Organum and the Samaritans.* Tel Aviv.

Reifenberg, Adolf
1950   *Ancient Hebrew Seals.* London.

Reifenberg, N.
1936   "Judische Lampen," *JPOS* 16: 166-79.

Reisner, George Andreu, et al.
1924   *Harvard Excavations at Samaria, 1908-1910,* vols. 1-2. Cambridge.

Rezvani, Medjid
1962   *Le Theatre et la Danse en Iran.* Paris.

Richard, Suzanne
1987   "The Early Bronze Age: The Rise and Collapse of Urbanism," *BA* 50/1: 22-43.

Richter, Gisela M. A.
1971   *Greek Art.* London-New York.

Rimmer, Juan
1969   *Ancient Musical Instruments of Western Asiatic Antiquities in the Department of Western Asiatic Antiquities.* London.

RlA
1932-.   *Reallexikon der Assyrologie und vorderasiatischen Archäologie,* ed. D. O. Edzard, vols. 1-8. Berlin-Leipzig-New York.

Roeder, Günther
1956   *Ägyptische Bronzenfiguren.* Berlin.

Romanoff, Paul
1944   *Jewish Symbols on Ancient Jewish Coins.* Philadelphia.

Rosenthal, Renate
1976   "Late Roman and Byzantine Bone Carvings from Palestine," *IEJ* 26/2-3: 96-103.

Roth, Cecil
1955   "Messianic Symbolism in Palestinian Archaeology," *PEQ* 86: 151-64.

Rothenberg, Beno
1972   *Timna: Valley of the Biblical Copper Mines.* London.

Rowe, Alan
1940   *The Four Canaanite Temples of Beth Shan.* Philadelphia.

Saalschuetz, J. L.

1829   *Geschichte der Würdigung der Musik bei den Hebräern.* Berlin.

Sachs, Curt (Kur)

1940   *The History of Musical Instruments.* New York.

1942   "Music in the Bible," in *The Universal Jewish Encyclopedia.* New York, pp. 46-48.

1943   *The Rise of Music in the Ancient World East and West.* New York.

1965   *Geist und Werden der Musikinstrumente.* Hilversum.

Sadokov, Rjurik

1970   *Muzikal'maya kul'tura drevnego Horezma* (The Musical Culture of the Ancient Horezm). Moscow.

Safrai, Shmuel, M. Stern, et al., ed.

1974-76 *The Jewish People in the First Century,* vols. 1-2. Philadelphia.

Saller, F. Sylvester John

1966   "Iron Age Tombs at Nebo, Jordan," *LA* 16: 165-298.

Salmen, Walter

1979/80 "Zur Ikonographie Musizierender jubelnder Frauen Alt-Israels," *Orbis Musicae* 7: 37-42.

1983   *The Social Status of the Professional Musician from the Middle Age to the 19th Century.* New York.

Sandler, Daniel

1980   "The Music Chapters of 'Shiltey hagiborim by Avraham Portaleone: Critical Edition.'" Ph.D. thesis, Tel Aviv University (Heb.).

Schaik, Martin van

1998   *The Marble Harp Players from the Cyclades.* Utrecht.

Schatkin, Margaret

1978   "Idiophones of the Ancient World," *Jahrbuch für Antike und Christentum* 21: 147-72.

Schmidt-Colinet, Constanze

1981   *Die Musikinstrumente in der Kunst des Alten Orients: Archaeologisch-philologische Studien.* Bonn.

Schott, S.

1950   *Altägyptische Liebeslieder.* Zurich.

Schroer, Silvia

1987   *In Israel gab es Bilder* (= *OBO* 74). Freiburg, Göttingen.

Schumacher, Gottlieb, and Carl Watzinger
1929   *Tell-el-Mutesellim,* vol. 2. Leipzig.

Shur, Nathan
1992   *History of the Samaritans.* Frankfurt am Main.

Schwabe, Mosche, and Baruch Lifshitz
1974   *Beth She'arim,* vol. 2: *The Greek Inscriptions.* Jerusalem.

Seewald, Otto
1934   *Beiträge zur Kenntnis der Steinzeitlichen Musikinstrumente Europas.*
            Wien.

Seidel, Hans
1956-57   "Horn-Trompete im Alten Israel unter Berücksichtigung der
            'Kriegsrolle' von Qumran," *Wissenschaftliche Zeitschrift der Karl-
            Marx-Universitat Leipzig,* Gesellschafts- und
            Sprachwissenschaftliche Reihe 5, pp. 589-99.
1981   "Ps 150 und die Gottesdienstmusik in Altisrael," *Nederlands
            Theologisch Tijdschrift* 35: 89-100.
1989   *Musik in Altisrael: Untersuchungen zur Musikgeschichte und
            Musikpraxis Altisraels anhand biblischer und ausserbiblischer Texte.*
            Frankfurt am Main–Paris.

Sellers, Ovid R.
1941   "Musical Instruments of Israel," *BA* 4/3: 33-47.

Sendrey, Alfred
1969a   *Bibliography of Jewish Music.* New York.
1969b   *Music in Ancient Israel.* London.

Sepphoris
1988   "Prize Find: Mosaic Masterpiece Dazzles Sepphoris Volunteers,"
            BAR 14/1: 30-33.

Seyrig, Henri
1939   "Antiquites syriennes — La grande statue parthe de Shami et la
            sculpture palmyrenienne," *Syria* 20: 177-83.

Shank, Hershel
1979   *Judaism in Stone.* New York.

Shea, William M.
1981   "Artistic Balance among the Beni Hasan Asiatics," *BA* 44/4: 219-28.

Shur, Nathan
1992   *History of the Samaritans.* Frankfurt am Main.

BIBLIOGRAPHY

Smith, Janet C., and Anne D. Kilmer
2000   "Laying the Rough, Testing the Fine," *Orient Archaeology* 6, pp. 127-40.

Smith, John Arthur
1984   "The Ancient Synagogue, the Early Church, and Singing," *ML* 65: 1-16.
1990   "Which Psalms Were Sung in the Temple?" *ML* 71: 167-86.
1998   "Musical Aspects of Old Testament Canticles in Their Biblical Setting," in I. Fenlow, ed., *Early Music History,* vol. 17. Cambridge, pp. 221-64.

Smith, Morton
1967   "Goodenough's Jewish Symbols in Retrospect," *JBL* 86: 53-68.

Smith, William Sheppard
1962   *Musical Aspects of the New Testament.* Amsterdam.

Soggin, Jan Alberto
1964   "'Wachholder Holz,' 2 Sam 6:5 gleich 'Schlaghoelzer, Klappern,'" *VT* 14: 374-77.

Soreq, Yehiam
1981   "Music in Judaism in the Second-Temple, Mishnaic, and Talmudic Eras." Ph.D. thesis, University of South Africa.

Spear, Nathaniel
1978   *A Treasury of Archaeological Bells.* New York.

Spektor, Johann
1964   "Samaritan Chant," *Journal of the International Folk Music Council* 16: 66-69.

Stager, Lawrence E.
1985   "The Archaeology of the Family in Ancient Israel," *BASOR* 260: 1-35.

Stainer, John
1914   *The Music of the Bible.* London (De Capo Press, London, 1970).

Staubli, Thomas
1991   *Das Image der Nomaden im alten Israel und in der Ikonographie seiner sesshaften Nachbaren* (= *OBO* 107). Freiburg, Göttingen.

Stauder, Wilhelm
1961a   *Die Harfen und Leiern Vorderasiens in babylonischer und assyrischer Zeit.* Frankfurt/Main.
1961b   "Zur Frühgeschichte der Laute," in *Festschrift Helmuth Osthoff, zum 65. Geburtstag.* Tutzing, pp. 15-25.

350

Stern, Ephraim

1982   *The Material Culture of the Land of the Bible in the Persian Period: 538-332 BC.* London.

1984   *Excavations at Tel Mevorach 1973-1976* (= *Qedem* 18). Jerusalem.

1993   "The Many Masters of Dor," *BAR* 20/1: 24-31 and 76; *BAR* 20/3: 39-49.

Stern, Menahem, ed.

1974-80   *Greek and Latin Authors on Jews and Judaism,* vols. 1-2. Jerusalem.

Stockmann, Doris

1986   "On the Early History of Drums and Drumming in Europe and the Mediterranean," in Cajsa S. Lund, ed., *Second Conference of the ICTM Study Group of Music Archaeology,* vol. 1. Stockholm, pp. 11-28.

Studia Phoenicia

1983-87   *Studia Phoenicia,* vols. 1-5. Leuven.

Sukenik, Eleazar

1932   *The Ancient Synagogue of Beth Alpha.* Jerusalem.

Susmann, Varda

1978   "Samaritan Lamps of the Third-Fourth Century A.D.," *IEJ* 28/4: 238-50.

1986/87   "Samaritan Cult Symbols as Reflected on Terra-cotta Lamps from the Byzantine Period," *Israel-Haam v'aretz* 22/4: 133-46 (Heb.).

Tadmor, Miriam

1982   "Female Cult Figurines in Late Canaan and Early Israel: Archeological Evidence," in *Studies in the Period of David and Solomon and Other Essays,* ed. Tomoo Ishida. Winona Lake, Ind., pp. 139-73.

1986   "Naturalistic Depictions in the Gilat Sculptured Vessels," *IMJ* 5: 7-12.

Tatton-Brown, Veronica

1989   *Cyprus and the East Mediterranean in the Iron Age.* London.

Tcherikover, Victor A.

1957   *Corpus papyrorum Judaicarum,* vol. 1. Cambridge, Mass.

TDOT

1974-   *Theological Dictionary of the Old Testament,* ed. G. J. Botterweck, H. Ringgren, and H.-J. Fabry. Grand Rapids.

Telgam, Rina, and Weiss, Ze'ev

1988   "Dionysos Leben einer Boden-Mosaik," *Qadmoniot* 21/3-4: 93-99.

THL

1986   *Treasures of the Holy Land: Ancient Art from the Israeli Museum.*
        New York: The Metropolitan Museum of Art, 1986.

Thomas, Edit B.

1970   *King David Leaping and Dancing: A Jewish Marble from the Roman
        Imperial Period.* Budapest.

Thomson, Peter

1936/37 "Ausgrabungen in Megiddo," *Archiv für Orientforschung* 11: 269-70.
1937-39 "Ausgrabungen in Megiddo," *Archiv für Orientforschung* 12:. 180-83
        and 408-10.

Tsafrir, Yoram, and Gideon Foerster

1987-88 "The Beth-Shan Project," in *Excavations and Surveys in Israel 1987/
        88,* vol. 6, pp. 7-43.

Tufnell, Olga, et al.

1953   *Lachish III: The Iron Age.* London-New York-Toronto.
1958   *Lachish IV: The Bronze Age.* London-New York-Toronto.

Turville-Petre, F.

1932   "Excavations in the Mugharet el-Kebarah," *JRAI* 62: 271-76.

Ugolino, Blasius

1767   *Thesaurus antiquitatum sacrarum . . . ,* Bd. 32. Venice.

Urbach, Ephraim E.

1959   "The Rabbinical Laws of Idolatry in the Second and Third Cen-
        turies in the Light of Archaeological and Historical Facts," in *IEJ* 9:
        149-65 and 229-45.

Vertkov, K., G. Blagodatov, and E. Yazo

1975   *Atlas of Musical Instruments of the Peoples Inhabiting the USSR.*
        Moscow.

Vogel, Martin

1966   *Apollonisch und Dionysisch: Geschichte eines genialen Irrtums.*
        Regensburg.

Vorreiter, Leopold

1972/73 "Westsemitische Urformen von Seiteninstrumenten," *Mitteilungen
        der Deutschen Gesellschaft für alt Musik des Orients* 11: 71-77.
1983   *Die schonsten Musikinstrumente des Altertums.* Frankfurt am Main.

VR

1987   *La Voie Royale: 9000 ans d'art au Royaume de Jordanie.* Musée du
        Luxembourg.

Webb, J. M.
1986   "The Incised Scapulae," in V. Karageorghis, ed., *Kition V.* Nicosia, pp. 317-28.

Wegner, Max
1963   *Griechenland* (= *MGB*, 2/4), Leipzig.

Weippert, Helga
1988   *Palästina in vorhellenistischen Zeit* (= *Handbuch der Archaeologie Vorderasiens*, 2/1). Munich.

Weiss, Ze'ev
1995   "Tarbut hapnay haromit vehašpa'tah 'al yehudey eretz-israel (The Roman Free-Time Culture and Its Influence on the Jews of Eretz-Israel)," *Qadmoniot* 38/1: 2-20.
2000   "The Sepphoris Synagogue Mosaic: Abraham, the Temple and the Sovereign God — They're All in There," *BAR* 26/5: 48-61 and 70.

Weiss, Ze'ev, and Ehud Netzer
1996   *Promise and Redemption.* Jerusalem.
1998   "Zippori 1994-95," in *Excavations and Surveys in Israel,* vol. 18, pp. 22-27.

Wellhausen, J.
1898   "Music of the Ancient Hebrews," in *The Book of Psalms: A New English Translation.* Stuttgart–New York, pp. 217-34.

Wenning, Robert
1987   *Die Nabataer-Denkmäler und Geschichte,* Freiburg-Göttingen.

Werner, Eric
1959 and 1984
    The Sacred Bridge: The Interdependence of Liturgy and Music in Synagogue and Church during the First Millennium, vols. 1-2. London and New York.
1960   "'If I speak in the tongues of men . . .': St. Paul's Attitude to Music," *JAMS* 13: 18-32.
1976   *Prolegomenon — Contributions to the Historical Study of Jewish Music.* New York, pp. 1-36.
1980   "Jewish Music," in *NGD,* vol. 9, pp. 614-34.

Wiese, André
1990   *Zum Bild des Königs auf ägyptischen Siegelamuletten* (= *OBO* 96). Freiburg-Göttingen.

Winter, Urs
1983   *Frau und Gottin: Exegetische und ikonographische Studien zum*

weiblischen Gottesbild im Alten Testament und dessen Umwelt (= *OBO* 53). Freiburg-Göttingen.

Winternitz, Emmanuel
1967   *Musical Instruments and Their Symbolism in Western Art.* New York.

Wulstan, David
1971   "The Earliest Musical Notation." *ML* 52: 365-82.
1974   "Music from Ancient Ugarit," in *Revue d'Assyriologie et l'Archéologie Orientale* 68: 125-28.

Yadin, Yigael
1955   *Der Kampf der Sohne des Lichtes und der Sohne der Finsternis.* Jerusalem.

Yadin, Yigael, et al.
1958, 1960, and 1961
          Hazor I-IV. Jerusalem.

Yasser, Joseph
1960   "The Magrepha of the Herodian Temple: A Five-fold Hypothesis," *JAMS* 13/1-3: 24-42.

Yavin, S.
1979   "L'ma'amaro shel N. Avigad 'bat hamelech'" (To the Article of N. Avigad, 'The Daughter of the King')," *Qadmoniot* 49-50/1-2 (Heb.).

Zaqzuq, A. R., and M. Duchesne-Guillemin
1970   "La Mosaique de Mariamine," *Annales archéologiques arabes syriennes* 20/1-2: 93-125.

Zayadine, Fawzi
1970   "Die Gotter der Nabataer," in Lindner, 1970, pp. 108-17.

Ziegler, Charlotte
1979   *Catalogue des Instruments de Musique Egyptiens.* Paris.

Zimmerman, Heidy
2000   *Tora und Shira: Untersuchungen zur Musikauffassung des rabbinischen Judentums.* Bern-Oxford-Wien.

Index of Subjects and Names

355

Index of Scripture References

Index of Scripture References

Index of Scripture References